Understanding Hate Crimes

Hate crimes and lesser acts of bigotry and intolerance seem to be constants in today's world. Since 1990, the federal government has published annual reports on hate crime incidents in the United States. While the reported numbers are disturbing, even more devastating is the impact of these crimes on individuals, communities, and society.

This comprehensive textbook can serve as a stand-alone source for instructors and students who study hate crimes and/or other related acts. It invites the reader to consider relevant social mores and practices as well as criminal justice policies as they relate to hate crimes by presenting this subject within a broad context.

Carolyn Turpin-Petrosino is Professor of Criminal Justice in the College of Humanities and Social Sciences at Bridgewater State University. She served on the Massachusetts Juvenile Justice Advisory Council during the Romney Administration. As a result of her research and writings on hate crime, she was invited to Capitol Hill in 2002 to participate in a Congressional Briefing on the state of hate crime research and public policy in the United States. She recently co-authored a book, *American Corrections*, now in its second edition. In addition, she has published several articles and book chapters on hate crimes in the areas of the history of hate crime in the United States, affiliation dynamics and recruitment practices of hate groups, and the nature and scope of anti-Black hate crimes. Her next project focuses on communities, collective efficacy, and community response to hate crimes.

Turpin-Petrosino challenges us to engage with some of the fundamental questions associated with hate crimes, and to think more critically about their nature, causation, and implications. Written accessibly and authoritatively throughout, this text underlines the importance of seeing hate crime as a human problem which requires interventions beyond simply the immediate or the obvious.

Neil Chakraborti, Director of the Leicester
Centre for Hate Studies, University of Leicester, UK

In the last two decades or so hate crime has become a significant global cause for concern. Drawing upon her own vast experience and expertise in the area, Carolyn Turpin-Petrosino has written a fascinating and accessible book that offers a comprehensive and wide-ranging overview of the complex field of hate crime. She offers insightful analysis of not just the harmful effects of hate, but also of the motivations and profiles of offenders, both from a US and international perspective. I've no doubt *Understanding Hate Crimes* will become a key texts for academics, students, and practitioners.

Jon Garland, Reader in Criminology,
University of Surrey, UK

Thoughtful, well-written, and broad in scope, this book provides a strong overview of hate crime. Researchers and students in a variety of disciplines will find this text enlightening and accessible. Professor Turpin-Petrosino brings a fresh perspective to a topic still badly in need of more study.

Phyllis B. Gerstenfeld, J.D., Ph.D.,
California State University, Stanislaus, USA

Understanding Hate Crimes

Acts, motives, offenders, victims, and justice

Carolyn Turpin-Petrosino

Routledge
Taylor & Francis Group

LONDON AND NEW YORK

First published 2015
by Routledge
711 Third Avenue, New York, NY 10017

and by Routledge
2 Park Square, Milton Park, Abingdon, Oxon OX14 4RN

Routledge is an imprint of the Taylor & Francis Group, an informa business

British Library Cataloguing-in-Publication Data
A catalogue record for this book is available from the British Library

Library of Congress Cataloging in Publication Data
Petrosino, Carolyn
Understanding hate crimes: acts, motives, offenders, victims, and justice /
Carolyn Petrosino.—1 Edition.
pages cm
1. Hate crimes—United States. 2. Violence—Psychological aspects.
3. Criminal psychology—United States. I. Title.
HV6773.52.P487 2015
364.150973—dc23
2014036287

ISBN: 978-0-415-48400-8 (hbk)
ISBN: 978-0-415-48401-5 (pbk)
ISBN: 978-0-203-88369-3 (ebk)

Typeset in Times New Roman
by Swales & Willis Ltd, Exeter, Devon, UK

MIX
Paper from
responsible sources
FSC
www.fsc.org FSC® C013604

Printed and bound by CPI Group (UK) Ltd, Croydon, CR0 4YY

Contents

Figures

Tables

Foreword

It is often said that racism "is as American as apple pie." But that is an insipid metaphor because it disrespects a dark history of how White Europeans conquered North America by devastating the native population and how they then built their new nation's economy on the backs of kidnapped Africans who had been turned into chattel slaves. In perhaps the most poetic Presidential inaugural speech of all time, on March 4, 1865, Abraham Lincoln wondered aloud why God saw fit to send the slaughter of the Civil War to the United States. His conclusion: that slavery was a kind of original sin for the United States, and all Americans had to do penance for it. Nineteen days later, Lincoln was killed by the racist John Wilkes Booth.

One hundred and fifty years have passed since Lincoln's assassination and his admonition for penance is all but forgotten. From the White House and Congress to the federal courts and corporate boardrooms, racism is seldom discussed. What has not changed, however, is the pervasive character of racism in American crime and violence. Few criminologists pay attention to this problem. Yet according to the FBI, 5,800 hate crimes are committed each year in the United States. Sixteen hate crimes occur each day; one hate crime is committed every ninety minutes. Barack Obama, the nation's first African-American President, is the target of some thirty assassination threats a day. Still, criminologists ignore this dangerous form of criminality.

Thankfully, Carolyn Turpin-Petrosino has our pedagogical back. Herein lays a comprehensive review of the hate crime phenomenon covering its historical breadth, its structural correlates, its perpetrators, and its victims. This book will not only sound an alarm in college classrooms across the country, it may well inspire a generation of students to do their part in seeking penance for our nation's original sin.

Mark S. Hamm

Preface

Teaching a course on hate crime is no easy task. Personally, I don't think it should be. The subject itself is disturbing on many levels. But many subjects in criminology, such as homicide, terrorism, and sex crimes, are disturbing. Hate crimes, however, are particularly harmful because they are designed to not only injure the direct victim, but to send a message to the group the victim represents. The questions that a course on hate crime must tackle are equally disturbing. How is it that the possession of a certain social or biological characteristic such as race or disability becomes condemnatory? How is it that some people come to vilify other members of the human family, not because of personal experience and factual data, but because of flawed and destructive ideologies they hold onto out of fear and ignorance? But teaching such a course is invaluable for students and instructors alike, as hate crimes serve as a barometer on the state of social relationships in an increasingly multicultural world, and contributes to discussions about social justice and egalitarianism.

Instructors of hate crime courses are often challenged when teaching to facilitate student understanding of the nature of these crimes, and all of the larger societal issues that these offenses reflect. When I taught a hate crimes course in 1995, there were few published works on the subject, and even fewer extensive single source writings. I spent a lot of time searching for course materials that would adequately address the myriad complexities of hate crime. Subsequently, I accumulated disparate writings that had to be structured into a coherent framework for my students. That experience serves as my primary motivation for writing this book. I wanted to write a comprehensive introductory text for instructors and students that covers the major aspects of hate crime. The text, therefore, not only covers the who, what, where, and why of hate crime, but it also includes the history, legal background, criminology, and official statistics relevant to these offenses.

A second motivation for the book was to emphasize the very human nature of hate crimes. It is sometimes too easy for researchers to speak of crime, criminals, and victims as a collection of statistics, theories, study findings, and policies. Although it is important to examine crime using rigorous social science methods, it is equally vital to not lose sight of hate crime as a *human* problem; with *human* actors, *human* offenders, *human* victims, and consequently, *human sufferings*.

I hope this text adequately conveys the human side of hate crime and that readers see themselves in *both* the perpetrators and the victims of hate crime.

There are at least three themes that reverberate throughout most of the book's nine chapters: (1) that the hate crime perpetrator is quite *ordinary*; (2) that the major ideology driving hate crime is the "us versus them" worldview and; (3) that the control and prevention of hate crime rests in addressing its obvious cause—bigotry.

Understandably, we often view perpetrators of hate crime, or any violent crime, as an aberration, as individuals who are very different from the average, law-abiding citizen. But in reality, ordinary law-abiding persons have a lot more in common with hate crime perpetrators than they would dare to suspect. How? We are all subject to various prejudices and bigoted notions. The difference is that the hate crime perpetrator acts upon these notions. But the underlying "motivation" or driving force for the hate crime perpetrator may not be that different from the ordinary person's sexist, anti-Semitic, or racist beliefs.

Chapter 8 International perspectives demonstrates that this strong inclination towards constructing an "us versus them" world view is not just an American phenomenon. I deliberately chose the examples of bigoted and hate-motivated acts highlighted in Chapter 8 to show how remarkably commonplace this marginalization of the other is, even in societies with vastly different cultures, customs, and traditions.

The last theme, which addresses how to counter hate crime, is covered in several chapters, including Chapter 5 (Perpetrators: what do we know about them?), Chapter 6 (Victims: who are they?), and the aforementioned Chapter 8. What readers should recognize from these chapters are universal motivations that prompt hate crime: prejudice, fear, insecurity, ignorance, and a sense of entitlement. If these factors are the primary motivations which also transcend differences in gender, class, race, nationality, and culture, then the strategies to address hate crime must focus on these motivations. In the book, I highlight some of these strategies, including education, community-based initiatives, coalition building, and the exercise of political courage by elected officials.

Finally, I frequently conclude my classes by challenging students to now make a difference; which is the obligation of those privileged to an education. I emphasize the challenge to consciously reject the tendency, sometimes ingrained in all of us, to see the world through the "us versus them" lens, but to endeavor to seek and recognize the commonalities across peoples and cultures. I hope this book will encourage readers to learn from our persistent social shortcomings, and to determine to bridge differences with understanding.

Acknowledgements

For the students who continue to enroll in my hate crimes classes—thank you for the questions, comments, and insights that you've provided overall the last twenty years. Keep them coming!

I want to thank my husband Tony for his relentless encouragement during these several years. He tolerated my absences as I stole time away to write. He also acted as a sounding board for my rhetorical questions and entertained my many "a-ha!" moments throughout the writing process. You are my biggest supporter and I appreciate you more than you know! To my amazing children, Erica and Elliot; I am inspired to write this book for you both. It is my ardent prayer that the world in which you will raise your children will become more self-aware and more loving day by day.

Finally, I most hope that this book honors the legacy of my parents. They lived in a world that sought to remind them daily and in various ways that they were somehow less competent and less deserving because of their brown complexion. Despite what they encountered, they showed my siblings and I who we really were, our true value, that we were full of raw talent and intelligence, and had unlimited potential. We each understood our value and maintained our dignity and pride in ourselves as African-Americans. How did that happen at the time when the United States was still under its own apartheid system? My parents demonstrated what it was to be a warrior against these injustices without shouting or raising clenched fists. They determined to just "be." They were spiritual giants of strength, grace, and truth. Thank you, Ben and Erie Turpin.

Carolyn Turpin-Petrosino

1 Introduction

An overview

Crime is a staple of the news. The public is fed a daily diet of assorted illicit acts such as a corrupt official engaging in conspiracy and extortion, a domestic violence incident that leaves the victim in a coma and children in foster care, or a home invasion where criminals suddenly break into a residence, terrorize and then rob the owners, or worse. What of the OxyContin trafficking ring which has successfully eluded police despite breaking into multiple area drug store chains? From incidents of road rage to warring rival gangs, the public is inundated with crime stories.

All crime requires proper attention, clear understanding, and effective responses from the criminal justice system and that is no less true when it comes to hate crime. Over the last twenty-five years, hate incidents and hate crimes have repeatedly come to the attention of the public. Some see these types of crime as no more serious than the next, while others argue that hate crime, unabated, threatens our very democracy. But what exactly is the nature of hate crime? How is hate crime different from other crimes and how is it defined by law? Does geographical location impact the nature or meaning of a hate crime act? Do hate crime laws as a whole differ from civil rights laws or do they basically address the same unlawful behavior? When hate speech transpires, does that mean that a hate crime has occurred? How trustworthy are hate crime statistics? In reality, there are countless questions about the nature and attributes of hate crime. As such, it would take a series of monographs to adequately address these and other questions. This chapter humbly addresses the fundamental aspects of hate crime. The objective here is to inform the reader and to clarify commonly misunderstood perceptions of these crimes.

What is hate crime?

On November 18, 2008, a young woman went to enter a convenience store in Worcester, Massachusetts, to pick up a few items while her boyfriend waited in the car. Normally such mundane tasks occur speedily and without incident; this time would be different. Suddenly, two men violently confronted her, spewing racial epithets, slurs, and began to physically assault her. The ferocity of the attack was such that witnesses inside the convenience store believed the young woman's life was in danger and with much effort they pulled her inside the store. Then the two men turned to attack the victim's boyfriend, but he quickly drove off. Even after the police arrived, one of the attackers *continued* to scream racial epithets and make physical threats against the young woman. This attack came out of nowhere. It was instantaneous, violent, and unprovoked (Eagan, 2008). The police classified this as a hate crime. The attackers, who were two White males, assaulted the victims, who were Black—because of their perceived race. Their motivation was not to randomly harass others, to rob for financial gain, or to assault the next person in sight due to uncontrolled rage. The attack was racially motivated and this incident is representative of the nature or character of hate crime.

Individuals commit crimes for a variety of reasons: frustration and anger, drug or alcohol addiction problems, financial distress, greed, impulsiveness, to satisfy a lust for evil, psychological problems, boredom, or just plain poor judgment. Still another motivation for committing crime is bias or hatred. Bias crime, more commonly referred to as hate crime, refers to those offenses that are committed due to the perpetrator's prejudiced or hostile attitudes toward a particular social group represented by the victim. Most commonly, the offender's hostility is triggered by his or her perception of the victim's ethnicity, race, national origin, religion, sexual orientation, disability, or gender. But to hold prejudiced attitudes alone is not a crime. A hate crime is comprised of at least two components, (1) the predicate or base criminal offense, such as harassment or intimidation, aggravated assault, malicious damage, arson, or even murder, and (2) evidence that the perpetrator's actions are motivated by prejudice or animus against the group represented by the victim. The following incident reflects the two components: on November 24, 2013 in Fulshear, Texas, Conrad Alvin Barrett attacked a 79-year-old man via the infamous "knockout" game (Dinan, 2013). These are random, vicious, and unprovoked attacks that are usually committed by young adults upon unsuspecting victims. The victim in this case sustained a broken jaw and the loss of three teeth. According to reports, what made this a hate crime and not the typical "knockout" assault was the evidence that the perpetrator sought to purposely target a Black person. The perpetrator videotaped the crime as well as stating his bias motivation to commit it. In this case, the perpetrator was a White male and the victim was Black. However, the perpetrator's race is of little importance relative to the bias motivation which triggers the crime. But the essential components are present: (1) the criminal offense (aggravated battery) and (2) evidence of a bias motivation (perpetrator heard on tape stating his interest in attacking a Black person).

To the perpetrator, the victim is representative of a social group that he or she dislikes intensely or despises. Discovering why the perpetrator possesses this negative attitude or what germinated his or her bigotry is not relevant to the crime itself. Rather, the fact that the prejudiced attitude drives or motivates the offender's action — in whole or in part—is essential. The victim is targeted because of his or her apparent membership, for example he or she shares common characteristics or attributes such as religion or sexual orientation with the social group, of which the perpetrator strongly disapproves. It is not always clear to law enforcement which bias is at work in a hate crime. A victim could hold *multiple* memberships involving two or more groups (or in fact none) that are hated by the perpetrator. For example, the victim could be both Asian *and* homosexual, or Hispanic *and* an immigrant, or disabled *and* Jewish. In such situations, despite the fact that the victim could be legitimately ascribed membership to more than one group, it is the perpetrator's *perception* of who the victim is—rightly or wrongly—that determines the hate motive or motives.

Hate crimes are committed throughout the United States with regularity but are not as prevalent as ordinary crimes. The US Justice Department's 2012 Uniform Crime Report indicated the estimate of 10,189,900 offenses reported to law enforcement. By comparison, the number of reported hate crime offenses for the same year is miniscule, just 5,796. Clearly, hate crimes do not occur to the same extent as conventional crimes. As a result, some believe that such crimes are not a serious problem because they are relatively rare events or that these crimes are a throwback of the past and more of an anomaly today. Some also make the argument that special laws to address hate crimes are not necessary and even counterproductive—a viewpoint that will be discussed in Chapter 3 (Jacobs & Potter, 1998). However, terrorist acts are also rare, but because of the extraordinary ramifications of such acts, they are not only the subject of intense study but also the focus of special legislation and government policy.

Hate-motivated crimes can range from the intentional destruction of property to violent aggravated assaults and even murder. The more typical of these acts is reflected in the following accounts:

> Norwalk, CT. Oct. 13, 2009—Robert Wolf, 48, was charged with intimidation based on bigotry and third-degree assault for allegedly spitting in a woman's face and calling her a derogatory name for Latinos.
>
> (SPLC, 2009a)

> Tinley Park, Ill. Nov. 7, 2009—Valerie Kenney, 54, was charged with a hate crime for allegedly yanking the headscarf of a Muslim woman two days after the Fort Hood shootings.
>
> (*Brooklyn Daily Eagle*, 2010)

> Ivaylo Ivanov . . . spray-painted swastikas and anti-Semitic slogans throughout Brooklyn Heights . . . while assembling . . . illegal guns and bombs inside his . . . home. "Kill All Jews," "SS + Jew = Soap," . . . pamphlets papered parked cars . . . Ivanov pled guilty . . . to possession of a weapon . . . and criminal mischief as a hate crime. He was . . . sentenced to an 18 year(s) of incarceration.
>
> (Brooklyn Heights Blog, 2010)

The basic fundamentals of hate crime also include the distinctive manner in which it causes harm. A victim is targeted by the perpetrator because of a perceived attribute that is an essential element of their identity and not easily obscured. Therefore, for the victim of a hate crime, there is no real ability to mitigate vulnerability.

Whereas, a victim of a house burglary can install alarms and deadbolt locks or purchase a watchdog to reduce the likelihood of future targeting and victimization, hate crime victims cannot simply detach from that which makes them Jewish, Hispanic, Gay or Black. This reality is summarized well by Frederick M. Lawrence (1999, 40), "this heightened sense of vulnerability caused by bias crimes is beyond that normally found in crime victims . . . It is an attack from which there is no escape." In addition, because the majority of hate crime acts are aimed at individuals who are from groups that historically have been subjected to institutionalized discriminatory treatment, harm effects are exacerbated and reverberate old fears; evoking a collective memory of past pains and mistreatment.

Conceptualizations and statutory definitions of hate crime

As previously stated there are two necessary components of a hate crime, the predicate criminal offense and the perpetrator's demonstration of animus toward the victim due to their perceived status. Most hate crime laws articulate these components in statutory language. Nevertheless there are a variety of different conceptualizations and statutory features that are found among hate crime laws.

The US Department of Justice defines hate crime as, "a criminal offense committed against a person, property, or society that is motivated, in whole or in part, by the offender's bias against a race, religion, disability, sexual orientation, or ethnicity/national origin" (US Department of Justice Hate Crime Statistics Act 2004, Appendix A, (b)(1)). In this definition, the base offense is prioritized with the bias element following. This definition also requires that even if a bias motive is only partially at work in a crime, it is still considered a hate crime. The state of California's hate crime statute mirrors this definition:

> California Penal section 422.55 states, 'a criminal act committed, in whole or *in part*, because of one or more of the following actual or perceived characteristics of the victim: 1) disability, 2) gender, 3) nationality, 4) race or ethnicity, 5) religion, 6) sexual orientation, 7) association with a person or group with one or more of these actual or perceived characteristics.'
>
> (Office of the Attorney General, July 2008)

However, the California statute includes the category "association" with those who are targeted as a result of their perceived characteristics. This expands California's ability to use their hate crime statute to prosecute cases where individuals are targeted due to their mere affiliation with members of a group hated by the perpetrator.

Most states include the protected categories of race, ethnicity, religion, and sexual orientation. But just as California included "association," other states also include less common protected categories. For example, New York's Hate Crimes Act of 2000 (485.05) not only includes religion, but also "religious practice," and "ancestry" as bias categories. Recently disability has been added as a bias category. Alabama includes it among its protected categories, and further delineates it as either physical or mental disability (Section 13A-5-13). This state also adds interesting language to its statute by describing the justification as well as the limits of its hate crime statute. It references incitement by groups like the Ku Klux Klan and others, which have a history of carrying out hate-motivated violence. According to California State University at San Bernardino's Center for the Study of Hate and Extremism: Alabama 2: The Legislature finds and declares the following:

1   It is the right of every person, regardless of race, color, religion, national origin, ethnicity, or physical or mental disability, to be secure and protected from threats of reasonable fear, intimidation, harassment, and physical harm caused by activities of groups and individuals.
2   It is not the intent, by enactment of this section, to interfere with the exercise of rights protected by the Constitution of the State of Alabama or the United States.
3   The intentional advocacy of unlawful acts by groups or individuals against other persons or groups and bodily injury or death to persons is not constitutionally protected when violence or civil disorder is imminent, and poses a threat to public order and safety, and such conduct should be subjected to criminal sanctions.

One finds different terminology incorporated in Utah's hate crime law. The statutory language found in 76-3-203.3 includes a noticeable emphasis on the intimidation of the victim:

2   (a) A person who commits any primary offense with the intent to intimidate or terrorize another person or with reason to believe that his action would intimidate or terrorize that person is subject to Subsection (2)(b).
3   "Intimidate or terrorize" means an act which causes the person to fear for his physical safety or damages the property of that person or another. The act must be accompanied with the intent to cause or has the effect of causing a person to reasonably fear to freely exercise or enjoy any right secured by the Constitution or laws of the state or by the Constitution or laws of the United States.

Utah has apparently determined to eschew the inclusion of specific protected categories, preferring to emphasize the intent of the perpetrator to threaten or terrorize the victim.

This brief review provides a sense of the variation found in hate crime statutes. But these differences are not unexpected. Differences in cultural and social norms and local politics, including the discourse and negotiations that occurs among politicians, policymakers, citizen advocacy groups, other interest groups and the voting public, all play a role in defining crime in general and hate crime in particular (Lawrence, 1999; Petrosino, 1999; Jacobs & Potter, 1998, Jenness & Broad, 1997). These dynamics help forge the differences seen among state hate crime laws. For example, although gender and disability are included as protected categories in New Jersey's hate crime laws, Delaware, New Jersey's close neighbor to the south, does not include gender. Ohio, another neighboring state of New Jersey, lists race, color, religion, or national origin, but not gender, disability, or sexual orientation. Criminalized acts are the product of multiple social forces that subsequently forge a set of laws. Perry (2001) and Hall (2005) respectively identify these vagaries by noting, "crime is . . . socially constructed and means different things to different people at different times, and what constitutes a crime in one place may not in another" (Perry, 2001 as cited in Hall, 1). As Perry suggests, crime is therefore relative and historically and culturally contingent . . . this is particularly true of hate crime" (Perry, 2001 as cited in Hall, 1).

Scholars also construct various definitions or theoretical conceptualizations of hate crime. Early efforts focused on *describing* aspects of hate crime. These endeavors emphasized the bias motive of perpetrators, their demographic profiles, and the violent nature of these acts. There were also significant contributions made in describing the operational elements of these crimes (Hamm, 1994; Levin & McDevitt, 1993; Levin, 1999; Gerstenfeld, 2004). Initial observations by researchers included the view that hate crimes were at times typical juvenile acts committed by youngsters seeking a thrill or peer approval (Levin & McDevitt, 1993). Others describe hate crimes as political acts with consequences that far exceed the immediate injury of the victim (Hamm, 1994, Petrosino, 1999, Perry, 2001). The most serious of these acts are viewed by some as having the potential to destabilize government itself (Dees & Corcoran, 1996).

Some theoretical definitions of hate crimes include the assertion of a *dynamic* quality that has significant repercussions beyond that of the crime for the victim, the perpetrator, and even for society (Bowling, 1993; Perry, 2001; Petrosino, 2002). These definitions contend that the action of hate crimes has a practical and deeply symbolic meaning. The perpetrator has constructed a world view that requires him or her to "defend" against an imagined threat. This "defense" in the hate crime perpetrator's mindset is acted out each time an attack on a "threatening" victim/enemy occurs. The perpetrator is messaging to the victim and his or her community that they have crossed a social boundary that will not be tolerated; they have violated a standard in the perpetrator's social world and therefore pose a threat that must be addressed. Thus, the hate crime act is 100 percent pragmatic— it directly punishes the victim physically and psychologically, and it is equally symbolic—it represents and enforces the social relationship and social ordering constructed by the perpetrator.

The differences among hate crime statutes and to some degree, the differences among scholarly or academic definitions clearly reflect the complexities surrounding hate crime as a social problem. Bigotry, racism, homophobia, anti-Semitism, ethnocentrism and the rest of the *isms* have occurred since the beginning of humankind. But as policymakers, criminal justice officials, social service providers, community activists, and academics further comprehend the intricacies of hate crime, the more likely theoretical definitions and hate crime laws themselves will become increasingly refined.

Why did hate crime laws come into being?

Hate-motivated acts have long existed, but what were the driving forces that led to modern hate crime legislation? As the Civil Rights Movement of the 1950s and 1960s gained momentum and public attention, it also ignited a resurgence of activity from the USA's leading hate group at the time, the Ku Klux Klan (Levin, 2009; Sims, 1996). During that era, as institutionalized discriminatory and racist practices were uncovered and publicized, the more the federal government enacted laws—civil rights laws—as a response to punish those behaviors. The Civil Rights Act of 1964 (The Act), sought to discourage racially motivated discrimination.

It prohibited state and municipal governments from denying access to public facilities on grounds of race, religion, gender, or ethnicity. The Act also outlawed discrimination in "hotels, motels, restaurants, theaters, and all other public accommodations engaged in interstate commerce." This law propounded that discrimination based on race, color, or national origin will not be acceptable in any program that receives federal funds and asserted that such racially motivated discrimination (and other included biases) will be circumscribed by the federal government. Similar laws like the Civil Rights Act of 1968, the Civil Rights Restoration Act of 1988, and the Civil Rights Act of 1991, all served as the precursors to modern hate crime legislation. These laws were used to impact discrimination motivated by race, religion, gender and ethnicity and firmly established the intent of the government to intervene and suppress racial and other hate-motivated acts committed by institutions and citizens.

In spite of these legislative developments, the 1980s saw an increased visibility of neo-Nazi skinheads, various White nationalists, Klansmen and other racialist groups in the United States. This should not be taken to mean that individuals and groups committed to the ideals of White supremacy and other similar ideologies of power and privilege laid dormant between the Civil Rights era through to the 1980s. No. There are several substantive works that describe with detail the ongoing efforts and activities of those dedicated to this philosophy *since* World War II (Zeskind, 2009; Barkun, 1994; Lee, 2000). But, the noticeable activeness of hate groups in the 1980s was also commensurate with a clear increase in hate-motivated criminal activity. As a result of this disturbing trend and calls from civil rights organizations like the Southern Poverty Law Center (SPLC), the Anti-Defamation League (ADL), and others, the Congress enacted the Hate Crimes Statistics Act of 1990 (HCSA). This federal law, which was the first to employ the term "hate crime," requires the US Attorney General to collect, maintain and publish data on crimes reported that evidenced prejudice based on race, ethnicity, religion, and sexual orientation. This data is published annually by the Federal Bureau of Investigation's Uniform Crime Reports program. The protected categories in the HCSA were expanded to include disabilities, with the enactment of the 1994 Violent Crime Control and Law Enforcement Act. Passage of state hate crime laws were advocated by the Anti-Defamation League and were further supported by the ADL's model hate crime statute which withstood court challenges (see Box 1.1).

Box 1.1 ADL—Model Hate Crime Statute originally drafted in 1981

1   Institutional Vandalism

- A person commits the crime of institutional vandalism by knowingly vandalizing, defacing or otherwise damaging:

  ○ Any church, synagogue or other building, structure or place used for religious worship or other religious purpose;
  ○ Any cemetery, mortuary or other facility used for the purpose of burial or memorializing the dead;
  ○ Any school, educational facility or community center;
  ○ The grounds adjacent to, and owned or rented by, any institution, facility, building, structure or place described in subsections (i), (ii) or (iii) above; or
  ○ Any personal property contained in any institution, facility, building, structure, or place described in subsections (i), (ii) or (iii) above.

- Institutional vandalism is punishable as follows:

  ○ Institutional vandalism is a _____ misdemeanor if the person does any act described in subsection A which causes damage to, or loss of, the property of another.
  ○ Institutional vandalism is a _____ felony if the person does any act described in Subsection A which causes damage to, or loss of, the property of another in an amount in excess of five hundred dollars.
  ○ Institutional vandalism is a _____ felony if the person does any act described in Subsection A which causes damage to, or loss of, the property of another in an amount in excess of one thousand five hundred dollars.
  ○ Institutional vandalism is a _____ felony if the person does any act described in Subsection A which causes damage to, or loss of, the property of another in an amount in excess of five thousand dollars.

2   Bias-Motivated Crimes

- A person commits a Bias-Motivated Crime if, by reason of the actual or perceived race, color, religion, national origin, sexual orientation, or gender of another individual or group of individuals, he violates Section _____ of the Penal code (insert code provisions for criminal trespass, criminal mischief, harassment, menacing, intimidation, assault, battery, and or other appropriate statutorily proscribed criminal conduct).
- A Bias-Motivated Crime under this code provision is a _____ misdemeanor/ felony (the degree of criminal liability should be at least one degree more serious than that imposed for commission of the underlying offense).

(continued)

(continued)

3   Civil Action for Institutional Vandalism and Bias-Motivated Crimes

- Irrespective of any criminal prosecution or result thereof, any person incurring injury to his person or damage or loss to his property as a result of conduct in violation of Sections 1 or 2 of this Act shall have a civil action to secure an injunction, damages or other appropriate relief in law or in equity against any and all persons who have violated Sections 1 or 2 of this Act.
- In any such action, whether a violation of Sections 1 or 2 of this Act has occurred shall be determined according to the burden of proof used in other civil actions for similar relief.
- Upon prevailing in such civil action, the plaintiff may recover:

    o   Both special and general damages, including damages for emotional distress;
    o   Punitive damages; and/or
    o   Reasonable attorney fees and costs.

- Notwithstanding any other provision of the law to the contrary, the parent(s) or legal guardian(s) of any unemancipated minor shall be liable for any judgment rendered against such minor under this Section.

4   Bias Crime Reporting and Training

- The state police or other appropriate state law enforcement agency shall establish and maintain a central repository for the collection and analysis of information regarding Bias-Motivated Crimes as defined in Section 2. Upon establishing such a repository, the state police shall develop a procedure to monitor, record, classify and analyze information relating to crimes apparently directed against individuals or groups, or their property, by reason of their actual or perceived race, color, religion, national origin, sexual orientation or gender. The state police shall submit its procedure to the appropriate committee of the state legislature for approval.
- All local law enforcement agencies shall report monthly to the state police concerning such offenses in such form and in such manner as prescribed by rules and regulations adopted by state police. The state police must summarize and analyze the information received and file an annual report with the governor and the appropriate committee of the state legislature.

(continued)

(continued)

- Any information, records and statistics collected in accordance with this subsection shall be available for use by any local law enforcement agency, unit of local government, or state agency, to the extent that such information is reasonably necessary or useful to such agency in carrying out the duties imposed upon it by law. Dissemination of such information shall be subject to all confidentiality requirements otherwise imposed by law.
- The state police shall provide training for police officers in identifying, responding to, and reporting all Bias-Motivated Crimes.

(Source: ADL)

Since the passage of the HCSA in 1990, nearly every state, with the exceptions of Wyoming, Georgia, Arkansas, South Carolina, and Indiana, has some legislation aimed at punishing hate-motivated behavior. Wyoming does have laws that are more in keeping with criminal civil rights laws, which prohibit discrimination— Wyo. Stat. paragraph 6-9-102 states, "No person shall be denied the right to life, liberty, pursuit of happiness or the necessities of life because of race, color, sex, creed or national origin." What also increased state responses to hate-motivated crime were several high profile crimes that occurred in the late 1980s through the 1990s that brought national attention to the ugly nature of hate crimes. In 1989, Black teenager Yusef Hawkins was killed in a racially motivated shooting in Bensonhurst, New York, a predominately White community. Both James Byrd Jr, and Matthew Shepard were brutally murdered in 1998, in different areas of the country, due to their race and sexual orientation, respectively. All three of these deaths triggered public outrage; each brought public demonstrations and marches that vowed to bring pressure to legislatures to pass laws to stem these types of tragic crimes.

How do hate crime laws differ from federal civil rights laws?

Rev. Henry Harris, reported that . . . he and . . . his family watched for 35 minutes as white diners . . . who arrived after him were escorted to tables at a Cracker Barrel restaurant in Arkansas. He and his family wound up in the smoking section with other African-American patrons . . .

(*USA Today*, 2010)

After investigating multiple similar complaints, the US Justice Department filed a lawsuit against Cracker Barrel. Its complaint alleges that Cracker Barrel violated Title II of the Civil Rights Act of 1964 by engaging in a pattern or practice of discrimination against African-American customers and prospective customers on the basis of their race or color:

Cracker Barrel segregated customers by race; allowed white servers to refuse to wait on African-American customers; and seated or served white customers before seating or serving similarly situated African-American customers. The lawsuit further alleged that, in many cases, managers directed, participated or acquiesced in those practices.

(*USA Today*, 2010)

What is alleged to have happened to Rev. Harris and other Black families illustrates a violation of federally protected civil rights. The Civil Rights Act Title II states:

> SEC. 201. (a) All persons shall be entitled to the full and equal enjoyment of the goods, services, facilities, and privileges, advantages, and accommodations of any place of public accommodation, as defined in this section, without discrimination or segregation on the ground of race, color, religion, or national origin.

Public accommodations include, but are not limited to, hotels, inns, movie theaters and restaurants—such as the Cracker Barrel restaurant whereas, the type of actions criminalized by state and local hate crime laws are represented by acts like the following reported by the SPLC:

> Ronald Allen Bramlett, a 65-year-old white man, was charged with felony aggravated assault, criminal threats and an enhancement of an alleged hate crime for allegedly calling a Black teenager racial slurs and threatening him with a knife.
> (SPLC, 2010)

These two examples help us to understand similarities and differences in acts that violate federal civil rights laws and those that violate state hate crime laws as well as the intent of both sets of laws. Both civil rights and hate crime laws: (1) seek to inhibit discriminatory acts that are motivated by race, religion, national origin and ethnicity; (2) seek to protect the constitutionally protected rights of citizens; (3) provide specific sanctions for behaviors that violate these laws; and (4) identify the discriminatory aspect of the action as a central component of this prohibition. There are at least three general differences between these laws. First, federal civil rights acts are only applicable when there is a bias motivation to interfere with an individual engaging in activities that are constitutionally protected (using public accommodations or places of entertainment, seeking employment, or using a facility of interstate commerce (trains, buses). Federal civil rights laws protect victims targeted due to a status condition and who are participating in a federally protected activity. Second, hate crime statutes address the targeting of individuals because of their race, ethnicity, and so on, *regardless* of the victim's activity. These laws protect victims targeted because of their group membership. Finally, federal civil rights laws are handled by federal prosecutors in federal courts, whereas state and local hate crime laws are administered by the local district attorney and state or lower level courts.

Hate speech is not hate crime

Many may find hateful speech to be repugnant and distressing, but such speech is not a crime in the United States. It is often protected by the Constitution despite the intent of the speaker to wound and denigrate the individual and/or group the speech is directed against. The Framers of the Constitution held that the right to free speech is necessary for a free society and therefore cannot be interfered with by government. The First Amendment reads, in part, "Congress shall make no law . . . abridging the freedom of speech." Nevertheless, the Constitution does allow some restrictions on speech under certain circumstances. To illustrate this point, Justice Holmes wrote, "The most stringent protection of free speech would not protect a man in falsely shouting fire in a theater and causing a panic" (*Schenck v. United States*, 249 U.S. 47, 39 S. Ct. 247, 63 L. Ed. 470 [1919]). Expressions that under certain circumstances may trigger, facilitate, or encourage harmful acts are less likely to receive First Amendment protections.

Example of protected hate speech

White Supremacists March in Jena:

> Klansmen and white nationalists brandished nooses and chanted "If it ain't white, it ain't right" during a racist march and rally in Jena, La., organized by the Nationalist Movement on Martin Luther King Jr. Day.

(SPLC, 2008)

Matsuda (1993, 36), define hate speech as speech that (1) has a message of racial inferiority, (2) is directed against a member of a historically oppressed group, and (3) is persecutory, hateful, and degrading. While hate speech is often in the form of verbal communication directed toward a target or expressed in a public forum during a hate rally, there are other forms of speech less recognized. Symbolic speech is nonverbal expression that conveys an idea. In the world of racialists and White supremacists, nonverbal expressions include the wearing of symbols such as Nazi regalia like swastikas, the iron cross or lightning bolts. Even cross burning may be considered protected speech but other times, it would not. For example, *Virginia v. Black*, 538 U.S. 343, 123 S. Ct.1536. 155 L. Ed.2d 535 (2003) involved a cross burning aimed at terrorizing an African-American family. A Virginia criminal statute had outlawed cross burning "on the property of another, a highway or other public place . . . with the intent of intimidating any person or group." The court upheld the statute and emphasized that the First Amendment would protect *some* types of cross burnings, such as those done at political rallies. However, when the cross burning targeted individuals for the purposes of criminal intimidation, the First Amendment would not be triggered (Cornell University Law School).

Despite the differences between hate speech and hate crime, hate speech may be interpreted by law enforcement as an indicator of a suspected hate crime. For example, an assault and battery may be identified as bias motivated if words or other forms of expression used by the assailant communicate hate or animus for the group represented by the victim." Frederick Lawrence offers one of the clearest explanations of the difference between hateful but protected speech and hate crime:

> The basic distinction . . . lies in the underlying motivation of the actor . . . racist speech is expression, a form of behavior that, however offensive, is protected . . . in our legal system. Speech advocating racial superiority is . . . the expression of an opinion. Burning a cross on the lawn of a Black family, [a form of expression] bias aside, is still at least trespass . . . Free expression protects the right to express offensive views but not the right to behave criminally. Speech that is intended to frighten someone . . . is a verbal assault that may be punished. Bias-targeted behavior that is intended to create fear in its targeted victim is a bias crime, whether the behavior is primarily verbal or physical. . . . Racially targeted behavior that vents the actor's racism . . . constitutes racist speech that is protected by the First Amendment.
>
> (Lawrence, 1999, 83)

While it is true that hate speech is generally protected by the First Amendment, it is also true that these are socially damaging expressions with the potential to seed and strengthen bigoted notions in others. Moreover, the use of the Internet, by racialists and other extremists, to spread hate-filled ideologies exponentially increases the potential social harm. However, the use of the Internet by hate groups and like-minded individuals once again is protected by the First Amendment. But using the Internet to directly threaten a targeted individual or organization is criminal and is not protected speech. Law enforcement officers and prosecutors must be careful in their determination of whether a hate crime has occurred, as opposed to an incident of protected hate speech (Bell, 2002).

A hate incident is not a hate crime

There are acts that occur which are clearly motivated by prejudice or hatred, but they are not illegal. For example, the *Pittsburgh Tribune Review* reported that in January 2010 a student at a junior high school in Pittsburgh, Pennsylvania, wore a mask depicting Barack Obama to a school basketball game and carried an empty bucket of Kentucky Fried Chicken. Although the student was removed from the gymnasium and disciplined by school officials, this act is not considered a hate crime (*Pittsburgh Tribune Review*, January 19, 2010, *Race Relations Newsletter*, dtd. January 19, 2010). Likewise, racist pamphlets were found in several locations in and around Hayden, Idaho. The hate literature was left on lawns or placed at public gathering spots (*Coeur d'Alene Press*, January 19, 2010, *Race Relations Newsletter*, dtd. January 19, 2010). Unless this activity violated a littering or trespassing ordinance, it is not a hate crime. Both of these incidents describe bigoted behaviors that are repugnant and offensive—but they are not illegal. As mentioned earlier, a hate crime must involve a criminal offense (for example, assault, malicious damage) that is motivated by bias.

The term "hate crime" is appropriate

According to the US Department of Justice, the term "hate crime" was coined by journalists and DOJ staff during the preparation of the bill to propose the Hate Crimes Statistics Act, which was subsequently incorporated in the statutory language. Many began to adopt the expression and use it to refer to this crime category. More recently, there have been those who assert that the term is inaccurate and that the phrase "bias crime" is perhaps more appropriate (Chakraborti & Garland, 2009; Jacobs & Potter, 1998). They reason that the term "hate crime" overreaches and makes assumptions about the motives of the perpetrator. The term suggests that for such a crime to occur, the perpetrator's actions must be driven by detestation and loathing of what the victim represents. Moreover, this perspective observes that it is not hatred but prejudice toward the victim *because of* his or her membership in a group for which the perpetrator feels contempt (Ehrlich, 1992; Lawrence, 1999; Hall, 2005). This understanding is represented in the following statement offered by the Prejudice Institute (Ehrlich, paragraph 4):

> In actual fact, "hate" as a strong, negative emotional response is not necessarily involved. Many ethnoviolent incidents are committed impulsively, or as acts of conformity, or as calculated acts of intimidation designed to achieve specific ends of the perpetrator.

However, even with the recognition that not all hate crime perpetrators are driven by intense hatred, it is nevertheless arguable that the term "hate crime" *is* appropriate and may be a more accurate term with respect to the experiences of the *victims* of such attacks. Consider the nature of the victims' experiences in the following accounts of alleged hate crime acts:

- Eric Patten was sentenced to 30 days in jail for punching and pushing two women after yelling anti-gay epithets at them in May (SPLC, 2009b).

- Darrel James Allen, a 23-year-old Black man, was charged with a hate-crime battery causing injury, robbery, assault and violation of civil rights for yelling racial slurs and punching a Latino man unconscious (SPLC, 2009c).
- Swastikas and the letters "KKK" were carved into a Black woman's car door and scrawled on her cubicle at work (SPLC, 2009d).
- Racial taunts were directed at African-American players on an opposing team during a basketball game at a high school in Anaheim, California. An audio recording of the game confirms that when a Black player touched the ball, members of the crowd made monkey noises (Orange County Register, January 17, 2009, *The Race Relations Reporter. Weekly Bulletin.* January 17, 2009).
- A Black professor at Fort Lewis College in Durango, Colorado, received a note in his office mailbox that contained a swastika. Later, the door to his office was set on fire. Police believe the incidents may be related (*Durango Herald*, October 4, 2008, *The Race Relations Reporter. Weekly Bulletin.* October 15, 2008).

Taking into account the nature of these acts and their real and symbolic meanings, one may question whether the term "bias crime" characterizes them sufficiently from the *victim's standpoint.* The deeply personal nature of these attacks all say to the victim that because of what you are, you are not entitled to exercise your right to liberty, to expect personal safety and security, nor to assume the privileges of citizenship (Parks & Jones, 2008). Whether the attacker is fully conscious of the destructive nature of his or her actions or has the requisite scorn that would qualify as "hatred" from a social psychology point of view, *the end result is the same.* It is akin to criminals who choose to use either a real or fake gun during the commission of a crime. Some of them have the intention to kill the victim, while others may wish only to intimidate the victim. But in the end, the victims are all terrified and believe that their lives may be coming to an end.

To be selected for victimization without provocation (merely because of what you represent to the attacker) certainly must have the impact of *being hated.* Those who investigate sexual violence usually identify rape as rape. Although the perpetrator's intent may be to dominate and exercise power over the victim, these crimes are not referred to as first or second degree *domination*; they are called what they are, correctly referencing the victim's experience of rape. Hate is what the victim experiences at the hands of the perpetrator and therefore "hate crime" may be a more fitting term than "bias crime." Ehrlich (1992, 5) acknowledges that the term "bias crime" possesses an "antiseptic quality." This quality may possibly diminish how victimization is viewed by utilizing "bias crime," a term that is more clinical and dispassionate than "hate crime," which is more reflective of the harm caused.

Public attitudes toward hate crimes and hate crime laws

Behaviors deemed threatening to the public welfare are often proscribed by law. Although the intent of these laws is to protect the public, sometimes public sentiment is mixed toward the crime, the law and/or the punishment it requires. Some view hate crime legislation as unnecessary, even counterproductive (Jacobs & Potter, 1998). Still, some studies show that there is public support for the existence of these laws, particularly when the victims of these crimes belong to historically oppressed groups (Steen & Cohen, 2004). There is also evidence that suggests that attitudes toward hate crime laws are influenced by personally held biases. For example those with anti-Jewish or anti-homosexual sentiments are less supportive of hate crime laws (Johnson & Byers, 2003; Lyons, 2006). This literature, which is not extensive, indicates that attitudes toward majority and minority social groups are predictive of support toward hate crime legislation.

Newspaper coverage and portrayals of hate crime incidents may also influence the public's perception. Since hate crimes are largely about efforts to control social place and order, newspapers may indirectly impact this aim depending on whether and how they cover these incidents. In other words, to the extent that the media gives insufficient attention to these crimes, the public may intuit that they hold less importance. Gross and Goldman (2003) compared the coverage of mainstream newspapers of anti-gay hate crime with that of a gay newspaper. While they found more coverage of anti-gay hate crimes in the gay newspaper, they also found that some mainstream papers presented these incidents in a manner similar to the gay newspaper. However, a more thorough and systematic examination of the coverage of hate crimes by major newspapers would contribute significantly to this under-researched area. Results could better explain whether and how media portrayals shape public opinion on hate crime in a more definitive way.

About hate crime statistics

Prior to the passage of the HCSA, there were very few jurisdictions that quantified bias or hate-motivated crimes. The Boston Police Department was the first to document racially motivated crimes, having done so since 1978 (Lawrence, 1999). It is also the first police department to establish a Community Disorders Unit and is recognized for its early commitment to educate and train officers and others about this emerging crime problem (Levin & McDevitt, 1993; Levin & McDevitt, 2002). Other early efforts to track hate crimes were undertaken by advocacy groups such as the Anti-Defamation League and the Southern Poverty Law Center. Notwithstanding these attempts, determining hate crime prevalence prior to 1990 is elusive due to the absence of a standardized data collection system during that time.

Official hate crime data primarily come from two sources, the FBI's Uniform Crime Reporting Program (UCR) and the National Crime Victimization Survey

(NCVS), which is administered by the Bureau of Justice Statistics. These data have different collection points. UCR hate crime data is based on crime statistics reported by state and local law enforcement agencies; whereas NCVS is based on hate crime victimization experiences reported in surveyed households. The limitations of both data sources are well known. Although UCR reflects crimes reported to police, it does not capture unreported crimes. For a variety of reasons, some hate crime victims do not contact police and report crimes. Generally speaking, racial minority communities and homosexuals historically have had strained relationships with law enforcement and see police as potentially unresponsive to their victimization. Or worse, they believe that police would exacerbate their distress with apathetic and discourteous treatment. In addition, although the vast majority of police departments participate in the UCR, there is not yet 100 percent participation. According to the Leadership Conference on Civil Rights Education Fund (LCCREF), "at least 21 agencies in cities with populations between 100,000 and 250,000, did not participate in the FBI data collection effort in 2007" (2009, 7). Also, since hate crime statutes and reporting protocols vary across jurisdictions, what is reported will contain vagaries and will not reflect a consensus or a standardized recognition of hate crime. Thus a crime that occurs in Illinois may be statutorily defined, but the same act in Georgia may not be and therefore would not be recorded by police as a hate crime. Thus the UCR only represents a fraction of the hate crimes that have occurred (see Table 1.1).

The NCVS was developed to address non-reporting problems by going directly to people and interviewing them regarding their crime victimization experiences. Even though this provides an excellent opportunity to capture information about unreported hate crimes, the NCVS has other inherent problems. For example, individuals may inaccurately recall an experience, unconsciously add features to the event or fail to remember significant aspects. Understanding bias motives is challenging even for trained law enforcement personnel, and therefore it may be an even larger hurdle for ordinary citizens. NCVS interviewees are asked to identify the type of bias they believed motivated their attack. Once again, misperceptions or mistaken interpretations could impede accurate accounts even with interviewees offering indicators that they believe corroborate their perceptions. Moreover, there may not be a clear understanding of the difference between a hate crime and a hate incident to the interviewee, and what is described may only be an embellished incident. Finally, there may be hesitancy in discussing a hate crime experience to NCVS interviewers, particularly if a gay male, lesbian woman or transgendered victim has not made their sexual orientation or gender identity public.

Now that we understand the differences between UCR and NCVS as sources of official crime statistics, as well as their respective limitations, how do these sources report hate crime prevalence? The average yearly number of hate crimes reported by the UCR for years 2000–5 is 7,926. But the NCVS reports that the average number, for the time period of July 2000 through to December 2003 (a shorter time period), is 191,000 (Bureau of Justice Statistics, 2005).

This considerable difference suggests that NCVS *may* be capturing as much as 24 times the number of hate crimes than is reflected in UCR reports. These realities make clear that a single source of national data cannot be viewed as sufficient to gauge the true scope of hate crime prevalence.

The National Incident Based Reporting System (NIBRS) is an additional government source of information on reported hate crimes. NIBRS collects more detailed information on reported crime events (up to 53 data elements recorded) and thus has the capacity to provide more in depth information (see Table 1.2). Beyond information describing the base crime, bias or hate motive, victim and perpetrator attributes, NIBRS includes information regarding the location of the crime and the relationship between the victim and the perpetrator, time of day of the incident, and victimization patterns. More importantly, it reports incident-specific factors and thus provides context-rich data that goes beyond the aggregate data of the UCR.

Examples from the data sources

Table 1.1 Hate crimes statistics 2008: incidents, offenses, victims, and known offenders by bias motivation

Bias motivation	Incidents	Offenses	Victims[1]	Known offenders[2]
Total	**7,783**	**9,168**	**9,691**	**6,927**
Single-bias incidents	**7,780**	**9,160**	**9,683**	**6,921**
Race:	**3,992**	**4,704**	**4,934**	**3,723**
Anti-White	716	812	829	811
Anti-Black	2,876	3,413	3,596	2,596

Source: http://www.fbi.gov/ucr/hc2008/data/table_01.html. Retrieved October 2, 2010

Notes:
1 The term *victim* may refer to a person, business, institution, or society as a whole.
2 The term *known offender* does not imply that the identity of the suspect is known, but only that an attribute of the suspect has been identified, which distinguishes him/her from an unknown offender.

NCVS data—2005

- Most hate crimes described by victims accompanied violent crimes—a rape or other sexual assault, robbery, or assault (84 percent). The remaining 16 percent were associated with property crimes—burglary or theft.
- Victims reported a major violent crime—a rape, robbery, or an assault in which a victim was injured or threatened with a weapon—in a third of hate incidents.
- In about half of hate crimes, the victim was threatened verbally or assaulted without either a weapon or an injury being involved.

(Source: BJS, 2005)

Table 1.2 NIBRS data (1995–2000): number of incidents by location and bias motivation

	Race	Religion	Ethnicity	Sexual orientation	Disability	Unknown	Total
Air/Bus/Train terminal	17	3	3	5	1		29
Bank/Savings and loan	9	1	1	1			12
Bar/Nightclub	79	4	27	36	1		147
Church/ Synagogue/ Temple	14	116	2	4		1	137
Commercial/ Office building	152	56	18	15			241
Construction site	17	4	3	2			26
Convenience store	58	7	14	6	1		86
Department/ Discount store	50	6	6	7			69
Drug store/Drs office/Hospital	25	2	4	4	2		37
Field/Woods	42	10	8	5		2	67
Government/ Public building	69	18	9	11			107
Grocery/ Supermarket	34	5	11	9			59
Highway/Road/ Alley	739	61	134	100	6		1,040
Hotel/Motel/etc.	46	2	8	5			61
Jail/Prison	62	2	3	4			71
Lake/Waterway	9	1	3	1	1		15
Liquor store	3		2	1			6
Parking lot/ Garage	300	53	64	62	6		485
Rental stor. facil.	6	4	1	7			18
Residence/home	1,131	215	207	305	23	3	1,884
Restaurant	90	6	14	17			127
School/College	382	110	66	107	4	3	672
Service/Gas station	44	11	12	8	1		76
Specialty store (TV, Fur, etc.)	44	12	7	4		2	69
Other/unknown	218	38	31	26	1		314
TOTAL	3,640	747	658	752	47	11	5,855

Source: www.as.wvu.edu/~jnolan/analysis.html (Accessed February 10, 2010)
Note: Unit of count—Incident

Other sources of information on hate crime incidence

A number of agencies and organizations publish statistics on hate crimes. Mandated by the Jeanne Clery Act of 1990 (*Clery Disclosure of Campus Security Policy and Campus Crime Statistics Act)*, the Department of Education monitors the compliance of colleges and universities that are required to publish information on crime data. These data also includes hate crimes (US Department of Education, 1998). Founded in 1913, the early focus of the Anti-Defamation League (ADL) was on exposing anti-Semitism and to advocate for the fair treatment of Jewish people. Today the ADL addresses bigotry and intolerance in general and supports civil rights for all people. The organization audits and publishes yearly anti-Semitic incidents in the United States. Co-founded in 1971 by Morris Dees and Joe Levin, the Southern Poverty Law Center (SPLC) remains focused on advocating for minorities and the poor to ensure that civil rights laws would be actualized. Combining the tools of education and the courts, the SPLC brings civil suits against hate crime perpetrators and provides educators and others resources on teaching bridge building and innovative diversity initiatives. The SPLC also publishes information on hate incidents and hate crimes, *For the Record*, through the *Intelligence Report* publication. Similar efforts were made by *The Journal of Blacks in Higher Education*'s, *The Race Relations Reporter. The Reporter*, which is no longer available, was a weekly disseminated electronic newsletter that provided a variety of articles and commentary primarily on education policies and court decisions that impact African-American and other racial groups. It also chronicled racial incidents in *Recent Racial Incidents in the United States*, which listed brief summaries of racial incidents reported in US newspapers.

Distinct from other victim advocacy organizations, the National Coalition of Anti-Violence Programs (NCAVP) is committed to addressing violence against sexual minorities and HIV-affected persons even when the violence is perpetrated by members of those communities. Similar to the ADL, the NCAVP provides a number of informational resources to assist communities responding to these incidents. It also annually publishes a report on anti-LGBTQ violence (see www.avp. org). One of the more recent advocacy groups, the Asian American Justice Center, which was founded in 1991, monitors anti-Asian trends in the USA and offers assistance in combating these behaviors and promotes civil rights for all groups. It publishes comprehensive reports of anti-Asian incidents (see 2002_Audit of Violence Against Asian Pacific Americans.pdf). While the efforts of these organizations may contribute to the further understanding of prevalence, none demonstrate a well-vetted methodology to establish good baseline data that would enable comparative or other analyses.

Where hate crimes occur

Descriptive data from a number of sources provide information on when and where hate crimes have occurred. NIBRS reports the following:

- 32 percent of all hate crimes reported in NIBRS 1997–1999 occurred in a residence.
- 28 percent in an open space such as parking garages, parking lots or streets.
- 19 percent in a commercial/retail business or public building.
- 12 percent in a school or college.
- 30 percent or more of racial, ethnic, and disability-motivated incidents occurred in an open space.
- Of sexually motivated incidents, 41 percent occurred at a residence, 23 percent in an open space, 16 percent at a school or college and 15 percent at a commercial/retail business or public building.
- One-third of religious-motivated incidents occurred at an educational or religious institution.
- Weapons were reported to have been used in 18 percent of all violent hate crimes.
- Victims age 17 or younger were most likely to be victimized during the day, as nearly two-thirds of these incidents occurred between 7 a.m. and 6 p.m., with a peak between 2 p.m. and 4 p.m.
- Violent hate crimes involving victims age 18 to 24 were more likely to occur in the late evening, between 10 p.m. and 1 a.m., with a peak around midnight.

(BJS, 2001, 6)

These data mostly show that as a crime category, hate crimes are not very dissimilar from conventional crime events when it comes to place and time factors (Victims of Crime). In particular, children and younger teenagers or often victimized between 2 p.m. and 4 p.m., when adult supervision is most likely to be lacking (after school and before parents arrive home from work). However, young adults (aged 18–24) are more likely to be targeted during late evening.

Christopher Lyons (2007) examined the structural conditions of communities and the likelihood of racially motivated hate crimes to occur in them and reported instructive conclusions. In testing social disorganization theory, resource competition theories and the defended community perspective, Lyons found that anti-Black motivated incidents were more likely to happen in organized communities with established informal social control mechanisms in place, and less likely in deteriorating communities undergoing economic strain and uncertainty. His findings support the historical observation of coordinated resistance to Blacks attempting to integrate White communities. In socially organized and economically sound White communities, resources are marshalled and used to message to Blacks that they are unwelcome in that area. Thus, hate crimes carried out to defend the community against the threat of *intruding* Blacks would happen in middle-class, upper-class, and even affluent White neighborhoods. A related observation is made by Ed Dunbar (2004) who examined the patterns of hate crime in Los Angeles. Dunbar found that African-Americans and persons of Asian-Pacific descent were more likely to be victimized by hate crime while in their own neighborhoods. However, despite the fact that targeting occurred in the communities in which they resided, these victims were also living in areas where Blacks and Asians were less than 20 percent of the population. In such environments, they were very visible and therefore more easily targeted.

Hate crime settings—the workplace and the campus

In the preceding section we reviewed elements of where hate crimes occur, including time and place, location, and the reality of the neighborhood as a relevant context for hate crime occurrence. We now turn to two additional settings, the workplace and the college campus to gain a sense of how and why hate crimes occur in these environments.

The workplace setting

What is meant by hate crime at the workplace? Does this simply refer to victims being targeted by White supremacists while at work or because they do work? Do such acts require that the perpetrators be employees at the same workplace? Or could it only reflect the place at which the crime occurs—that the defining element is that the victim is at work or leaving the workplace at the time of the attack? The US Department of Labor's Occupational Safety and Health Administration (OSHA) defines workplace violence as: "violence or the threat of violence against workers. It can occur at or outside the workplace and can range from threats and verbal abuse to physical assaults and homicide."

This definition suggests that workplace violence is merely indicative of where the crime occurs. It is not required to mean that the crime occurs *because of* the workplace. However the US Department of Agriculture offers a more specified definition

> A number of different actions in the work environment can trigger or cause workplace violence. It may even be the result of non-work-related situations such as domestic violence or "road rage." Workplace violence can be inflicted by an abusive employee, manager, supervisor, co-worker, customer, family member, or even a stranger.

There may be a greater connection, however, between the place of employment, the victim, and the perpetrator in hate crimes. As mentioned earlier, hate crime is frequently about efforts to control social place, both real and symbolic. Perhaps for some perpetrators, contending with a new female, Muslim, or homosexual supervisor is too much to tolerate. Presently, too little is known about hate crime in the workplace. It is another area that requires systematic and sustained examination. The following two examples illustrate hate crimes that occurred in, around, or because of the workplace.

The Alfred P. Murrah Federal Building in Oklahoma City, Oklahoma housed over 500 employees. It was home to various federal offices including the Federal Bureau of Investigation (FBI), the Bureau of Alcohol, Tobacco, and Firearms (ATF), the Drug Enforcement Administration (DEA), the Social Security Administration and others, as well as a day care center. The building and its employees was targeted by Timothy McVeigh, who set off a strategically placed truck bomb killing 168 individuals, 19 of which were children, on April 19, 1995. Clearly an act of domestic terrorism, this act arguably is also an example of workplace hate crime. McVeigh was strongly motivated by animus towards the US federal government and all that it symbolized to a mindset immersed in anti-government, militia, and White supremacist ideologies (Levitas, 2002). He attacked federal employees due to his hatred of the government and its representatives. It appears that he attacked them in, around, and certainly because of the workplace and what it represented to him.

On July 28, 2006, the Jewish Federation of Greater Seattle building was the scene of a workplace hate crime in Seattle, Washington. Naveed Afzal Haq entered the building armed with semi-automatic handguns. He shot six people, killing one because of his hatred for Israel and Jews. Among the multiple felonies charged was malicious harassment, the state's felony charge for hate crime (*The Seattle Times*, 2006). In this instance, the perpetrator selected this work site because of what it represented and his focus on targeting Jews.

Both of these events are examples of the most violent workplace hate crimes; other workplace incidents are less severe. "SANFORD, NORTH CAROLINA: The owner of a grocery store in Sanford, North Carolina, made racial comments and threatened to kill a Black couple if they did not leave the store. The proprietor reportedly said, "You niggers are trespassing. Those people only come in a store to steal." The store owner was arrested and charged with ethnic intimidation (*The Race Relations Reporter*, December 23, 2009). In 2009, 168 Black and Hispanic employees of Colorado's Albertson Supermarket chain were awarded nearly $9 million dollars in a class action lawsuit filed by the Equal Employment Opportunity Commission. The lawsuit described reprehensible incidents of racial harassment, taunting, unequal treatment and other unconscionable acts. Racist graffiti was commonplace; drawings depicting Blacks lynched; hanging stuffed animal monkeys were routinely placed in the work spaces; and the word nigger was scrawled on walls. Hispanics were directly referred to as 'border jumpers' and subjected to poor treatment. A Black male employee suffered an on the job injury, his leg crushed by a piece of equipment. He was left in that condition for 30 minutes on the floor and was told that's what he deserved for being Black (7News Denver). These bias motivated acts occurred in or around the workplace but are illustrative of the more typical hostile acts that occasionally take place in these settings.

The college and university campus setting

Institutions of higher education generally seek to empower students; to help them realize their potential and to equip them with the skill sets necessary for success in their chosen fields. These are not environments where one would expect to see crimes motivated by bigotry and hatred. However, as indicated earlier, these settings are not immune. In fact, the US Department of Justice has brought civil rights actions against non-students, former students and current students who have committed hate crimes against other students. The following cases reported by the Center for the Prevention of Hate Violence (2001) illustrate the nature of these crimes on US campuses:

> **United States v. Samar.** James Samar, a college student, was indicted on three counts of using threats of force to interfere with the federally protected rights of three students attending a small Massachusetts college. Samar used anti-Semitic slurs, threatened two fellow students, and threatened to kill one fellow student. In addition, he delivered photographs of holocaust victims to one student and stated, among other things, that the photographs were "a reminder of what happened to your relatives because they too made a mockery of Christianity." Samar entered a plea agreement (3).

> **United States v. Little.** The defendant, Robert Allen Little, was charged with igniting a homemade pipe bomb in the dorm room of two African-American students on a campus in Utah. The bomb caused extensive damage to the building and destroyed the belongings of both students. After the bombing, Little returned to the dorm and left a threatening and racist note on the door of another African-American student. Little was sentenced to 12 years in prison, fined $12,000, and ordered to pay restitution (4).

These examples are representative of the most serious and rarest campus hate crimes. More common are incidents that do not rise to the level of a crime and are at best, acts of prejudice. The Department of Justice describes such acts as mostly "degrading language and slurs by . . . students directed toward people of color, women, homosexuals, and Jews" (US Department of Justice, 2001, 6).

Are hate crimes really distinctive crimes?

In what ways might hate crimes be considered different from conventional crimes? *In the perpetrator's intent.* Some perpetrators commit hate crimes without possessing a well-formed ideology that fuels these actions. Rather, they seek peer approval, or thrill and exhilaration from harassing and attacking others viewed as weak and vulnerable (Levin & McDevitt, 2002). However, other perpetrators have a focused intent, even an agenda to intimidate, threaten, and ultimately control the individual victim, and to message the members of the victim's community (Hamm, 1994; Miethe & McCorkle, 1998). For these perpetrators, their crimes are committed in order to conform the social landscape to that which subordinates racial, sexual, ethnic, religious, and other minority communities while ensuring the "superiority" of White heterosexual males (Perry, 2001). Ultimately, hate crimes seek to compromise the civil liberties of targeted victim groups. This aim is unlike traditional crime.

In the nature of its impact on the victim. Garcia & McDevitt (1999), Herek, et al. (2002), McDevitt, et al. (2001) and others have reported on the perceived seriousness of hate crime victimization and related issues according to victims. Much of the literature underscores the fact that the trauma experienced, both physical and psychological, is more deleterious than that suffered by victims of comparable non-hate crime acts.

In the nature of its impact on the victim's community. The repercussions of hate crime attacks extend well beyond that of the immediate victim. The victim's community becomes more aware that safety is less sure as persons who share their skin color, sexual orientation, ethnicity, religion, or disability are targeted. Moreover, if members of the victim's community begin to alter their habits and not venture into certain locations or they begin to travel in groups for safety, moving quickly through areas where they now feel less welcomed, then a major concession has occurred and the perpetrator has won a battle. These communities have become more wary, more distrustful, and more isolated.

Its historical relevance. Hate crimes further distinguish themselves in two important areas: (1) the historical continuity of hate crime victimization of racial minorities, Jews, Hispanics, and homosexuals; and (2) the complicity of main-stream institutions and cultural practices in the victimization of these groups (Petrosino, 1999; Boeckmann & Turpin-Petrosino, 2002). Given these factors, the harm factor in hate crimes is evidently distinctive from non-bias crimes.

As a result of these four distinguishing characteristics, hate crimes may possess qualities that well justify their criminalization and punishment as a unique category of crime.

Chapter summary points

- Hate crimes are offenses committed due to the perpetrator's prejudice against a particular group represented by the victim. The most common categories of prejudice include ethnicity, race, national origin, religion, sexual orientation, disability, or gender. Hate crimes are comprised of two components, (1) the predicate or base offense, and (2) the perpetrator's prejudice against the group represented by the victim.
- While a victim may hold *multiple* memberships to two or more targeted groups, it is the perpetrator's *perception* of the victim that determines the hate motive.
- The majority of hate crime acts are aimed at individuals from social groups that have been historically subjected to institutionalized discriminatory treatment.
- Hate crime laws were enacted to address a disturbing increase in hate-motivated criminal acts during the 1980s in the United States.
- There are several differences between federal civil rights laws and hate crimes statutes. Essentially, federal civil rights laws are applicable when there is interference with an individual engaging in constitutionally protected activities; whereas hate crime statutes address the harming of individuals because of their race, ethnicity, and so on, *regardless* of the victim's activity. Federal civil rights laws are handled by federal prosecutors in federal courts, whereas state and local hate crime laws are administered by the local district attorney and state level or lower courts.
- Hate speech is generally protected by the First Amendment. However, speech that directly threatens a targeted individual or organization is criminal and is not protected speech.
- There are acts that are clearly motivated by prejudice, even hatred, but they are not illegal. A hate crime must involve a criminal offense (for example, assault, malicious damage) that is motivated by bias.

- The term "hate crime" is appropriate. The deeply personal nature of these attacks and the intense disregard of the victim's humanity all say to the victim that they are the victim of intense animus or hatred and not simply bias.
- National hate crime data primarily come from two sources, Uniform Crime Reports (UCR) and the National Crime Victimization Survey (NCVS). There are limitations in both data sources. The UCR reflects only reported crimes, and despite a high number of police agencies participating in the program, there is not yet 100 percent participation. The NCVS data is based on victimization surveys of a national sample of households. Limitations include the failure of interviewees to recall facts accurately (or at all) or confusion or misinterpretation of an event and the reluctance to divulge a victimization experience to an interviewer.
- Hate crimes are distinct from conventional crimes in the following areas: (1) the perpetrator's intent; (2) impact on the victim; (3) impact on the victim's community; and (4) historical relevance.

Case study 1.1 Citizens' band radio and hate crime

When is talk just talk and when is it a crime, especially a hate crime? The Ninth US Circuit Court of Appeals clarified that when it upheld the conviction of Bradley Smith whose words and actions constituted a hate crime. Smith, as well as the victim, Alfred Henderson were participants in the citizens' band (CB) radio culture of Modesto, California. But Smith used CB radio to threaten Henderson, an African-American and his family. Smith would routinely use racial slurs (N-word) and epithets aimed at Henderson; he also threatened to burn a cross on his property, throw Molotov cocktails on the property, sexually abuse his wife and then to lynch him by hanging. These threats persisted over two years and culminated with Smith again taunting and threatening harm to Henderson, his wife and the rest of his family, and that he and a number of Whites were going to come to his home to attack them. Henderson then called the police, and Smith and a group of other Whites did come to the house. Smith's motivation was to intimidate the Henderson family and encourage them to move out of the community. Eventually they did just that. Although the Stanislaus County prosecutor declined to pursue charges against Smith, federal prosecutors did. Smith was convicted and sentenced to six and a half years for civil rights violations.

(Source: www.sfgate.com/cgi-bin/article.cgi?f=/c/a/2010/
02/12/BAVI1C0T8B.DTL, Accessed February 14, 2010)

Discussion questions

1   Identify what elements in this action indicate that a hate crime had occurred.
2   Why didn't the First Amendment protect Smith's comments over the CB radio?
3   Do you agree that federal prosecutors should have filed charges, even when the county district attorney chose not to?

Bibliography

7News Denver. (n.d.). December 15, 2009. Albertsons Settles $8.9 Million Racial Discrimination Lawsuits. Available from www.thedenverchannel.com/news/albertsons-settles-8-9-million-racial-discrimination-lawsuits [Accessed March 5, 2015].

Anti-Defamation League (ADL). (n.d.). Available from www.adl.org/99hatecrime/text_legis.asp [Accessed March 29, 2010].

Barkun, M. (1994). *Religion and the Racist Right: The Origins of the Christian Identity Movement.* Chapel Hill, NC: The University of North Carolina Press.

Bell, J. (2002). *Policing Hatred: Law Enforcement, Civil Rights, and Hate Crime.* New York: New York University Press.

Bowling, B. (1993). Racial Harassment and the Process of Victimisation. *British Journal of Criminology,* 33(2), 231–50.

Brooklyn Daily Eagle (February 2, 2010). Available from www.brooklyneagle.com/categories/category.php?category_id=4&id=33379 [Accessed March 26, 2010].

Brooklyn Heights Blog (February 25, 2010). *Ivanov Gets 18 Years for Bombs, Hate Crimes.* Available from http://brooklynheightsblog.com/archives/16654 [Accessed January 8, 2014].

Bureau of Justice Statistics Special Report (BJS). (2001). Hate Crimes Reported in NIBRS 1997–1999. September 2001. NCJ 186765.

Bureau of Justice Statistics Special Report. (BJS). (2005). *Hate Crimes Reported by Victims and Police.* November 2005. NCJ 209911. Available from http://bjs.ojp.usdoj.gov/content/pub/pdf/hcrvp.pdf [Accessed October 2, 2010].

Center for the Prevention of Hate Violence, University of Southern Maine. (2001). Hate Crimes On Campus: The Problem and Efforts to Confront It. Bureau of Justice Assistance Monograph. Hate Crime Series #3. October. NCJ 187249.

Center for the Study of Hate and Extremism. (n.d.) Selected Hate Crime Laws in Various States: Alabama—Section 13A-5-13. Available from http://hatemonitor.csusb.edu/resources/hate_crime_law_A_L.htm [Accessed January 30, 2010].

Chakraborti, N. & Garland, J. (2009). *Hate Crime: Impact, Causes and Responses.* Los Angeles, CA: Sage.

Cornell University Law School. (n.d.). Legal Information Institute. Virginia v. Black. Available from www.law.cornell.edu/supremecourt/text/01-1107 [Accessed on March 5, 2015].

Dees, M. & Corcoran, J. (1996). *Gathering Storm. America's Militia Threat.* New York: HarperCollins Publishers.

Dinan, S. (2013). Feds Charge White Man with Hate Crime in First "knockout" Prosecution. *The Washington Times.* December 26. Available from www.washingtontimes.com [Accessed February 7, 2015].

Dunbar, E. (2004). Community Factors in Hate Crime Victimization. Paper presented at the 112th Annual Convention of the American Psychological Association in Honolulu.

Eagan, Jennifer. (2008). *City Leaders Condemn Alleged Hate Crime in Worcester.* Available from www.necn.com/pages/landing?blockID=136934&tagID=21150 [Accessed March 22, 2010].

Ehrlich, H. J (n.d.). Understanding Hate Crimes. The Prejudice Institute. Available from http://prejudiceinstitute.com/understandinghatecrimes.html [Accessed March 5, 2015].

Ehrlich, H. J. (1992). The Ecology of Anti-Gay Violence. In G. M. Herek & K. T. Berrill (eds.) *Hate Crimes: Confronting Violence Against Lesbians and Gay Men.* Newbury Park, CA: Sage Publications.

Garcia, L. & McDevitt, J. (1999). *The Psychological and Behavioral Effects of Bias and Nonbias Motivated Assault.* Washington, DC: US Department of Justice, National Institute of Justice.

Gerstenfeld, P. B. (2004). *Hate Crimes: Causes, Controls, and Controversies.* Thousand Oaks, CA: Sage Publications.

Gross, K. & Goldman, S. (2003). Framing Hate: A Comparison of Media Coverage of Anti-Gay Hate Crime in the Washington Post and Washington Blade. Paper presented at the annual meeting of the American Political Science Association. Philadelphia, PA.

Hall, N. (2005). *Hate Crime*. Portland, OR: Willan Publishing.

Hamm, M. S. (1994). *American Skinheads: The Criminology and Control of Hate Crime*. Westport, CT: Praeger Publishers.

Herek, G. M., Cogan, J. C., & Gillis, J. R. (2002). Victim Experiences in Hate Crimes Based on Sexual Orientation. *Journal of Social Issues,* 58(2), 319–39.

Jacobs, J. B. & Potter, K. (1998). *Hate Crimes: Criminal Law & Identity Politics.* New York: Oxford University Press.

Jenness, V. & Broad, K. (1997). *Hate Crimes: New Social Movements and the Politics of Violence.* New York: Aldine de Gruyter.

Johnson, S. D. & Byers, B. D. (2003). Attitudes Toward Hate Crime Laws. *Journal of Criminal Justice*, 31(3), 227–35.

Lawrence, F. M. (1999). *Punishing Hate: Bias Crimes under American Law*. Cambridge, MA: Harvard University Press.

Leadership Conference on Civil Rights Education Fund (LCCREF). (2009). Confronting the New Faces of Hate: Hate Crimes in America. Published by the Leadership Conference on Civil Rights Education Fund, Washington, DC.

Lee, M. A. (2000). *The Beast Reawakens: Fascism's Resurgence from Hitler's Spymasters to Today's Neo-Nazi Groups and Right-Wing Extremists*. New York: Routledge.

Levin, B. (1999). Hate Crimes: Worse by Definition. *Journal of Contemporary Criminal Justice*, 15(1), 6–21.

Levin, B. (2009). The Long Arc of Justice: Race, Violence, and the Emergence of Hate Crime Law. In B. Perry (ed.) *Hate Crimes: Understanding and Defining Hate Crime*, Vol. 1 (pp. 1–22). Westport, CT: Praeger.

Levin, J. & McDevitt, J. (1993). *Hate Crimes: The Rising Tide of Bigotry and Bloodshed*. New York: Plenum Press.

Levin, J. & McDevitt, J. (2002). *Hate Crimes Revisited: America's War on Those Who Are Different*. Boulder, CO: Westview Press.

Levitas, D. (2002). *The Terrorist Next Door: The Militia Movement and the Radical Right*. New York: St. Martin's Press.

Lyons, C. J. (2006). Stigma or Sympathy? Attributions of Fault to Hate Crime Victims and Offenders. *Social Psychology Quarterly*, 69(1), 39–59.

Lyons, C. (2007). Community (Dis)organization and Racially Motivated Violence. *American Journal of Sociology*, 113(3), 815–63.

Matsuda, M. J. (1993). Public Response to Racist Speech: Considering the Victim's Story. In M. J. Matsuda, C. R. Lawrence III, R. Delgado, and K.W. Crenshaw (pp. 17–51). *Words That Words: Critical Race Theory Assaultive Speech, and the First Amendment*. Boulder, CO: Westview.

McCorkle, R. C. & Miethe, T. D. (1998). The Political and Organizational Response to Gangs: An Examination of a Moral Panic in Nevada. *Justice Quarterly* 15, 41–64.

McDevitt, J., Balboni, J., Garcia, L., & Gu, J. (2001). Consequences for Victims: A Comparison of Bias and Non Bias Motivated Assaults. *American Behavioral Scientist*, 45(4), 697–713.

Nolan III, J.J., Menken, C., & McDevitt, J. (2005). NIBRS Hate Crimes 1995–2005, Juvenile Victims and Offenders. Washington, DC. Office of Juvenile Justice and Delinquency Prevention, US Department of Justice.

Office of the Attorney General. (July 2008). California's Department of Justice. Hate Crime in California 2007. Available from http://ag.ca.gov/cjsc/publications/hatecrimes/hc07/preface07.pdf [Accessed January 30, 2010].

Parks, G. S. & Jones, S. E. (2008). "Nigger": A Critical Race Realist Analysis of the N-Word Within Hate Crimes Law. *The Journal of Criminal Law and Criminology*, 98 (4), 1305–52.

Perry, B. (2001). *In the Name of Hate: Understanding Hate Crimes*. New York: Routledge.

Petrosino, C. (1999). Connecting the Past to the Future: Hate Crime in America. *Journal of Contemporary Criminal Justice*, 15, 22–47.

Petrosino, C. (2002). Hateful Sirens . . . Who Hears Their Song? An Examination of Student Responses to Hate Groups and their Recruitment Practices. *Journal of Social Issues,* 58(2), 281–302.

Race Relations Reporter, The (n.d.). Available from www.jbhe.com/rrr/rrr.html [Accessed February 14, 2010].

Seattle Times, The (2006). Available from http://seattletimes.nwsource.com/html/localnews/2003170287_webhaq02.html [Accessed February 14, 2010].

Sims, P. (1996). *The Klan*. Lexington, KY: University Press of Kentucky.

Southern Poverty Law Center. (SPLC) (2008). Nationalist Movement Rally. Intelligence Report, Spring 2008, Issue No. 129. Available from http://www.splcenter.org/get-informed/intelligence-report/browse-all-issues/2008/spring/nationalist-movement-rally [Accessed March 4, 2015].

Southern Poverty Law Center. (SPLC) (2009a). Hate Incidents. Connecticut. Available from http://www.splcenter.org/get-informed/hate-incidents?year=2009&state=CT   [Accessed March 4, 2015].

Southern Poverty Law Center. (SPLP (2009b). Hate Incidents. Massachusetts. Available from http://www.splcenter.org/get-informed/hate-incidents?page=2&year=&state=MA [Accessed March 5, 2015].

Southern Poverty Law Center. (SPLC) (2009c). Hate Incidents. California. Available from http://www.splcenter.org/get-informed/hate-incidents?page=19&year=&state=CA [Accessed March 5, 2015].

Southern Poverty Law Center (SPLC). (2009d). Hate Incidents. Washington. Available from http://www.splcenter.org/get-informed/hate-incidents?page=4&year=&state=WA [Accessed March 5, 2015].

Southern Poverty Law Center. (SPLC) (2010). Hate Incidents. California. Available from http://www.splcenter.org/get-informed/hate-incidents?year=2010&state=CA [Accessed March 4, 2015].

Steen, S. & Cohen, M. A. (2004). Assessing the Public's Demand for Hate Crime Penalties. *Justice Quarterly*, 21(1), 91–124.

USA Today. (2010). Available from www.usatoday.com/money/companies/2004-05-07-cracker-barrel_x.htm [Accessed February 3, 2010].

US Department of Agriculture. (n.d.). Available from www.usda.gov/news/pubs/violence/wpv.htm [Accessed February 7, 2015].

US Department of Education. (1998). Amendments to the Higher Education Act of 1965. Available from http://www2.ed.gov/policy/highered/leg/hea98/sec486.html [Accessed on March 8, 2015].

US Department of Justice. (2001). Hate Crimes on Campus. Bureau of Justice Assistance. Hate Crimes Series #3. NCJ 187249. Available from https://www.ncjrs.gov/pdffiles1/bja/187249.pdf [Accessed March 5, 2015].

US Department of Labor's Occupational Safety and Health Administration (OSHA). (2002). OSHA Fact Sheet. Available from www.fbi.gov/ucr/hc2004/appendix_a.htm [Accessed February 1, 2010].

Victims of Crime. (n.d.) When And Where Does Violent Crime Happen? Available from www.libraryindex.com/pages/447/Victims-Crime-WHEN-WHERE-DOES-VIOLENT-CRIME-HAPPEN.html#ixzz0lSSh9UAP [Accessed February 7, 2015].

Zeskind, L. (2009). *Blood and Politics: The History of the White Nationalist Movement. From the Margins to the Mainstream*. New York: Farrar, Straus, and Giroux.

2 A history of hate in the United States

Perpetrators of hate crime see their victims as inherently inferior people. Intruders in their world who are unworthy or somehow undeserving of the equality, justice, or freedom guaranteed by the Constitution due to reasons of race, religion, sexual orientation, or other status condition. Should hate crimes achieve their intended effects, the civil liberties afforded to some segments of the US population would become moot or non-existent.

Hate-motivated acts are as much a part of America's past as other events that are usually written about in history books. There are many acts that occurred in the past that would well qualify as hate crimes had they occurred in the twenty-first century. As stated previously, hate crimes are crimes that manifest evidence of prejudice based on categories such as race, religion, sexual orientation, gender, ethnicity, and disability. Despite the fact that hate-motivated acts of the past were virtually identical to modern hate crimes in motive, intent, and sometimes in manner, for the most part they were not criminalized acts. Moreover, although hate-motivated acts have occurred in the United States for the last 400 years, what has society learned from them? Is there anything about those events that can shed light on modern hate crimes? This chapter provides a historical perspective of hate crime in the United States. Because the scope of this topic cannot be sufficiently addressed here, this chapter will only identify broad similarities between historical and modern hate-motivated acts and related factors. I also argue here that these historical events are very relevant to the understanding of present-day hate crime. In addition, this chapter explores the question of whether modern hate crimes are a consequence of historical hate crime patterns and whether such patterns are possibly predictive of developing trends in hate crimes.

A hate crime is a hate crime is a . . .

On a beautiful autumn afternoon, a group of individuals going about their daily routine were suddenly and viciously attacked in their own community by those who viewed the individuals as threatening. The aim of the attackers was to send a message: these individuals were not welcomed there, despite living separately, because of their *difference*, *inferiority*, and *dangerousness*. The attack nearly accomplished the murder of most of the male members of the group, including children.

This incident, the Haun's Mill massacre, occurred on October 30, 1838, in Caldwell County, Missouri. The victims were Mormons. The perpetrators were local militiamen, who may have been inspired to commit this act by Missouri's Governor who earlier issued an extermination order against Mormons (Denton, 2003). Although this event occurred over 150 years ago, it possesses characteristics of modern-day hate crimes. Mormonism was viewed with suspicion and those that practiced this religion were viewed as threatening. Mormons were attacked by individuals, citizen groups, and finally governments. They were persistently subjected to harassment and banishment, even their extinction was periodically sought. Today, Mormons number in the hundreds of thousands and they live peacefully throughout the United States; yet their history includes being the target of hate-motivated acts for decades. There are many historical incidents that resemble the hate crimes of today. The targeting of others due to their religion, ethnicity, race, or other perceived differences has been a common occurrence throughout American history (Feagin, 2001; Perlmutter, 1992).

America's past—when hate crimes were not

Many bias- or hate-motivated acts were not considered illegal during the distant past (Jordan, 1968; Miller, 1979; Petrosino, 1999; Stampp, 1956; Steinfield, 1973; Takaki, 1994a, 1994b; Wells-Barnett, 1969). The likely reasons for this includes the absence or limited constitutional or statutory protections afforded to victims, the devaluation of their very personhood according to the social norms of that time, and the direct role of governments and other legal authorities in hate-motivated actions (Petrosino, 1999). While acts such as assault, theft, murder, and rape were crimes under the common law, (which is the historical basis for American jurisprudence), these same acts were less likely to be viewed as criminal when motivated by racism, ethnocentrism, or classism (Hoffer, 1992; Jordan, 1968; Perlmutter, 1992). Few would argue that the common law was utilized to protect the poor or racial and ethnic minorities to the same extent as White native-born property-owning males (Mann, 1993; Perlmutter, 1992; Steinfield, 1973; Takaki, 1994a, 1994b; Walker, et al. 1996).

General characteristics of modern hate crime includes: (1) victims are more likely to be members of racial and or ethnic minority groups (Bureau of Justice Assistance, 1997; Hamm, 1994); (2) victim groups tend to be less advantaged economically and politically, relative to the majority group (Hamm, 1993); (3) prevailing cultural values and traditions situate victim groups as suitable for discriminatory and unequal treatment (Perry, 2001); and (4) victim groups are perceived as a serious threat to the quality of life of the dominant group (i.e., social hegemony, economic stability and/or physical safety); (Levin & McDevitt, 1993; Ridgeway, 1990; Herek, 1992; Hall, 2013). The historical incidents selected for this examination possess some of these attributes and are drawn from among the historical experiences of racial and ethnic minority groups in America. This approach aids comparative analysis efforts, an objective in this chapter. Nevertheless, it is important to state strongly that hate-motivated acts were not experienced solely by members of racial and ethnic minority groups (the Irish were also the victims of deplorable systematic discrimination, as were Catholics), however historical records describing the mistreatment of these groups is well documented in the literature due to the constancy and extreme nature of their victimization.

Historical incidents and the evolution of hate crime

Pre-Civil War

Many historians describe the early contacts between European settlers and Native Americans as non-violent and even mutually beneficial (Abbot, 1975). However, the relationship between these groups changed with the increasing efforts of colonists to homestead and take tribal land, often in unfair ways (Sanders, 1978; Spindler, 1972; Steinfield, 1973; Tebbel & Jennison, 1960). As Native Americans resisted White encroachment, interferences with their sovereignty, and the deceptive practices of colonists, they found themselves demonized (Harjo, 1998; Riding In, 1998). Anti-Indian sentiments became prominent in early American culture, political discourse and governmental policies. Jacksonian democracy, which shaped cultural and social practices and political thought from the 1820s to 1860s exemplifies these convergent social forces. Berlet and Lyons (2000) describe Jacksonian perspectives as advocating "an inclusive class ideology of White male egalitarianism with the hard racism of exclusion, terror, and suppression toward people of color" (42). Expansionist efforts during that time were rationalized by this chauvinistic ideology. This social climate facilitated egregious hate-motivated acts against Native Americans.

The near-genocide of the Yuki and Cheyenne Indians—anti-Native American acts

The Yuki of northern California numbered approximately 5,000 when first encountered by White settlers in 1848. By this time period in American history, atrocities and inhumane treatment was routinely committed against Native Americans by settlers, local authorities, and the US Cavalry in the form of kidnapping, theft, fraud, forced indentured servitude, sexual assault, starvation, and murder (Hendricks, 2006; Riding In, 1998). Targeting the Yuki for similar treatment, unfortunately, was not unusual. In fact, military records indicate interest in their extermination in order to increase White settlements (Gundersen & Smelser, 1994; Miller, 1979). With the execution of planned attacks authorized by California's Governor Peter Burnett, the Yuki lost 90 percent of their population in a 32-year period (Chalk & Jonassohn, 1990). The Cheyenne were victims of similar acts, as described in the 39th *U.S. Congressional Record*, 2nd session, Senate Report 156. The following is an account of a mass murder that occurred on November 28, 1864, as told by eyewitness Robert Bent:

When the troops fired, the Indians ran. . . . I think there were six-hundred Indians in all. . . . about sixty [men]. . . . I saw five squaws under a bank for shelter. . . . but the soldiers shot them all. . . . There seemed to be indiscriminate killing. . . . There were some thirty or forty squaws collected in a hole for protection; they sent out a little girl about six years old with a white flag. . . . ; she had not proceeded but a few steps when she was shot and killed. . . . I saw one squaw cut open with an unborn child. . . . I saw the body of a leader, with the privates cut off, and I heard a soldier say he was going to make a tobacco pouch out of them.

(Brown, 1970, 73)

Few would disagree that these acts were at least in part racially motivated. Evidence of racial animus toward Native Americans permeated American culture at that time, and these brutal acts clearly indicate a potent disregard of the victims' humanity (Berthrong, 1963). Sentiments toward Native Americans during that time are captured by the astounding fact that it was not until 1891 that the US Supreme Court declared that Indians were human beings (Kennedy, 1959).

The commodification of Black Africans: slavery—anti-Black acts

Early observations of Africa and African people were articulated through a Eurocentric perspective (Fredrickson, 1991; Jordan, 1968; Pieterse, 1992). When economic profit became a driving force for furthering the New World and slavery the crucial means, a particular image of the African was needed. African skin color and non-Christian religious practices made it simpler to cast the African as an uncivilized pagan and to associate Blackness with negativity, evil, and unworthiness (Jordan, 1968). It became the norm in White culture to associate being Black with the conditions of inferiority.

As early as 1625, being African became synonymous with being enslavable. However, the treatment of Africans in a debased and discriminatory manner predated institutionalized slavery in Colonial America. With the advent of legalized slavery in the colonies and the enactment of the Black Codes in 1640, Blacks became distinguished from all other groups in America (Morris, 1996). These consistent social and legal practices reinforced racial animus and prejudiced attitudes toward this group. Once slavery was well established, it received the legal status of perpetual (Jordan, 1968), making the loss of freedom lifelong and complete. The status of children born to slaves was clarified when slavery was defined by law as an inherited condition (Higginbotham, 1978). Despite the overwhelming totality of slavery as an institution, slaveholders employed various techniques to force Blacks to accept their condition. These techniques included acts of kidnapping, assault, torture, inhumane treatment (because slaves were viewed as chattel and not as human beings), rape, and psychological abuse. These acts were at least in part racially motivated and largely viewed as innocuous considering the prevailing social norms of that time.

Kearneyism—anti-Asian Acts

Asian laborers were invited to the United States in the 1800s as workers in large scale labor projects including the construction of the California Central railroad and the Transcontinental railroad (Healey, 1995). Initially viewed as an industrious people, the images of Asians soon deteriorated for several reasons. Ideas advocated by the eugenics movement (which began as earlier as the 1880s) centered on racial classifications and social practices needed to ensure a racially superior America. Non-European groups, such as Asians, did not fare well in these proposals. Some contended that the adult Mongoloid was equivalent to an adolescent Caucasian (Gould, 1981). In fact, many stereotypes used to depict Native Americans and Africans were also used against Asians:

> White workers called the Chinese "nagurs" [*sic*], and a magazine cartoon depicted a Chinese man as a bloodsucking vampire with slanted eyes, a pigtail, dark skin, and thick lips. Like blacks, the Chinese were described as heathen, morally inferior, savage, childlike, and lustful. Chinese women were condemned as a "depraved class" and said to resemble Africans.
>
> (Takaki, 1994b, 66)

The industrious nature of the Chinese, their ability to earn a wage, and even own a business incurred resentment from others. Their successes were viewed by many as threatening. Several states enacted laws during the 1800s to constrain Asian liberties. These statutes initially segregated them and culminated in an effort to banish Asians from the United States. The pervasiveness of anti-Asian sentiments during this period is well documented. Consider the sentiments expressed by President Theodore Roosevelt (1901–09) who believed that America should be preserved as a heritage for Whites and that Asians should not live here (Takaki, 1994b). The Native Sons of the Golden West, a nativist organization that vigorously sought to minimize the presence of racial minorities in California, is accredited with the following statement (Chronister, 1992): "the state of California should remain what it had always been and God himself intended it shall always be—the White Man's Paradise. . . . the 31st star shall never become dim or yellow" (pp. 40–41). Asian unemployment surged at the completion of the railways but was short-lived. Many took jobs that Whites declined, or they started their own businesses. While Asians found steady work, White unemployment became a growing problem. Labor leader Denis Kearney and others inflamed anti-Asian sentiments by consistently arguing that Chinese workers caused White unemployment (Steinfield, 1973). The scapegoating of Asians by Kearney, along with pre-existing norms of racial prejudice, created an atmosphere that prompted spontaneous acts of racially motivated violence. During this period Asian businesses were vandalized or destroyed and individuals were robbed, assaulted, and murdered. In 1871, 22 Chinese were hung by a mob in Los Angeles (Perlmutter, 1992). Because Asians lacked basic civil liberties, (see *People v. Hall*, 1854), little was done through the courts to respond to their victimization.

In fact, the murder of Asians became so casual that the print media frequently chose not to report its occurrence (Steinfield, 1973; Takaki, 1994b). These acts, which were motivated by ignorance, resentment, and racial animus were carried out with impunity and sent an unmistakable message to Asian communities.

Post-Civil War

Lynching: anti-Black acts

Named after Charles Lynch, who popularized the act during the eighteenth century, lynching, or lynch law, is the unlawful killing of an individual thought to have violated important social norms and/or the law. These extra-legal acts were usually carried out publicly by citizen mobs. Although Whites and other minorities were also lynched, (e.g. in the Southwestern part of the US more Mexican Americans were lynched than Blacks between 1865 and 1920, [Perlmutter, 1992]), overall Blacks were disproportionately the recipients of these actions. The victimization rate of Blacks in southern states is reported to have been 350 percent greater than that of Whites (Cutler, 1969; Dennis, 1984; Garraty & Foner, as cited in Levin, 2002; Wells-Barnett, 1969). Historical records reflect how easily Blacks were selected for lynching (Wells-Barnett, 1969): "John Hughes of Moberly (Missouri) and Isaac Lincoln of Fort Madison (S. Carolina) and Will Lewis in Tullahoma, Tenn. suffered death for no more serious charge than that they were 'saucy' to white people" (p. 17). The casual nature of Black lynching reveals the ubiquitous nature of the racial animus existing at that time. Perlmutter (1992) states that "lynching was so common it was impossible to keep accurate accounts" (p. 151). The following is an eyewitness report of a July 15, 1921, lynching in Moultrie, Georgia that was published in a local newspaper:

> Williams was brought from Moultrie on Friday night by sheriffs. . . . Saturday court was called. . . . The trial took half an hour. Then Williams, surrounded by fifty sheriffs armed with machine guns, started out of the courthouse door toward the jail. . . . 500 poor pecks rushed the sheriffs, who made no resistance. . . . They tore the negro's clothing off. . . . The negro was unsexed, as usual, and made to eat a portion of his anatomy. . . . The negro was chained to [a] stump. . . . The pyre was lit and a hundred men, women, old and young. . . . joined hands and danced around the negro while he burned.
>
> (Steinfield, 1973, 40–42)

Ku Klux Klan: the first hate group (first and second eras)

The idea of Black equality and participation in the democratic process through the vehicles provided by Reconstruction was repugnant to many White Southerners. To hinder these developments, a group of veterans of the Confederate army formed the Ku Klux Klan in 1866 in Pulaski, Tennessee. A secret society, the Klan utilized violent terroristic tactics to stop Blacks from exercising newly gained civil liberties and to restore White control over every major aspect of Black life. Black community leaders as well as sympathetic Whites where particularly targeted. In practicing these strategies, the Klan laid the foundation for the White supremacist movement in the United States. Historically, the Klan demonstrated three distinct periods of onset activity, which occurred in 1866, 1915, and 1954. During the first period, the Klan is suspected of having murdered over 1,500 Blacks in Georgia alone (Berlet & Lyons, 2000). The second period saw an increase in Klan membership with new members from among the more affluent and educated. Estimates of membership indicate a peak of nearly five million during this period (Dobratz & Shanks-Meile, 1997; Potok, 2001). Despite the Klan's ability to wield political influence, even on the national level, as well as obtaining a measure of respectability in the eyes of many, members frequently engaged in violent hate-motivated behavior. Only now, Roman Catholics, Jews, and other Whites who were empathetic to the plight of Blacks and others were added as legitimate targets.

The Leo Frank Lynching and related incidents—anti-Semitic acts

Anti-Semitic attitudes existed in the USA as far back as the Civil War (Diner, 2004). Since then, the scapegoating of Jews, the establishment of Jewish quotas, the portrayal of Jewish religious practices as sinister, and the committing of various discriminatory acts against them were commonplace. As mentioned earlier, the resurgence of the Ku Klux Klan, beginning in 1915, saw the targeting of Jews residing in the South and Midwest: "A whole new breed of hatemonger developed on the American scene [at that time] that thrived on the spread of hate propaganda against Jews" (Steinfield, 1973, 162).

The National Pencil Company in Atlanta, Georgia was the site of the rape and murder of 14-year-old employee Mary Phagan. Despite dubious evidence, Jewish owner Leo Frank was charged with her murder and placed on trial. As the trial was conducted, local newspapers waged blatant anti-Semitic campaigns against Frank. He was convicted and sentenced to death, but his sentence was later commuted to life by Georgia's governor. An action not well received by many. On August 16, 1916, while Frank was housed in Milledgeville Prison, a group of 25 men entered, overpowered guards, and removed him. After driving to Marietta, Georgia, the group lynched Frank by hanging. His murder was representative of the stark determination and boldness of those motivated by anti-Semitism and hatred.

Residential move-in violence—racially motivated acts

Beginning in the 1890s, Blacks began to leave the rural areas of the South for northern cities. A half million relocated during World War I, and approximately six million more followed after the war through the 1960s (Meyer, 2000). Along with the potential for a better life, migration also meant that victimization would no longer occur just in the South. Most Blacks settled in major metropolitan areas in the North that were largely racially segregated. Black families made economic gains, but seeking better neighborhoods meant moving into predominately White residential areas, which was met with great resistance. When White initiatives, such as opportunistic zoning regulations, improvement associations, and race-restrictive covenants, failed to maintain segregated neighborhoods, threats and violence was the next strategy employed. Black families were frequently subjected to racially motivated harassment and intimidation. Meyer (2000) provides an account of the notes received by a Black family that moved into a White area of Brooklyn:

> If you move into that house, one warned, it will be the worst days [*sic*] work that you ever did. . . . You should know better than to move where you are not wanted. Another letter came from the Klan. There are five of us for each Nigger on Staten Island.
>
> (Meyer, 2000, 34)

Detroit saw appalling racial violence as Black families attempted to settle into more pleasant neighborhoods occupied by White families. Meyer notes (2000, p. 37), "In early July, a mob of about 1,000 whites gathered to taunt the family of John Fletcher, which had recently moved to a white block on the city's west side. Demonstrators yelled, 'lynch him. Lynch him.'" Chicago violence was far worse than that which occurred in New York and Detroit. Fifty-eight racially motivated bombings occurred in the city between 1917 and 1921. Perpetrators targeted persons due to race and used threats and violence to attempt to maintain the status quo of racial segregation.

The civil rights era

The Ku Klux Klan's third era—resisting Black equality

Prior to *Brown v. the Board of Education* (1954), Black life was encumbered by two US Supreme Court decisions: *Dred Scott v. Sandford* (1857) and *Plessy v. Ferguson* (1896). In the *Scott* decision, the court established that people of African descent could never be citizens of the United States and were little more than objects of property. Approximately 40 years later, the *Plessy* decision established the legal doctrine of separate but equal, prescribing segregated public facilities. Together, these decisions codified and affirmed White supremacy and Black subordination in America. However, the *Brown* decision upended both *Scott* and *Plessy*. The Supreme Court decision in *Brown* announced that segregation was inherently unequal and violated the equal protection clause of the 14th Amendment. The modern Civil Rights Movement thus began, as well as the resurgence of hate-motivated crimes.

Backlash from *Brown* took many forms, such as the publication of the 1956 Southern Manifesto. Signed by 100 US senators and congressmen from eleven southern states, the manifesto stated that the signing members were committed to "resist forced integration by any lawful means" (Dudley, 1996, 70). The fear that integration would lead to "racial mixing" and in turn the demise of the White race, was a common belief among many in the United States. Alabama governor John Patterson reiterated his commitment to fight the *Brown* decision in his 1959 inaugural speech:

> I will oppose with every ounce of energy I possess. . . . any mixing of the white and Negro races in the classrooms of this state. . . . Any attempt by the federal government or anyone else to integrate the schools of this state by force would cause turmoil, chaos and violence.
>
> (Dudley, 1996, 78)

These pivotal Supreme Court decisions that first denied and then established the civil rights of Black Americans reflect the turbulence surrounding the very idea of Black equality in the USA. With the *Brown* decision and the start of the Civil Rights Movement, racially motivated crimes occurred more frequently between 1954 and 1965. Much of the violence was Klan activity and included, according to the US Justice Department, "seventy bombings in Georgia and Alabama, 30 Negro church burnings in Mississippi, the sadistic castration of a black man in Birmingham, ten racial killings in Alabama, plus the . . . murders of three civil rights' workers in Mississippi" (Sims, 1996, 95). This spree of violence is the third onset period of the Klan. The Mississippi White Knights were responsible for the most egregious terrorist attacks during this time. Klan leaders urged their members to engage in strategic attacks against civil rights participants. Consequently "there were 80 racially motivated assaults, including 35 shootings, 20 church arsons, and five murders" (Bullard, 1993; Chalmers, 1981 as cited in Levin, 2002, 235).

The modern age of hate crimes

The fundamental elements that form the social conditions that facilitate hate crimes arise from historical patterns of racial and ethnic discrimination and violence. Today, hate crimes range from malicious damage to property, verbal threats and intimidation, to assaults and murder—all predicated on the perpetrator's hostility toward the social group represented by the victim. Most modern hate crimes are relatively consistent in presentation, but there are emerging patterns that may have implications not just for today—but also for the evolving nature of these crimes. These patterns include the growing commonality of the globalization of hate groups, the exploitation of the US military by hate groups, the violent nature of younger participants in the hate movement, and the real potential for mass casualties in hate-motivated attacks. We now turn to take a brief look at each of these developments.

Globalization

As early as the 1960s, leaders of the American Nazi Party met periodically with European national socialists (Simonelli, 1999). Today, the Internet makes contact between hate groups effortless. According to some reports, members of US-based hate groups are associating more frequently with their European counter-parts (Anti-Defamation League, 1995; Southern Poverty Law Center, 2001). The Federal Bureau of Investigation (FBI) has long reported links between American hate groups and Middle-Eastern state-sponsored terrorist organizations (Levin & McDevitt, 1993; Sloan, 1997). These efforts towards building and strengthening international relationships is encouraged by pan-Aryanism, an ideological belief in the hate movement that describes a world-wide struggle of Whites against the "destructive" forces of Jews, racial minorities, and the evils of capitalism (Rock-well, 1967).

Exploitation of the military

High-profile crimes involving White supremacists serving in the US military uncovered a number of alarming developments. First, the strategy of some hate groups to locate near military bases in order to actively recruit servicemen and women; second, that there are neo-Nazis and other White supremacists who were actively serving in the US military and; third, that the military chain of command would often disregarded these events, even the displaying of Nazi flags and other similar regalia in living quarters (Leyden & Cook, 2008). David Holthouse (2006) stated in a recent article published in the *Intelligence Report*:

> In 1996, following a decade-long rash of cases where extremists in the military were caught diverting huge arsenals of stolen firearms and explosives to neo-Nazi and white supremacist organizations, conducting guerilla training for paramilitary racist militias, and murdering non-white civilians . . . , the Pentagon finally launched a massive investigation and crackdown. One general ordered all 19,000 soldiers at Fort Lewis, Wash., strip-searched for extremist tattoos. But that was peacetime. Now, with the country at war in Iraq and Afghanistan, and the military under increasingly intense pressure to maintain enlistment numbers, weeding out extremists is less of a priority. Recruiters are knowingly allowing neo-Nazis and white supremacists to join the armed forces, and commanders don't remove them from the military even after we positively identify them as extremists or gang members, said Department of Defense investigator Barfield.

The FBI has documented the presence of former and current US military personnel in the White supremacist movement. They report that "military experience is found throughout the White supremacist movement as the result of recruitment campaigns by extremist groups and self-recruitment by veterans sympathetic to White supremacist causes. Extremist leaders seek to recruit members with military experience in order to exploit their discipline, knowledge of firearms, explosives, and tactical skills and access to weapons and intelligence," (3). In addition, the FBI has documented instances were military personnel have "volunteered" their "professional resources," for the cause (4) (see Figure 2.1).

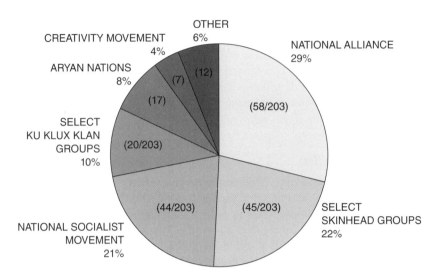

(REPORTING ON 203 PERSONS FROM OCTOBER 2001–MAY 2008)

OTHER
6%
CREATIVITY MOVEMENT
4%
ARYAN NATIONS
8%
(7)   (12)
(17)
SELECT
KU KLUX KLAN
GROUPS   (20/203)
10%
NATIONAL ALLIANCE
29%
(58/203)
(44/203)   (45/203)
NATIONAL SOCIALIST
MOVEMENT
21%
SELECT
SKINHEAD GROUPS
22%

(U) Service: F[3] White Supremacist Extremist subject major group dase files. Individuals have been categorized according to most recent group affliation. In cases of concurrent multiple group affliations, persons have been identified with the group with which they are most actively involved.

Figure 2.1 Distribution of military experience in post-9/11 White supremacist extremism

Currently the military touts a zero-tolerance policy regarding enlisted personnel participating in hate groups as a result of the fallout from the hate-motivated crimes committed by ex-serviceman Timothy McVeigh (Oklahoma City bomber) and enlisted men James Burmeister and Malcolm Wright (Ft. Bragg/Fayetteville murders) (Kifner, 2006; Potok, 2006).

Extremist groups seek to recruit those actively serving as well as those who have been discharged. Individuals with a military background have been trained in weaponry, explosives, combat skills, and may also have access to arsenals.

Youth involvement

According to the Bureau of Justice Statistics' National Incident-Based Reporting System, nearly 40 percent of hate crime offenders are under the age of twenty-five. Neo-Nazi skinheads, who are among the most violent hate crime perpetrators (Dobratz & Shanks-Meile, 1997; Hamm, 1993), also have the youngest memberships (Hamm, 1993; Wooden, 1994). Leaders of racist skinhead groups have directly appealed to youth through music. The Anti-Defamation

League reports that these groups at times target high school newspapers to place ads for free music downloads (ADL, 2009). Those that respond to the offer are then exposed to White power music and the not very subtle bigoted messages it contains. According to the ADL report, this has occurred in high schools located in California, Indiana, and Montana. Such strategies have the objective of recruiting youth "to become soldiers in the war for White racial survival" (5). An example of the messaging embedded is viewed in the title of the CD, *Smashing Rainbows: Rock Against Homosexuality*, and in the name of a song in this collection, *Killer of Faggots* by Evil Incarnate. The song includes the repeated use of slurs against Blacks and gays and calls for their violent killing. Despite the contemptible nature of such lyrics that are routinely found in this genre, White power music has several distributors and an audience who financially support it.

Potential for mass destruction

Modern hate crime perpetrators have the capacity to cause large-scale destruction single-handedly. In 1989, Patrick Purdy acquired a semi-automatic assault rifle and shot Asian children (as he saw the Asian community as responsible for the difficulties in his life) during recess in their Stockton, California elementary school. Purdy wounded 30 children and killed 5 (Levin & McDevitt, 1993). Fifteen years later, in 2004, Demetrius Van Crocker with White supremacist involvement, was arrested for attempting to buy from an undercover agent ingredients for Sarin nerve gas along with C-4 explosives (SPLC, 2001). It is reported that he remarked, "it would be a good thing if somebody could detonate some sort of weapon of mass destruction on Washington, D.C." (paragraph 63). An odorless and colorless agent, Sarin can be released into the air; and with sufficient exposure, it can cause devastating consequences, including many deaths. Crocker was sentenced to 30 years. In 2003, federal agents found a considerable arsenal held by William Krar in Noonday, Texas. The cache included 500,000 rounds of ammunition, multiple pipe bombs, remote-control briefcase bombs as well as hate literature (SPLC, 2001). In addition, Krar managed to acquire sodium cyanide along with the tools needed to weaponize it. Police described this as "a sodium-cyanide bomb capable of killing thousands" (*Christian Science Monitor*, December 29, 2003). Finally, in December 2008, police discovered in the home of shooting victim and neo-Nazi James G. Cummings, "a cache of radioactive materials," in his efforts "to build a radioactive dirty bomb, along with literature on how to build such a deadly explosive. Authorities reported that Cummings was very upset by the election of Barack Obama" (SPLC, 2001, paragraph 71). Clearly the capabilities of some hate groups or lone wolfs to acquire dangerous weapons show their threat potential. We now turn to examine similarities between historical and modern hate-motivated acts.

Comparing past and present patterns

Before identifying distinctions among historical incidents, it is important to review the social conditions that appear to facilitate hate-motivated acts, both historical and modern. These conditions include the existence of: (1) dominant groups with cultural, political, and economic advantages that are not available to other groups; (2) subordinate groups lacking in the aforementioned resources and possess a lesser social standing according to the dominant groups; (3) a mainstream culture that ignores, devalues, demeans or mocks the cultural traditions of minority groups; (4) an underlying fear or suspicion of subordinate groups, which includes the notion that their existence negatively impacts the quality of life of others; and (5) authorities that fail to recognize and/or sufficiently address these dynamics, which inevitably lead to hate-motivated acts. The historical hate-motivated acts discussed earlier reflect these conditions, as do modern hate crimes. Keeping these social conditions in mind, the following summaries reflect distinctions among the historical examples that nevertheless gave rise to the evolving nature of hate-motivated acts.

Summary: pre-Civil War

- Victim groups were viewed as either interfering with or necessary to governmental policies. The intent to grow the nation geographically and economically placed the freedom and dignity of Native Americans, Africans, and Asians on a collision course with government objectives.
- Majority groups generally supported racially motivated discriminatory government policies as such policies also reflected the social norms and cultural beliefs of that time.
- The confluence of the preceding factors produced conditions that facilitated innumerable destructive outcomes, including fatalities brought by hate-motivated acts. As a result, the so-called hate crimes from this period mostly resembled pogroms. Native Americans were almost totally obliterated, Africans endured perpetual bondage and spontaneous lynching, and Asians were murdered because of their ability to survive economically.

The most egregious racially motivated acts during this time period were carried out almost exclusively by governmental bodies or agents acting on behalf of local, state, or federal authorities and not extremist groups.

Summary: post-Civil War

- Victim groups were targeted by smaller entities that were less likely to be directly connected to government authorities.
- Perpetrators organized under the banner of White supremacy for the first time. The modern hate movement was born in 1866 with the formation of the Ku Klux Klan in Pulaski, Tennessee.

- The Klan formed in reaction to efforts by the federal government to move toward de facto equality and to address discriminatory and other mistreatment perpetrated against victim groups. This pattern of reacting against efforts toward social (and political) equality of subordinate groups would be repeated during the civil rights period.
- Hate-motivated acts committed during this period were terroristic in nature as perpetrators utilized violence or threats of violence to achieve sociopolitical objectives.
- Finally, the intent of hate crime was not genocidal, as was found in the pre-Civil War era, but rather to intimidate, control, and oppress victim groups.

Summary: civil rights era

- Hate-motivated crimes committed during this period, particularly as a result of the Civil Rights Movement, reveal the conspicuous involvement of law enforcement and other governmental authorities in these actions. Several bombings and murders directly involved local officials and government agents (e.g., Neshoba County, Mississippi law enforcement and other personnel were involved in the 1964 murders of civil rights workers Michael Schwerner, James Chaney, and Andrew Goodman).
- With law enforcement officials either taking an active role in hate crimes or protecting perpetrators, the level of vulnerability for victim groups was more pronounced. In these instances, the law enforcement community victimized those targeted by hate-motivated acts, rather than protected them.

Summary: post-civil rights era

- With the availability of an assortment of lethal weaponry, including automatic assault weapons, "how to" Internet sources on killing methods, the existence of paramilitary training camps, greater access to deadly explosives, ammunition, and potentially deadly chemical agents, today's hate crime perpetrator can accomplish a high level of destruction within a very brief period of time.
- US military personnel are occasionally implicated in the hate movement; active and former servicemen and women are highly sought for recruitment due to their training in hand-to-hand combat, marksmanship and knowledge of explosives.
- This period sees the involvement of younger and more violent hate crime perpetrators than those from earlier periods.

Growing acceptance of extremist ideology

Even more disturbing is the quiet acquiescence to and adoption of extremist views in some corners of mainstream political platforms and ideologies (Hagan, 1997; Horowitz, 1996; Levin & McDevitt, 1993; McLemee, 1997). Self-avowed White supremacist Tom Metzger considered by some to be the leading force behind the revitalization of the racist skinhead movement in the United States (Hamm, 1994), sought to enter into mainstream politics early in his career. He supported Republican Presidential Candidate Barry Goldwater in 1964, George Wallace in 1968, and he found agreement in much of Ronald Reagan's campaign platform. Metzger ran for a congressional seat in 1980 and his extreme views were present in his political vision (Hamm, 1993). He nevertheless won his primary with 55,000 votes and became the Democratic candidate for US Congress, only to lose in the general election.

More recently the Tea Party movement, a grassroots populist movement (which gained public attention in 2009) which has captured the imagination and participation of many in Middle America, contains some racist, homophobic, and xenophobic elements. During the contentious debate on health care reform, Tea Party protestors gathered at the Capitol to express their concerns. Both racist behavior and speech was observed among the group: "a racist Tea Partier spat on Rep. Emanuel Cleaver, an African-American Democrat from Missouri. Another African-American congressman, Rep. André Carson, remembered the nasty atmosphere: "They were shouting the N-word. It was like a page out of a time machine." Openly gay Congressman Barney Frank was reportedly heckled with anti-gay slurs during the same rally (*Washington Post*, March 20, 2010).

The social conditions of the past are deeply etched into the social and cultural norms of today and are evidenced by the following: first, the continual existence of hate-motivated crime, which now has a nearly 400-year history in the United States; second, the composition of perpetrator–victim groups remains largely unchanged over time; and third, the general factors that motivate hate crime also remain consistent in spite of social progress. These observations indicate that the problem of hate crime will not be eradicated any time soon. But lessons can be learned from this history. The most apparent is that dominant social and cultural dynamics must begin to dismantle the security blanket of tacit approval and make animus towards others due to perceived status unsupportable.

Chapter summary

- Hate-motivated acts of the past are as much a part of the fabric of the USA's history as those events that are more commonly found in American history books.
- There are many acts that occurred in the past that would well qualify as hate crimes had they occurred in the twenty-first century.
- Discrimination or hate-motivated acts were not considered illegal during the distant past. The reasons for this includes the absence of legal protections for victims, the devaluation of their personhood according to the social norms of that time, and the direct role of governments and other authorities in hate-motivated acts.
- General characteristics of modern hate crime include the following: (1) victims are more likely to be members of racial and or ethnic minority groups; (2) victim groups tend to be disadvantaged economically, politically, and

socially relative to the majority group; (3) prevailing cultural norms and traditions situate victim groups as suitable for discriminatory treatment; and (4) victim groups are perceived as a threat to the quality of life of the dominant group.

- History is replete with events that could be characterized as hate-motivated crimes, particularly (but not exclusively) for Native Americans, African slaves and subsequently African-Americans, and Asians, both Chinese and Japanese.
- The Klan laid the foundation for the White supremacist movement in the United States. Collectively, Klan groups had three periods of onset activism, in 1866, 1915, and 1954, respectively.
- The resurgence of the Ku Klux Klan in 1915 saw the targeting of Jews residing in the South and Midwest and the exploitation of anti-Semitic propaganda.
- The 1980s saw a surge in hate-motivated criminal activity across the United States concurrent with a growth in neo-Nazi extremist groups. It is during this post-civil rights period that these acts are first referred to as hate crimes.
- More recent incidents of modern hate crimes (completed or attempted) and/or hate group activity may have implications for future developments of this crime. These characteristics include the increasing globalization of hate groups, exploitation of the US military, younger participants in the hate movement, and a capacity for more sophisticated and lethal methods of attack heighten the potential for mass casualties in hate-motivated attacks.
- Historical hate-motivated acts vary in nature and manifest themselves differently in accordance to the cultural and sociopolitical features of a given time period.
- The history of hate-motivated acts suggest two critical indicators: (1) when dominant cultural values and social practices undermine the equality of minority and other marginalized groups and (2) when government and other institutions of formal social control fail to effectively address these social practices, then the resulting environment facilitates hate-motivated acts.
- The social conditions of the past are deeply etched into the social and cultural norms of today and are evidenced by: the continual existence of hate crime; the composition of perpetrator–victim groups remains relatively unchanged; and, the general factors that motivate hate crime also remain stable despite social progress.
- More effective interventions and prevention initiatives will help to diminish the potential danger found in modern hate crime. What is required is a commitment to disrupt the patterns that we have consistently viewed throughout history and today.

Case study 2.1 The murder of Lenuel Penn

Lemuel A. Penn was an assistant superintendent of education in the District of Columbia's public schools. He was also a lieutenant colonel in the Army Reserves. Lt. Col. Penn was murdered on July 11, 1964, near Athens,

Georgia, as he was driving from Fort Benning, Georgia, to Washington, DC. The four Ku Klux Klan members who shot Penn were later convicted in federal court of violating his civil rights. It was the first such conviction under the 1964 Civil Rights Act.

(Source: Papers of the FBI Investigation of the Lemuel A. Penn Murder, www.lib.uiowa.edu/spec-coll/MSC/ToMsc550/MsC507/msc507.html)

The murder

In the early hours of July 11, 1964, a sedan carrying U.S. Army Reserve officers Charles E. Brown, John D. Howard, and Lemuel Penn departed Fort Benning outside Columbus and headed north for Washington, D.C. After two weeks of active army reserve training, the men were returning home to resume their civilian routines as educators in the District of Columbia school system.

. . . neither Penn nor his passengers noticed the . . . station wagon that followed the men out of town. The pursuing vehicle was trailing the officers . . . but pulled alongside their sedan as it crossed the Broad River Bridge near the Madison-Elbert County line. Two shots were then fired from inside the station wagon, and Penn was killed instantly.

The trial

Georgia governor Carl Sanders declared that he was "ashamed for myself and the responsible citizens of Georgia that this occurrence took place in our state." After weeks of investigation, state prosecutors brought first-degree murder charges against two local White men, Cecil Myers and Joseph Howard Sims. Despite considerable evidence indicating their guilt, an all-White jury in Madison County acquitted both men on September 4, 1964.

Federal authorities remained committed to bringing Penn's murderers to justice. FBI agents had uncovered enough evidence, they believed, to secure a guilty verdict in a federal court. On the basis of the recently enacted Civil Rights Act of 1964, federal authorities charged Sims, Myers, and four other local Klansmen, Herbert Guest, James S. Lackey, Denver Phillips, and George Hampton Turner, with violating the federal law, which made it illegal for two or more persons to conspire to abridge or threaten another person's civil rights.

Criminal proceedings against the men began on June 27, 1966, two years after Penn's murder. Though four of the defendants were found innocent, Sims and Myers were both convicted on conspiracy charges and sentenced to ten years apiece in the federal penitentiary.

(Source: "Lemuel Penn Murder" by Edward A. Hatfield from the *New Georgia Encyclopedia* www.newgeorgiaencyclopedia.com/nge/Article. jsp?path=/HistoryArchaeology/SunbeltGeorgia/People-7&id=h-3611)

Discussion questions

1   Considering the conditions that facilitate hate-motivated acts, why do you think Lemuel Penn and his two colleagues were targeted by the Ku Klux Klan?
2   What was the significance of Governor Sanders' statement about public shame?
3   Some of the defendants were acquitted in the criminal trial. What social dynamics may have made that outcome unsurprising?
4   What factors caused the Ku Klux Klan to go into decline during the late 1960s, considering the indicators that facilitate hate crime?

Bibliography

Abbot, W. W. (1975). *The Colonial Origins of the United States, 1607–1763.* New York: Wiley.

Anti-Defamation League (ADL). (1995). *The Skinhead International: A Worldwide Survey of Neo-Nazi Skinheads.* New York: Author.

Anti-Defamation League (ADL). (1996). *Danger: Extremism. The Major Vehicles and Voices on America's Far-Right Fringe.* New York: Author.

Anti-Defamation League. (2009). Neo-Nazis Use Deceptive Music Downloads to Attract Young People to White Supremacy. Available from http://archive.adl.org/presrele/neosk_82/5681_82.html#.VPyjjjIcTIU [Accessed on March 8, 2015].

Barkan, S. E. & Cohn, S. F. (1994). Racial Prejudice and Support for the Death Penalty by Whites. *Journal of Research in Crime and Delinquency*, 31, 202–9.

Berlet, C. & Lyons, M. N. (2000). *Right-Wing Populism in America: Too Close for Comfort.* New York: Guilford Press.

Berthrong, D. J. (1963). *The Southern Cheyennes.* Norman, OK: University of Oklahoma Press.

Brown, D. (1970). *Bury My Heart at Wounded Knee: An Indian History of the American West.* New York: Holt, Rinehart & Winston.

Bullard, R. D. (1993). Confronting Environmental Racism: Voices from the Grassroots. *Economic Geography*, 72(2), 230–2.

Bullard, S. (ed.) (1993). *Free at Last: A History of the Civil Rights Movement and Those Who Died in the Struggle.* Montgomery, AL: Southern Poverty Law Center.

Bureau of Justice Assistance. (1997). *A Policymaker's Guide to Hate Crimes.* NCJ 162304. Washington, DC: US Department of Justice Office of Justice Programs.

Chalk, P. & Jonassohn, K. (1990). *The History and Sociology of Genocide: Analyses and Case Studies.* New Haven, CT: Yale University Press.

Chalmers, D. A. (1981). *Hooded Americanism: The History of the Ku Klux Klan.* New York: Franklin Watts.

Christensen, L. (1994). *Skinhead Street Gangs.* Boulder, CO: Paladin Press.

Christian Science Monitor. (December 29, 2003). *The Terror Threat at Home, Often Overlooked—As the Media Focus on International Terror, a Texan Pleads Guilty to Possessing a Weapon of Mass Destruction.* By Kris Axtman, Staff writer. Available from www.csmonitor.com/2003/1229/p02s01-usju.html [Accessed April 30, 2010].

Chronister, A. (1992). Japan-Bashing: How Propaganda Shapes Americans' Perception of the Japanese. Unpublished master's thesis, Lehigh University, Bethlehem, PA.

Cutler, J. E. (1969). *Lynch-Low: An Investigation into the History of Lynching in the United States*. Chicago, IL: Negro Universities Press.

Dennis, D. (1984). *Black History*. New York: Writers and Readers.

Denton, S. (2003). *American Massacre: The Tragedy at Mountain Meadows, September 11, 1857*. New York: Knopf.

Diner, H. (2004). *The Jews of the United States*. Los Angeles, CA: University of California Press.

Dobratz, B. A. & Shanks-Meile, S. (1997). *White Power, White Pride! The White Separatist Movement in the United States*. Baltimore, MD: Johns Hopkins University Press.

Dred Scott v. Sandford, 60 U.S. 393 (1857).

Dudley, W. (ed.) (1996). *The Civil Rights Movement: Opposing Viewpoints.* San Diego, CA: Greenhaven Press.

Feagin, J. R. (2001). *Racist America: Roots, Current Realities, and Future Reparations*. New York: Routledge.

Federal Bureau of Investigation. (2008). *White Supremacist Recruitment of Military Personnel Since 9/11.* Intelligence Assessment Report.

Federal Bureau of Investigation. (1964). *FBI Investigation of the Lemuel A. Penn Murder Papers*. Iowa, IA: University of Iowa Libraries, Iowa City.

Fredrickson, G. M. (1991). *White Supremacy: A Comparative Study in American and South African History*. New York: Oxford University Press.

Garraty, J. A. & Foner, E. (eds.) (1991). *The Reader's Companion to American History.* Boston, MA: Houghton Mifflin.

Gould, S. J. (1981). *The Mismeasurement of Man*. New York: W. W. Norton.

Gundersen, J. R. & Smelser, M. (1994). *American History at a Glance* (5th ed.). New York: HarperCollins.

Hagan, F. E. (1997). *Political Crime: Ideology and Criminality*. Needham Heights, MA: Allyn & Bacon.

Hall, N. (2013). *Hate Crime* (2nd ed.). London: Routledge.

Hamm, M. S. (1993). *American Skinheads: The Criminology and Control of Hate Crime*. Westport, CT: Praeger.

Hamm, M. S. (1994). Conceptualizing Hate Crime in a Global Context. In M. S. Hamm (ed.) *Hate Crime: International Perspectives on Causes and Control* (pp. 173–94). Cincinnati, OH: Anderson.

Harjo, S. S. (1998). Redskins, Savages, and Other Indian Enemies: An Historical Overview of American Media Coverage of Native Peoples. In C. R. Mann & M. S. Zatz (eds.) *Images of Color Images of Crime* (pp. 30–46). Los Angeles, CA: Roxbury.

Harris, L. M. (2003). *In the Shadow of Slavery: African Americans in New York City, 1626–1863*. Chicago, IL: University of Chicago Press.

Hate Crime Statistics Act, 28 U.S.C. Paragraph 534 (1990).

Hatfield, E. A. (August 5, 2013). Lemuel Penn Murder. *The New Georgia Encyclopedia*. Available from www.newgeorgiaencyclopedia.com/nge/Article.jsp?path=/HistoryArchaeology/SunbeltGeorgia/People-7&id=h-3611 [Accessed August 27, 2014].

Healey, J. F. (1995). *Race, Ethnicity, Gender and Class: The Sociology of Group Conflict and Change*. Thousand Oaks, CA: Sage.

Hendricks, S. (2006). *The Unquiet Grave: The F.B.I. and the Struggle for the Soul of Indian Country*. New York: Thunder's Mouth Press.

Herek, G. (1992). The Social Context of Hate Crimes: Notes on Cultural Heterosexism. In G. Herek and K. T. Berrill (eds.) *Hate Crimes: Confronting Violence Against Lesbians and Gay Men* (pp. 89–101). Newbury Park, CA: Sage.

Higginbotham, A. L., Jr. (1978). *In the Matter of Color: Race and the American Legal Process: The Colonial Period*. New York: Oxford University Press.

Higginbotham, A. L. (1996). *Shades of Freedom*. New York: Oxford University Press.

Hoffer, P. C. (1992). *Law and People in Colonial America*. Baltimore, MD: Johns Hopkins University Press.

Holthouse, D. (2006). A Few Bad Men. *Intelligence Report*, 122, 1–6.

Horowitz, C. (1996). Anti-semitic violence is increasing. In P. A.Winters (Ed.), *Current Controversies Series: Hate Crimes* (pp. 18–24). San Diego, CA: Greenhaven.

Jacobs, J. B. & Potter, K. (2000). *Hate Crimes: Criminal Law & Identity Politics*. New York: Oxford University Press.

Jordan, W. D. (1968). *White Over Black: American Attitudes Toward the Negro, 1550–1812*. Chapel Hill, NC: University of North Carolina Press.

Kane, P. (2010). Tea Party Protesters Accused of Spitting on Lawmaker, Using Slurs. *Washington Post*. March 20, 2010. Available from www.washingtonpost.com/wp-dyn/content/article/2010/03/20/AR2010032002556.html [Accessed February 8, 2015].

Kennedy, S. (1959). *Jim Crow Guide to the U.S.A.: The Laws, Customs and Etiquette Governing the Conduct of Nonwhites and Other Minorities as Second-Class Citizens*. Westport, CT: Greenwood Press.

Kifner, J. (2006). White Supremacists Enlisting in Military, Watchdog Report Says Aryan Nations Graffiti in Baghdad. *San Francisco Chronicle*, July 7, p. A-9.

Levin, B. (2002). From Slavery to Hate Crime Laws: The Emergence of Race and Status Based Protection in American Criminal Law. *Journal of Social Issues*, 58, 227–46.

Levin, J. & McDevitt, J. (1993). *Hate Crimes: The Rising Tide of Bigotry and Bloodshed*. New York: Plenum Press.

Leyden, T. J. & Cook, M. B. (2008). *Skinhead Confessions: From Hate to Hope*. Springville, UT: Sweetwater Books.

Mann, C. R. (1993). *Unequal Justice: A Question of Color*. Bloomington, IN: University of Indiana Press.

McLemee, S. (1997). The Militia Movement is Dangerous. In C. P. Cozic (Ed.), *The Militia Movement. At issue. An Opposing Viewpoints Series* (pp. 50–58). San Diego, CA: Greenhaven Press.

Meyer, S. G. (2000). *As Long as They Don't Move Next Door: Segregation and Racial Conflict in American Neighborhoods*. New York: Rowman & Littlefield.

Miller, Y. P. (1979). *Ukomno'm: The Yuki Indians of Northern California*. Socorro, NM: Ballena Press.

Morris, T. D. (1996). *Southern Slavery and the Law, 1619–1860*. Chapel Hill, NC: University of North Carolina Press.

Perlmutter, P. (1992). *Divided We Fall: A History of Ethnic, Religious, and Racial Prejudice in America*. Ames, IA: Iowa State University Press.

Perry, B. (2001). *In the Name of Hate: Understanding Hate Crimes*. New York: Routledge.

Petrosino, C. (1999). Connecting the Past to the Future: Hate Crime in America. *Journal of Contemporary Criminal Justice*, 15, 22–47.

Pieterse, J. N. (1992). *White on Black: Images of Africa and Blacks in Western Popular Culture*. New Haven, CT: Yale University Press.

Plessy v. Ferguson, 163 US 537 (1896).

Potok, M. (2001). The New Internationalism. *Intelligence Report*, 103, 1.

Potok, M. (2006). Extremism and the Military. *Intelligence Report*, 122, 1.

Rockwell, G. L. (1967). *White Power*. Dallas, TX: Ragnarok Press.

Ridgeway, J. (1990). *Blood in the Face*. New York: Thunder's Mouth Press.

Riding In, J. (1998). American Indians in Popular Culture: A Pawnee's Experiences and Views. In C. R. Mann & M. S. Zatz (eds.) *Images of Color Images of Crime* (pp. 15–29). Los Angeles, CA: Roxbury.

Sanders, R. (1978). *Lost Tribes and Promised Lands: The Origins of American Racism.* Boston, MA: Little, Brown.

Schmaltz, W. H. (1999). *Hate: George Lincoln Rockwell and the American Nazi Party.* Washington, DC: Brassey's.

Simonelli, F. J. (1999). *George Lincoln Rockwell and the American Nazi Party*. Champaign, IL: University of Illinois Press.

Sims, P. (1996). *The Klan* (2nd ed.). Lexington, KY: University Press of Kentucky.

Sloan, S. (1997). An Unholy Alliance: The Internationalization of Domestic Terrorism. *Intelligence Report*, 85, 10–11.

Southern Poverty Law Center (SPLC). (2001). Hands Across the Water. *Intelligence Report*, 103, 14–23.

Spindler, W. H. (1972). *Tragedy Strikes at Wounded Knee and Other Essays on Indian Life in South Dakota and Nebraska*. Vermillian, SD: University of South Dakota Press.

Stampp, K. M. (1956). *The Peculiar Institution: Slavery in the Ante-Bellum South.* New York: Vintage.

Steinfield, M. (1973). *Cracks in the Melting Pot: Racism and Discrimination in American History* (2nd ed.). New York: Glencoe Press.

Takaki, R. (1994a). *Issei and Nisei: The Settling of Japanese America*. New York: Chelsea House.

Takaki, R. (1994b). *Journey to Gold Mountain: The Chinese in 19th-Century America*. New York: Chelsea House.

Tebbel, J. & Jennison, K. (1960). *The American Indian Wars*. New York: Harper & Row.

US Department of Justice. (n.d.). *Hate Crime—Overview, 2007–2008*. Available from www.fbi.gov/hq/cid/civilrights/overview.htm [Accessed November 11, 2010].

Walker, S., Spohn, C., & DeLone, M. (1996). *The Color of Justice.* New York: Wadsworth.

Wells-Barnett, I. B. (1969). *On Lynchings: Southern Horrors, a Red Record, Mob Rule in New Orleans*. New York: Arno Press.

Wood, R. (1999). The Indigenous Nonracist Origins of the American Skinhead. *Youth & Society*, 31(2), 131–51.

Wooden, W. S. (1994). *Renegade Kids, Suburban Outlaws*. New York: Wadsworth.

3   The evolution toward modern hate crime laws

Introduction

New laws are sometimes controversial. This can be said for hate crime laws. Proponents of hate crime legislation argue that such laws are needed to punish this behavior and to symbolize values underlying an inclusive and diverse democracy. However, opponents assert that these laws are not necessary; that there are sufficient criminal statutes to respond effectively to hate-motivated crime. Moreover, opponents contend that instead of ameliorating the existence of bigotry and prejudice in society, hate crime laws may exacerbate these attitudes by instigating resentment over so-called "identity politics" (Jacobs & Potter, 1998). But oppositional arguments may lose their appeal to some when the etiology of hate crime laws are placed in a historical and legal context. This author contends that the historical perspective of hate crime law help the understanding of why such laws are legitimate, have utility, and are paramount to achieving and maintaining a free and secure society for all.

The evolution of hate crime law

The efforts of both federal and state legislatures to address hate-motivated crimes did not just begin in the twentieth century. Just as Chapter 2 provides a review of historical crimes and incidents that resemble modern hate crimes, we also find that in the past there were some efforts to respond to these acts by enacting laws. These early acts set the stage for hate crime laws. Among the most illuminating discussions of this area is that offered by legal scholar Brian Levin (2002). In his article, *From Slavery to Hate Crime Laws: The Emergence of Race and Status-Based Protection in American Criminal Law*, Levin meticulously identifies historical conditions that prompted legislative actions which would serve as building blocks for modern hate crime legislation.

Slavery and dealing with its aftermath

Since the justification of slavery in the USA was largely based on race, the remedies required to redress its damages likewise required the recognition of the effects of race-based oppression. The dismantling of slavery and the efforts needed to address its profound consequences prompted the initial use of the law as a means to *rectify* racially motivated actions and policies and to punish those who deliberately victimized others *because of* race. To that end, Levin begins with pointing to the significance of the Thirteenth, Fourteenth, and Fifteenth Amendments to the US Constitution. Each sought to remedy a race-based wrong:

> *Thirteenth Amendment (1865)*—abolished slavery. Slavery became synonymous with being Black.

> *Fourteenth Amendment (1868)*—established national citizenship for all persons born or naturalized in the US (including newly freed Blacks) and ensured their Constitutional protections. States were prohibited from depriving any person of life, liberty, or property without due process of law.

> *Fifteenth Amendment (1870)*—the right of citizens to vote shall not be denied or abridged by the United States or by any State on account of race, color, or previous condition of servitude.

Following the Emancipation Proclamation and the end of the Civil War, the sociolegal status of hundreds of thousands of Blacks was unclear. Race-based slavery was no more, but Black citizenship was not proclaimed either until the 1866 Civil Rights Act, which preceded the enactment of the Fourteenth Amendment.

Civil Rights Act of 1866, 14 Stat. 27 (1866)

> Be it enacted by the Senate and House of Representatives of the United States of America in Congress assembled, That all persons born in the United States and not subject to any foreign power, excluding Indians not taxed, are hereby declared to be citizens of the United States; and such citizens, of every race and color, without regard to any previous condition of slavery or involuntary servitude . . . shall have the same right, in every State and Territory in the United States, to make and enforce contracts, to sue, be parties, and give evidence, to inherit, purchase, lease, sell, hold, and convey real and personal property, and to full and equal benefit of all laws and proceedings for the security of person and property, as is enjoyed by white citizens, and shall be subject to like punishment, pains, and penalties, and to none other, any law, statute, ordinance, regulation, or custom, to the contrary notwithstanding.

This is the first federal law following the Civil War that purposed to address racially motivated acts targeting newly freed Blacks. The 1866 Civil Rights Act provided a penalty of a fine or incarceration to anyone who sought to interfere with Blacks exercising their rights as articulated in the law. Despite these and other efforts to support Black liberty and the privileges of citizenship, defiant southern authorities, the Ku Klux Klan, and even ordinary citizens fearful and resentful of these changes sought to harass, intimidate, and violently confront Blacks to prevent them from realizing the rights articulated in the Fourteenth and Fifteenth

Amendments in particular. To address the race-based reactionary violence, the federal government enacted the *Force Act of 1870* and the *Civil Rights Act of 1871* (also referred to as the *Ku Klux Klan Act of 1871*). These laws provided civil and criminal sanctions for those (whether government authorities or private conspiracies) who were guilty of interfering with or depriving citizens (including Black citizens) of their constitutional rights including suffrage. It was clear that the federal government was taking aim at Klan activities. One of the provisions of 42 U.S.C.A. paragraph 1985(3) states that "when two or more persons 'conspire or *go in disguise* on the highway or the premises of another, for the purpose of depriving . . . any person or class of persons of the equal protection of the law,' they may be sued by the injured parties." The disguise reference applied to the hooded garments that Klan members wore during their acts to terrorize Blacks.

While some efforts were made to put laws into place to address the targeting and victimization of Black citizens, laws to clarify and broaden their civil rights also occurred. Congress passed the *Civil Rights Act of 1875*, which provided equal public accommodations for African-Americans. It stated the following:

> That all persons within the jurisdiction of the United States shall be entitled to the full and equal enjoyment of the accommodations, advantages, facilities, and privileges of inns, public conveyances on land or water, theaters, and other places of public amusement; subject only to the conditions and limitations established by law, and applicable alike to citizens of every race and color, regardless of any previous condition of servitude.
>
> SEC. 2. That any person who shall violate the foregoing section by denying to any citizen . . . of every race and color, and regardless of any previous condition of servitude, the full enjoyment of any of the accommodations, advantages, facilities, or privileges in said section enumerated, or by aiding or inciting such denial, shall, for every such offense, forfeit and pay the sum of five hundred dollars to the person aggrieved thereby, . . . and shall also, for every such offense, be deemed guilty of a misdemeanor, and, upon conviction thereof, shall be fined not less than five hundred nor more than one thousand dollars, or shall be imprisoned not less than thirty days nor more than one year.
>
> (US Statutes at Large, Vol. XVIII, 335ff)

While each of the laws discussed above were designed to accomplish two things simultaneously—to ensure Black equality and to punish efforts to interfere with that objective, not all governing authorities agreed with those ends. Moreover, these laws mostly focused on state and local governments' infringement upon the rights of African-Americans and other citizens but not interference by private citizens. Thus these laws often are more akin to a stuttering gait rather than bold and confident moves toward progress. Nevertheless, these laws were precedent-like for criminalizing behaviors that were motivated by racial animus and or other related hostilities, causing the intentional targeting of victims due to their racial or other ascribed class-based characteristics (Hall, 2005; Higginbotham, 1996; Levin, 2002).

The years following emancipation were dangerous ones for Black Americans. They were subjected to many incivilities as well as summary lynching (from the time of emancipation, 1865, to the 1940s), particularly in southern states for exercising basic liberties. Lynching was carried out with impunity as law enforcement and other government powers rarely prosecuted those responsible. The federal government was powerless to intercede in these murders until the middle of the twentieth century due to the lack of federal anti-lynch laws. Several attempts were made to pass these laws from the 1920s to the 1940s. While anti-lynch bills would pass in the House of Representatives, they would fail to progress to a vote in the Senate due to filibusters or threats to filibuster by southern senators (NPR, 2005). Still, some states were more successful than the federal government in their efforts to combat this violence by passing anti-lynching and anti-masking laws that targeted the Klan. For example, African-Americans in West Virginia were able to effectively amass support for an anti-lynching measure. In 1921, the Capeheart Anti-Lynching bill was signed into law by Governor Ephraim Morgan. It stated in part:

> [a] "mob" or "riotous assemblage," [a] collection of individuals, five or more in number, assembled for the unlawful purpose of offering violence to the person or property of any one supposed to have been guilty of a violation of the law, or for the purpose of exercising correctional or regulative powers over any person or persons by violence and without lawful authority.
>
> . . . participation in such a mob or riotous assemblage is punishable by a fine ranging from a hundred to a thousand dollars and imprisonment of not less than 30 days nor more than 12 months. For damage on person or property, the crime is a felony punishable by imprisonment in the penitentiary. The person or persons damaged have an action against the city or county in which the damage is done up to $5,000.00. In case of lynching, where person lynched has been taken from state, county, of municipal officer, the county shall be subject to forfeiture of $5,000 for the dependents or estate of the deceased and action may be brought in any state court and mandamus issue for the execution of judgment even to the levying of a tax. County may then recover same from negligent officer by action on his bond.

A different type of racially motivated violence occurred when multiple waves of Blacks migrated from the rural south to northern urban centers, particularly following World War II. They were subjected to violence perpetrated by White mobs for moving into White neighborhoods, vying for jobs or due to rumors about Black on White crime (Tuttle, 1996; Lieberson & Silverman, 1965). Many of these attacks were precipitated by lies, fears, misrepresentations or gross exaggerations of local events.

Libel and slander are acts that defame another by written or verbal communications, respectively. Group libel is the defamation of a group of individuals based on their race, ethnicity, sexual orientation, religion, or other similar reasons. Illinois became the first state to criminalize group libel with the passage of the 1949 state law, 224a of the Illinois Criminal Code, Ill. Rev. Stat., 1949, c. 38, Div. 1, paragraph 471. The section provides:

> It shall be unlawful for any person, firm or corporation to manufacture, sell, or offer for sale, advertise or publish, present or exhibit in any public place in this state any lithograph, moving picture, play, drama or sketch, which publication or exhibition portrays depravity, criminality, unchastity, or lack of virtue of a class of citizens, of any race, color, creed or religion which said publication or exhibition exposes the citizens of any race, color, creed or religion to contempt, derision, or obloquy or which is productive of breach of the peace or riots.

Such laws, which target *a category of speech based on content*, would be subject to First Amendment scrutiny and tested. The Illinois law was also challenged in 1951 by Joseph Beauharnais. The founder of the White Circle League of America, Beauharnais was convicted under the law for distributing racist anti-Black literature on Chicago streets. An excerpt of the flier's content is instructive:

> "Wanted" One Million Self Respecting White People in Chicago to Unite under the Banner of the White Circle League . . . to oppose . . . Truman's . . . Civil Rights Program . . . to amalgamate . . . black and white races with the object of mongrelizing the white race!" The . . . League . . . is the only . . . white voice in America . . . in protest against negro . . . infiltrations into . . . white neighborhoods . . .
>
> (Leagle.com)

The US Supreme Court upheld the Illinois statute (and affirmed Beauharnais's conviction) in *Beauharnais v. Illinois* 343 U.S. 250 (1952). The court found that Beauharnais's speech was indeed the libel of a group and as such was not constitutionally protected speech. The significance of this statute and the Supreme Court's decision contributed to modern hate crime legislation by penalizing behaviors (not attitudes or thoughts) that denigrated a class of people due to their race, color, creed, or religion (Levin, 2002).

With racially and other hate-motivated violence occurring in the south and now the north, and rumblings of a developing Civil Rights Movement in the US, political leaders and social progressives advocated for the federal government to continue efforts to suppress these activities. Congress subsequently passed the *Civil Rights Act of 1957*. This law strengthened the civil rights division of the Justice Department and provided the Attorney General the authority to seek federal court injunctions against those who interfered with the right of African-Americans (or others) to vote (Cummings & Wise, 1971).

The Civil Rights Act of 1964 is arguably the single most important precursor to modern hate crime laws. Further strengthened in 1968 by the adding of criminal penalties to civil rights violations, it articulated civil rights that fall under federal protection. They include protection against unequal application of voter registration requirements, discrimination in public accommodations, state and municipal governments denying access to public facilities on grounds of race, religion, gender, or ethnicity, and segregated public schools (see Civil Rights Act of 1964 below).

Enumerated Federal Protections—Civil Rights Act of 1964

1   Prohibit racial or religious discrimination in public accommodations that affect interstate commerce, including hotels, motels, restaurants, cafeterias, lunch counters, gas stations, motion picture houses, theaters, and sports arenas.
2   Prohibit discrimination because of race, color, sex, religion, or national origin by employers or labor unions.
3   Bar voting registrars from adopting different standards for white, black or other applicants.
4   Permit the Attorney General to bring suit to enforce desegregation of public accommodations; and allow individuals to sue for their rights under the act.
5   Permit the executive branch of the Federal Government to halt the flow of funds to public or private programs that practice discrimination.
6   Extend the life of the Civil Rights Commission; create a Community Relations Service to conciliate racial disputes and an Equal Employment Opportunity Commission to enforce the fair employment section of the act.

(Cummings & Wise, 1971, 173)

The next significant legal advancement toward hate crime law is the *1968 Civil Rights Act (Title 18, U.S.C., Section 245)*, which makes it unlawful to "willfully injure, intimidate or interfere with any person, or to attempt to do so, by force or threat of force, because of that other person's race, color, religion or national origin *and* because of his/her activity in one of the federally protected activities." In addition, these activities include participating in a program or service provided by the government, attending a public school or college, traveling on a common carrier, patronizing a public accommodation, or participating as a juror. Title 18 further legitimized the use of the law to punish hate-motivated acts. The law provides punishments:

> fined or imprisoned not more than one year, or both; and if bodily injury results from the acts committed in violation of this section or if such acts include the use, attempted use, or threatened use of a dangerous weapon, explosives, or fire shall be fined under this title, or imprisoned not more than ten years, or both; and if death results from the acts committed in violation of this section or if such acts include kidnapping or an attempt to kidnap, aggravated sexual abuse or an attempt to commit aggravated sexual abuse, or an attempt to kill, shall be fined under this title or imprisoned for any term of years or for life, or both, or may be sentenced to death.

Additional laws were passed to provide the federal government the ability to intervene in hate or bias motivated acts such as the Fair Housing Act and the Church Arson Prevention Act. It is clear that each of these initiatives clearly established the ability of state and federal governments to legitimately criminalize hate-motivated acts.

Modern hate crime laws

From the 1860s to the 1960s, the federal government attempted to address hate-motivated attacks, which were primarily aimed at Black citizens, by criminalizing the hostile interference with constitutionally protected rights. These early laws provided a legal framework that informed post-civil rights era or modern hate crime legislation. To that end, early hate crime statutes were modeled after federal civil rights laws (Levin, 1999). But the contribution of the Anti-Defamation League's model hate crime statute paved the way for states to build laws that would withstand judicial review.

The 1981 Anti-Defamation League (ADL) model statute

Connecticut and Massachusetts were among the first states to pass hate crime laws before the 1980s (Lawrence, 1999; Levin, 2002). The slow start of most states to follow suit was likely due to the gradual recognition of hate crimes themselves, the political debate regarding how to respond to them, and finally the challenge of constructing sound crime bills. To encourage more states to pass hate crime legislation, the ADL drafted a model statute in 1981 that aided states in their efforts to enact similar laws. There were five components of the model statute: (1) identifying a hate crime as a two-tiered criminal act, the predicate or base offense and the element of animus toward the victim because of actual or perceived characteristics; (2) the enhanced penalty element; (3) institutional vandalism (as these acts are often directed towards groups due to bias); (4) availability of civil actions for hate crime victims; and (5) states collecting and maintaining hate crime data reported to law enforcement. While some states passed laws based on the ADL model, others preferred different approaches and passed hate crime statutes accordingly. But the vast majority of states (forty-five) and the District of Columbia with hate crime statutes include the penalty-enhancement feature. The majority of these jurisdictions (states plus DC) include race, religion, national origin, and ethnicity as protected categories; sexual orientation is included in 32, disability in 31, gender in 27, and gender-identity is included in 10 (ADL, The ADL Approach, 4). Many states also have institutional vandalism laws which address the destruction or defacement of private schools, houses of worship, meeting places, cemeteries or other similar institutions due to bias motives. Overall, the majority of states have laws to address hate crimes; at the time of this writing, 45 states plus the District of Columbia have hate crime laws. As mentioned earlier, five states do not and include Arkansas, Georgia, Wyoming, Indiana, and South Carolina. Members of Georgia's legislature have proposed hate crime bills consistently for the last several years, but with no successful outcomes.

The US Supreme Court decision in *Wisconsin v. Mitchell 508 U.S. 47* (1993) (which will be discussed later in the chapter) affirmed the constitutionality of the ADL model statute, including the enhanced penalty approach. Subsequently, most states today include penalty enhancement in their hate crime statutes. We now turn to the examination of the two court cases that placed the issue of the constitutionality of hate crime laws center stage: *R. A. V. v. City of St. Paul (90-7675), 505 U.S. 377* (1992) and *Wisconsin v. Mitchell (92-515), 508 U.S. 47* (1993).

The St. Paul, Minnesota hate crime ordinance (R.A.V. v. St. Paul), 1992

In June 1990, Robert A. Viktora (R.A.V.), Arthur Miller and several other teenagers burned a cross inside the fenced yard of a Black family that lived across the street from the house where they were staying. Viktora was charged under the St. Paul ordinance. The ordinance (Minnesota Legislation Code, paragraph 292.02, 1990) stated the following:

> Whoever places on public or private property a symbol, object, appellation, characterization or graffiti, including, but not limited to, a burning cross or Nazi swastika, which one knows or has reasonable grounds to know arouses anger, alarm or resentment in others on the basis of race, color, creed, religion or gender commits disorderly conduct and shall be guilty of a misdemeanor.

The trial court dismissed the charges, stating that the ordinance was overbroad and inappropriately interfered with the First Amendment rights of the defendant. The Minnesota State Supreme Court disagreed and reversed. The US Supreme Court did not concur with the State Supreme Court. The majority opinion written by Antonin Scalia stated that the ordinance is facially unconstitutional because it targets speech aimed at subjects of "race, color, creed, religion or gender." This is discriminatory as the ordinance chose to ban only certain symbolic conduct, that is, cross burning, when it was motivated by those categories identified in the law (race, color, creed, religion, or gender). But if this form of hostile expression, including the Nazi swastika and the like, is directed towards other reasons such as homophobia, political affiliation, or other social classifications, for example homelessness or public assistance recipient, the ordinance is silent. This results in content-based discrimination and is not permissible under the First Amendment (Cornell University Law School).

Thus St. Paul's attempt to enact a hate crime ordinance failed. As a result of the R.A.V. decision, any hate crime statutes that were constructed in a way that was similar to the St. Paul ordinance, were no longer viable. For example, the New Jersey State Supreme Court overturned the state's hate crime law in 1994 as a direct result of the *R.A.V v. St. Paul* decision; joining Maryland and Washington State. New Jersey, as with many other states, would come to rely on a different construction of its hate crime law; one that emphasized the intentional selection of victims due to their race, religion, or other perceived characteristics (*New York Times*, 1994).

The Wisconsin Bias Crime Statute (*Wisconsin v. Mitchell*), 1993

Wisconsin's hate crime statute differed substantially from the St. Paul ordinance. Whereas the St. Paul ordinance sought to criminalize specific speech content, Wisconsin's hate crime law focused on the *conduct* of hate crime perpetrators. Statute paragraph 939.645 (1991–92) includes the following:

> If a person does all of the following, the penalties for the underlying crime is increased as provided in sub. (2):(a) Commits a crime under chs. 939 to 948. (b) Intentionally selects the person against whom the crime under par. (a) is committed or selects the property that is damaged or otherwise affected by the crime under par. (a) in whole or in part because of the actor's belief or perception regarding the race, religion, color, disability, sexual orientation, national origin or ancestry of that person or the owner or occupant of that property, whether or not the actor's belief or perception was correct.
>
> (ADL, 2012. See the full description of Wisconsin's hate crime statute at https://docs.legis.wisconsin.gov/statutes/ statutes/939/IV/645)

After becoming angry from watching the movie *Mississippi Burning*, defendant Todd Mitchell incited a group of teenagers and young men to attack and beat a fourteen-year-old white boy who was nearby. Mitchell was convicted of aggravated assault but, as a result of the Wisconsin penalty enhancement statute, his sentence exposure was increased from two years to seven years. Subsequently, he received a four-year sentence. Mitchell appealed his conviction, arguing that the Wisconsin law infringed upon his First Amendment rights. The Wisconsin State Supreme Court agreed and reversed the conviction. The court reasoned that the penalty enhancement law inappropriately punishes hate thought (motive) and thus compromised First Amendment rights. But in 1993, the US Supreme Court upheld the Wisconsin statute and found that the statute proscribes conduct (and not expression), specifically the conduct of intentional and "discriminatory selection" of a victim based on race (Lawrence, 1999, 33). As Lawrence explained (1999, 33) "so long as Mitchell chose (the victim) on the basis of his race, his conduct would trigger the Wisconsin penalty-enhancement statute."

Levin (2009) summarizes the significance of the changes in hate crime law as represented by *R.A.V. v. St. Paul* and *Wisconsin v. Mitchell*. The court's decision in *Wisconsin v. Mitchell* "upheld the constitutionality of broadly applicable penalty enhancement laws for hate crime" (2009, 15). In addition, it resolved some of the central criticisms of hate crime laws. Offering three reasons for its decision in Wisconsin, the court stated, (15):

> First, while the government may not punish abstract beliefs, it has wide latitude to address (offender) motive. Second, the Court further found that

penalty enhancement laws . . . were aimed at discriminatory conduct and did not punish merely hateful expression." (Whereas,) "in R.A.V. the criminality depended not on the hostile use of a particular symbol, but on whether a designated disfavored viewpoint was conveyed by its use. Last, the Court addressed the severity of hate crime harms, stating that they are "thought to be more likely to provoke retaliatory crimes, inflict distinct emotional harm on their victims and incite community unrest.

(*Wisconsin v. Mitchell*, 1993, 487–88)

According to the 2009 report of the Leadership Conference on Civil Rights Education Fund, at least 45 states and the District of Columbia had passed hate crime statutes that utilize the penalty enhancement structure. The next significant hate crime law is named for the victims of two highly publicized and tragic hate crimes that occurred in the United States, Matthew Shepard and James Byrd, Jr. Murdered in the same year (1998), but in two different parts of the country, (Wyoming and Texas, respectively), these crimes galvanized a network of advocacy groups, national organizations, and progressive political leaders to support stronger measures to combat hate crime. At the time of these murders, the state of Wyoming and Texas could not prosecute these as hate crimes. Neither state had hate crime laws at that time. Neither could the federal government intervene and prosecute because sexual orientation was not a protected status. Nor could Byrd's matter evoke federal statues because he was not engaged in a federally protected activity at the time of his attack. The Matthew Shepard and James Byrd, Jr. Hate Crimes Prevention Act would address those deficiencies.

The Matthew Shepard and James Byrd, Jr. Hate Crimes Prevention Act, 2009

On October 28, 2009 President Barak Obama signed the Matthew Shepard and James Byrd, Jr. Hate Crimes Prevention Act into law and essentially broadened the ability of federal authorities to prosecute local hate crimes. Before the passage of the Shepard-Byrd Act, the federal government could only be involved in the prosecution of a hate crime if the victim was attacked (because of race, religion etc.), while engaged in a federally protected activity. This legislation creates a new federal criminal hate crimes statute, 18 U.S.C. paragraph 249. Section 249(a)(1), which eliminates the requirement of victim participation in federally protected activities (see 18 U.S.C. paragraph 245). In addition, local and state law enforcement authorities receive additional investigative and prosecutorial resources by working collaboratively with federal authorities. In states where the local authorities have insufficient resources to respond to a hate crime; or for some reason, elect to not prosecute the case, federal authorities would have the ability to enter into the picture and or provide additional funds and technical assistance to support the local authorities. There are also instances when a criminal defendant has committed several hate crimes in multiple jurisdictions. Under such circumstances, federal authorities are best situated to respond.

While state authorities could be concerned with the possibility of federal prosecutors trampling upon state sovereignty and taking over prosecutions, the law has built in procedures to ensure that federal involvement is based on valid grounds and that state authorities have agreed to its involvement in a state case. The "certification requirement" requires that "no prosecution of any offense described . . . may be undertaken by the United States, except under the certification in writing of the Attorney General or his designee, that:

1   such certifying individual has reasonable cause to believe that the actual or perceived race, color, religion, national origin, gender, sexual orientation, gender identity, or disability of any person was a motivating factor underlying the alleged conduct of the defendant; and

2   such certifying individual has consulted with State or local law enforcement officials regarding the prosecution and determined that—

3   the State does not have jurisdiction or does not intend to exercise jurisdiction;

4   the State has requested that the Federal Government assume jurisdiction;

5   the State does not object to the Federal Government assuming jurisdiction; or

6   the verdict or sentence obtained pursuant to State charges left demonstratively unvindicated the Federal interest in eradicating bias motivated violence.

7   a prosecution by the United States is in the public interest and necessary to secure substantial justice.

(Open Congress, S. 909)

The law also provides new protected status categories in federal hate crime law: gender, sexual orientation, gender identity, and disability. Thus the protected status categories under federal law now include race, color, religion, national origin, gender, sexual orientation, gender identity, and disability.

The Hate Crimes Prevention Act is not without its critics. Some fear that adding the protected categories of sexual orientation and gender identity brings about targeted censorship and compromises religious freedom (Leichman, 2009; Lofton, 2009). They theorize that religious leaders would be subject to arrest if they deliver sermons that suggest that homosexuality runs counter to God's prescription for marriage and the family. Others suggest that the law provides protections for pedophiles and other categories of sexually deviant behavior as a result of the gender identity category, which is probably the least familiar and therefore less understood. These concerns aside, the Matthew Shepard and James Byrd, Jr. Hate Crimes Prevention Act does not appear to include language that permits targeted censorship or censorship in general, nor is it situated to infringe upon the First Amendment protection of freedom of religion.

The first case charged under the Shepard-Byrd Act ended in a conviction. George Thompson, an employee of the Transportation Security Administration (TSA), was off duty when he committed the crime on May 4, 2010. According to reports, upon leaving his neighborhood bar, Thompson spotted the victim whom he assumed was Muslim because he was bearded. Witnesses stated that Thompson yelled at the victim, "You, Muslims, go back to your country." Asking the man if he was Somali, Thompson continued. . . . "You Somali, go back to your country." He physically assaulted the eighty-two-year old, hitting him, and then chased him, threatening to kill him. Police intervened. Thompson admitted to the attack as well as to yelling ethnic and anti-Muslim slurs. He supposedly was frustrated from difficulty in his neighborhood with Somali youth. On August 10, 2011, he was sentenced to six months in federal prison (DOJ, 2011). With the passage of the Shepard-Byrd Act, the federal government has increased its ability to become directly involved in what would otherwise be typical state and local hate crime occurrences.

Cross-burning and anti-mask laws

Laws that criminalize cross-burning and mask-wearing may be considered a subset of hate crime laws. Historically, these laws were a response to the violent campaigns of the Ku Klux Klan to intimidate and terrorize African-Americans and others and the particular manner in which these campaigns were carried out. What came to be the iconic images and symbols of the Klan had practical benefits. The wearing of hoods and robes not only evoked fear but also concealed the identity of the wearer. Cross-burnings have also been used throughout the years as a method to threaten others. The first documented incident of cross-burning by the Klan occurred in 1915 (Swanson, 2002). Although the Klan itself will argue that a burning cross is part of a ceremonial sacred ritual, they've also used it as a tool of aggression and promise of violence. It is because of the manner in which the hood wearing and cross-burning has been used that legislatures have sought to criminalize these actions under proper circumscribed conditions. The challenge to these laws is their ability to withstand First Amendment challenges. Wearing hoods or masks and cross-burning may be construed as expressive or symbolic speech. The First Amendment exists for the purpose of ensuring freedom of speech; even speech that many would find detestable.

Georgia's anti-mask law

In 1951, Georgia enacted the Anti-Mask Act OCGA paragraph 16-11-38. This law was prompted by the high level of violent actions, threats and harassment perpetrated by the Klan against targeted citizens of the state. The law provides the following:

A person is guilty of a misdemeanor when he wears a mask, hood, or device by which any portion of the face is so hidden, concealed, or covered as to conceal the identity of the wearer and is upon any public way or public property or upon the private property of another without the written permission of the owner or occupier of the property to do so.

(*State v. Miller*)

The law was careful to target *certain* mask-wearing behavior and not all. Mask-wearing during seasonal holidays, for physical safety at the workplace or during a sports activity, or for theatrical productions or celebrations such as Mardi Gras are exceptions and do not trigger the Act. The specific objective of the law is reflected in the Statement of Public Policy articulated in the law itself. The Anti-Mask Act reflects "the General Assembly's awareness of and concern over the dangers to society posed by anonymous vigilante organizations." It reads as follows:

All persons residing in the State are entitled to the equal protection of their lives and property. The law protects all, not only against actual physical violence, but also against threats and intimidations from any person or group of persons. The General Assembly cannot permit persons known or unknown, to issue either actual or implied threats, against other persons in the State. Persons in this State are and shall continue to be answerable only to the established law as enforced by legally appointed officers.

(*State v. Miller*)

This language clearly indicates that Georgia's Anti-Mask Act was in reaction to the lawless violent behavior of the Klan, which used the mask to conceal the identity of those implicated in criminal behavior. But the law was challenged in *State v. Miller*. Shade Miller was convicted under the Act for wearing Klan regalia including the traditional hood in public. He challenged the constitutionality of the Georgia law arguing that the law violated his freedom of speech among other encroachments upon his civil rights.

Although the trial court declared the Anti-Mask Act unconstitutional, the Georgia State Supreme Court in *State v. Miller* did not. The court referred to *United States v. O'Brien, 391 U.S. 367*, which affirmed that "the government may regulate conduct that has both speech and nonspeech elements, if the regulation furthers a substantial governmental interest that is unrelated to the suppression of free expression" and is minimal. The substantial governmental interest in the Act is the protection of the people of Georgia from "*terrorization by masked vigilantes*," while reassuring the free exercise of the civil rights of law abiding citizens. Governmental interests also includes supporting law enforcement in the apprehension of offenders. The identification of masked criminals by their victims is extraordinarily difficult, in addition to the paralyzing fear caused by such images. Moreover, the Georgia State Supreme Court stated that the Anti-Mask

Act was non-discriminatory and content-neutral as the law proscribed "menacing conduct" or the behavior of the mask-wearer rather than a particular message. The focus was on the intimidation or fear provoking aspect of the mask-wearer's behavior, which includes the concealment of the wearer's identity, which in turn evokes apprehension. The State Supreme Court reiterated that conviction requires that the context of the defendant's conduct must be considered. For example, it must be proved that the defendant wore the mask knowing or having reasonable knowledge that wearing the mask to intimidate or to threaten is not protected by the First Amendment. Miller or any Klansmen has the freedom to participate in organized public rallies, marches, to distribute leaflets and so on. The Anti-Mask Act does not interfere with this protected speech activity but rather forbids intimidating mask-wearing communicative conduct.

Virginia's cross-burning law

The Virginia legislature passed its cross-burning law, paragraph 18.2-423 (burning cross on property of another or public place with intent to intimidate); penalty; prima facie evidence of intent. The first version of this law was passed in 1950. The law states:

> It shall be unlawful for any person or persons, with the intent of intimidating any person or group of persons, to burn, or cause to be burned, a cross on the property of another, a highway or other public place. Any person who shall violate any provision of this section shall be guilty of a Class 6 felony. Any such burning of a cross shall be prima facie evidence of an intent to intimidate a person or group of persons.

Just as Georgia's Anti-Mask Act was challenged in court, so was Virginia's cross-burning law. In August 1998, Barry Black, the Imperial Wizard of the International Keystone Knights of the Ku Klux Klan, led a Klan rally in Carroll County, Virginia. To end the rally, the group circled a large cross approximately 25 feet high and burned it on private property with the owner's permission. Black was subsequently arrested and convicted under Virginia's cross-burning law. Several similar cases, in addition to Black's case, were appealed to the State Supreme Court challenging the constitutionality of Virginia's cross-burning law. That court held that the law was unconstitutional because it "selectively chooses only and all cross burnings because of its distinctive message," and is thus not content neutral but discriminatory. The court also stated that the pronouncement that the very occurrence of a cross-burning was prima facie evidence made the law overbroad and violated the First Amendment.

The state of Virginia petitioned the US Supreme Court, which subsequently reviewed the law and rendered a decision that clarified the issue. In *Virginia vs. Black 2003*, the court determined that a state *may* ban cross-burnings which are done *willfully* for the purpose of evoking fear and to intimidate. In this decision, the court acknowledges that the history of and social meaning surrounding cross-burning legitimizes state regulation. *However,* that portion of the Virginia law that stated that the burning of a cross in and of itself is sufficient evidence to establish the required intent was an overreach. As despicable as Klan cross-burning may be to some if not most individuals in a free society, the First Amendment permits such symbolic expression when done under appropriate (and legal) circumstances. The Klan and similar groups have the First Amendment protected right to use a burning cross as political speech, or as a symbol of group ideology and/or as a symbol of their organization or part of their rituals. To criminalize those aspects of cross-burning suppresses speech and violates the First Amendment. Therefore, while the Virginia law against cross-burning is valid, its provision of any act of cross-burning as prima facie evidence of intimidation is deemed unconstitutional and is struck down by the court.

State hate crime laws

In September 2005, the Congressional Research Service published a report on "State Statutes Governing Hate Crimes." The report identifies four types of state hate crime laws: "statutory provisions that outlaw destruction of religious institutions, criminalize bias motivated violence and intimidation, mandate training for state police officers in recognizing and reporting hate crimes, and also prohibit infringement on another person's civil rights" (Austin & Wallace, 2005, 4). Most state hate crime legislation will include one or more of these elements. There is variation and commonalities among state hate crime statutes. General differences may be found in how the hate crime offense is defined, the scope or comprehensiveness of the law, and the range in penalties. Some states utilize the civil rights legislative approach and conceptualize their hate crime laws as the interference with the exercise of a Constitutional right. For example Wyoming (Wyo. Stat. paragraph 6-9-102) criminalizes violations of civil or constitutional rights:

> 6-9-102. Discrimination prohibited; penalties.
> a   No person shall be denied the right to life, liberty, pursuit of happiness or the necessities of life because of race, color, sex, creed or national origin.
> b   A person who violates this section commits a misdemeanor punishable by imprisonment for not more than six (6) months, a fine of not more than seven hundred fifty dollars ($750.00), or both.

Other state laws use language that is similar to the ADL model statute: "offenses committed by reason of the actual or perceived race, color, religion . . . of another person or group of persons." Missouri state law 557.035 states: 1. For all violations of subdivision (1) of subsection 1 of section 569.100, RSMo, or subdivision (1), (2), (3), (4), (6), (7) or (8) of subsection 1 of section 571.030, RSMo, which the state believes to be knowingly motivated because of race, color, religion, national origin, sex, sexual orientation, or disability of the victim or victims, the state may charge the crime or crimes under this section, and the violation is a Class C felony.

Several states, such as California, have developed statutes that not only deal with the criminal offense, but in training and reporting issues as well. California— Cal Pen Code paragraph 422.6 criminalizes injury or threat to person or damage to property because of actual or perceived "race, color, religion, ancestry, national origin, disability, gender, or sexual orientation." The following components of California's hate crime laws reflect its comprehensive nature:

Cal Pen Code paragraph 666.7
Lists sentence enhancements for felony hate crimes and damage to property because the property is "associated with a person or group of identifiable race, color, religion, nationality, country of origin, ancestry, gender, disability, or sexual orientation."

Cal Pen Code paragraph 628.5
Establishes criteria for validating incidents of each crime description reported by schools.

Cal Pen Code paragraph 628.2
Covers compilation and distribution of reports of crimes committed on school grounds.

Cal Pen Code paragraph 628.1
Mandates development of reporting form for hate crimes, for use by all school districts and county offices of education.

Cal Pen Code paragraph 628
Establishes legislative intent to ensure collection of sufficient data and information about type and frequency of hate crimes and hate incidents on school campuses to combat such crime.

Cal Pen Code paragraph 594.3
Criminalizes vandalism of places of worship and interference with religious worship.

Cal Pen Code paragraph 422.95
Covers conditions of probation for hate crime perpetrators, including civil rights training and payments to organizations that help hate crime victims.

Cal Pen Code paragraph 422.75
Enhances penalty for felony committed because of victim's actual or perceived "race, color, religion, nationality, country of origin, ancestry, disability, gender, or sexual orientation."

Cal Pen Code paragraph 422.7
Specifies additional penalties to be imposed for "felony of intimidation because of specified beliefs or characteristics."

As discussed earlier, many state hate crime statutes include a penalty-enhancement element, which reflects the ADL model hate crime statute. It requires that crimes motivated by hate be subject to an increased or enhanced sentence. This component is triggered when the defendant intentionally selects the victim based upon his or her perceived membership in a group with characteristics that are included in the protected categories articulated in the state's law.

Wisconsin's hate crime law specifies the sentence enhancement feature:

a   If the crime committed . . . is ordinarily a misdemeanor . . . the revised maximum fine is $10,000 and the revised maximum period of imprisonment is one year in the county jail;

b   If the crime committed . . . is ordinarily a Class A misdemeanor, the penalty increase under this section changes the status of the crime to a felony and the revised maximum fine is $10,000 and the revised maximum period of imprisonment is 2 years;

c   If the crime committed . . . is a felony, the maximum fine prescribed by law for the crime may be increased by not more than $5,000 and the maximum period of imprisonment prescribed by law for the crime may be increased by not more than 5 years.

(Wisconsin State Legislature, paragraph 939.645)

In general, criminal laws vary from state to state. Therefore, it is not unusual to find distinctions among state hate crime laws. This variation is not only beneficial but it is also expected as the nature of hate crime itself manifests differently across counties, cities, states, and in different regions of the country.

The hate crime law controversy

Hate crime laws will continue to be viewed as a necessary tool by some and with certain skepticism by others. The disputed ideas surrounding hate crime laws may change, but never fully disappear. Despite the Supreme Court's decision in *Wisconsin v. Mitchell*, some will continue to argue that these laws punish thoughts and that it has opened the door to the concept of "thought police."

The recognition of hate-motivated acts in American society took hundreds of years to occur. The criminalization of that which used to be a cultural norm is a monumental step. The idea of prohibiting a crime because it is motivated by the animus of a social status or identity is unique from most other laws. Moreover, policing and punishing these crimes in a rational and effective manner are additional areas of disagreement. It is quite clear that this category of law will be viewed as controversial for the foreseeable future. We now turn to outline some of the more common arguments for and against hate crime laws.

Proponents of hate crime laws: a summary

1   *Hate crime laws are necessary because of the corrosive nature of hate crimes.* Some of the most important reasons why hate crime laws are needed were articulated in the US Supreme Court's decision in *Wisconsin v. Mitchell.* In it, the court describes the distinctive qualities of hate crime acts. For instance, the court mentioned that bias or hate motives are "depraved motives." The selection of the term "depraved" is meaningful— as it suggests that hate crimes are particularly repugnant acts. The court also pointed to the severe nature of hate crimes stating that they are "thought to be more likely to provoke retaliatory crimes, inflict distinct emotional harm on their victims, and incite community unrest" (Levin, 1999, 10).

2   *There is evidence that hate crimes tend to be more violent and injurious than non-biased violent crimes.* These acts tend to involve more violent assaults and cause serious bodily injury to victims in comparison to non-biased motivated assaults (Levin & McDevitt, 1993). Hate crimes also tend to involve multiple perpetrators in a single attack.

3   *The vast majority of hate crimes go unreported.* There are several contributing factors for the lack of reporting. One includes the belief that not much can or will be done by law enforcement to respond to the crime. Furthermore, the relationship between racial minority communities, the gay community, and local police authorities have been strained at best (Dunbar, 1997). Victims from these communities may be distrustful of law enforcement and are less enthusiastic about turning to them to report the crime.

4   *Another justification for hate crime laws is based on the impact these crimes have on victims* (Herek, et al. 1997). Collectively these crimes seek to create a social order that places white male heterosexuals in a permanent position of superiority, and all others in an inferior position. Thus, these crimes rail against the American ideals of justice, equality, and freedom for all.

Opponents of hate crime laws: a summary

1   *Hate crime laws infringe upon freedom of speech.* Despite evidence to the contrary, some continue to argue that hate crime laws punish thoughts or certainly pose a threat to the right to free speech. This concern is supported by the fact that what distinguishes a hate crime from a conventional crime lies in the bias or hate motive. Motive can be determined by forms of communication, whether expressive or symbolic, written or verbal. Yet, the decision in *Wisconsin v. Mitchell* (1993) reiterated that the statute did not criminalize speech, but conduct in the offender's intentional selection of a target due to race, religion, sexual orientation, gender or disability. This decision should have effectively diminished this concern. Nevertheless, there are hate crime

statutes that are not modeled after the Wisconsin law, which may contribute to continuing First Amendment concerns.

2   *Hate crime laws infringe upon freedom of religion.* There have been instances outside of the United States where religious teachers, pastors, Catholic bishops, and others have been "scrutinized" by authorities and even charged with a hate crime for speaking out against homosexuality (and other topics) within the context of biblical teachings. The Catholic Civil Rights League of Canada reports several such specific instances in the following online publication (Catholic Civil Rights League of Canada):

- Catholic Insight Magazine was the subject of a complaint to the Canadian Human Rights Commission due to material on its website critical of homosexual conduct. (The complaint was dismissed but is currently under appeal by the complainant.)
- Steven Boissoin, a Christian pastor was fined a total of $7,000 in 2008 and ordered never to speak or write publicly in future about homosexual conduct, after a complaint to the Alberta Human Rights Commission for a letter published in the Red Deer Advocate. Boissoin did win his appeal in December 2009.
- In 2002, the Saskatchewan Human Rights Commission ordered the Saskatoon Star Phoenix and Hugh Owens to each pay $1,500 to three complainants because of the publication of an advertisement that quoted Bible verses on homosexuality. Four years later, this was overturned by the Saskatchewan Court of Appeal after the court ruled that the message, though offensive, didn't reach the level of inciting hatred.

Conflicts like these fuel the anxieties of cautionary First Amendment advocates and those of faith communities who point to these incidents and warn that they serve as a bellwether for the United States (Black, 2009).

3   *Hate crime laws further the problem of identity politics.* Other opponents interpret hate crime laws as somehow advantaging minorities and work against the majority group and that this benefit violates the equal protection clause on the Fourteenth Amendment and plays to the interests of identity politics (Jacobs & Potter, 1998). This stance almost justifies why hate crime laws are needed. The interpretation of the historical victimization of minorities and subsequent laws to punish that behavior is in some way viewed as favoritism. Those expressing this view point think of racially motivated acts as only anti-Black, or anti-Hispanic and fail to see that racially motivated also includes anti-White motivated acts. This viewpoint also overlooks that in *Wisconsin v. Mitchell*, Mitchell the defendant, was a young African-American male who facilitated a group attack upon a Caucasian. The aim of hate crime laws is to punish discriminatory behavior and does not have the goal of prosecuting a particular group. The protective categories are exhaustive. Racially motivated includes a member of any race,

Black, Asian/Pacific Islander, American Indian/Alaskan Native and White. Religion-motivated crimes means a victim of any religion, not just Judaism or Christianity, but also Buddhism and Islam. Likewise, sexual orientation-motivated crime includes gays, lesbians, bisexuals, transgendered persons, and heterosexuals.

Chapter summary

- Legal scholars contend that the legal antecedents of modern hate crime legislation can be found in the Thirteenth, Fourteenth, and Fifteenth Amendments to the US Constitution. Each of these Amendments sought to remedy a race-based wrong. The significance and relevance of these and other federal laws is found in the stated objectives and language used, which has direct relevance to the goals of modern hate crime laws.
- As a result of the federal government's efforts to protect freed Blacks and support their participation as American citizens, defiant southern authorities, the Ku Klux Klan, and even ordinary citizens fearful of these changes, worked to harass, intimidate, and violently confront Blacks at those junctures where they sought to exercise freedom.
- Seeking to address race-based reactionary violence, the federal government enacted laws such as the Force Act of 1871 and the Ku Klux Klan Act, also of 1871. These laws provided civil and criminal sanctions for those who were guilty of interfering with or depriving citizens (including Black citizens) of their Constitutional rights.
- The clear intention of these laws was to provide the federal government with the legal means to police, protect, and punish those individuals and groups, particularly the Ku Klux Klan, who engaged in racially motivated interferences and other types of systematic victimizations. But more importantly, these laws were precedent-like for criminalizing behaviors that were motivated by racial animus and or other related hostility, causing the intentional targeting of victims due to their racial or other ascribed class-based characteristics (Hall, 2005; Higginbotham, 1996; Levin, 2002).
- A different type of racial violence occurred when multiple waves of Black migration from the rural south to northern urban centers occurred. Blacks were subjected to violence perpetrated by White mobs for reasons that ranged from moving into predominately White neighborhoods and/or competing for jobs or rumors about Blacks perpetuating crimes against Whites (Tuttle, 1996; Lieberson & Silverman, 1965).
- Group libel is the defamation of a group of individuals based on their race, ethnicity, sexual orientation, religion, or other similar reasons. Illinois became the first state to criminalize group libel with the passage of the 1949 state law which criminalizes the portrayal of "any race, color, creed, or religion," as a class of citizens who lack any virtue or as being "depraved" or as "criminals."
- The US Supreme Court upheld the Illinois statute in *Beauharnais v. Illinois* 343 U.S. 250 (1952), which criminalized the libel of a group and essentially

found that this type of speech is not constitutionally protected. The significance of this statute and the Supreme Court's decision contributed to modern hate crime legislation by penalizing behaviors that denigrated a class of people due to their race, color, creed, or religion (Levin, 2002).

- Early hate crime statutes were modeled after federal civil rights statutes (Levin, 1999). However, these laws would begin to resemble modern hate crime statutes with the aid of the Anti-Defamation's model hate crime statute. There were five components of the model statute including: (1) identifying a hate crime as a two-tiered criminal act, the predicate or base offense and the element of animus toward the victim because of actual or perceived characteristics; (2) the enhanced penalty element; (3) institutional vandalism (as these acts are often directed towards groups due to bias); (4) civil actions may be sought for damages; and (5) states should collect and maintain hate crime data reported to law enforcement.

- On October 28, 2009 President Barak Obama signed the Matthew Shepard and James Byrd, Jr. Hate Crimes Prevention Act into law and essentially broadened the ability of federal authorities to prosecute local hate crimes. The law also provides new protected status categories in federal hate crime law: gender, sexual orientation, gender identity, and disability.

- Hate crime laws will continue to be viewed with skepticism by some. The disputed notions surrounding hate crime laws change, but never fully disappear.

- Arguments to support hate crime laws include: (1) Hate crime laws are necessary because of the corrosive nature of hate crimes. (2) There is evidence that suggests hate crimes tend to be more violent and injurious than non-biased violent crimes. (3) The vast majority of hate crimes go unreported. There are several contributing factors for the lack of reporting. One includes the belief that not much can or will be done by law enforcement to respond to the crime. The existence of these laws helps to diffuse this perspective. (4) Another justification for hate crime laws is due to the nature of the impact these crimes have on their victims (Herek, et al. 1997). Thus, these crimes rail against the American ideals of justice, equality, and freedom for all.

- Arguments against hate crime laws include: (1) Hate crime laws infringe upon freedom of speech. Despite evidence to the contrary, some are concerned that hate crime laws punish thoughts or certainly pose a threat to the right to free speech and free expression. (2) Hate crime laws infringe upon freedom of religion. There have been instances outside of the United States where religious leaders and others have been the subject of investigation by authorities and subsequently charged with a hate crime for teachings critical of homosexuality within the context of biblical teachings. These instances fuel the anxieties of cautionary First Amendment advocates and those of faith communities who point to these incidents as a bellwether for the United States. (3) Hate crime laws further the problem of identity politics. Other opponents interpret hate crime laws as somehow advantaging minorities and work against the majority group. However, racially motivated crimes address victims of any race.

Case study 3.1 California assembly passes new hate crimes bill

Author: Equality California

Published on Apr 30, 2010

SACRAMENTO, Calif. April 29, 2010 - Today the California State Assembly passed the Hate Crimes Protection Act (AB 1689) in a 44-25 vote. Sponsored by Equality California . . . , the bill would exempt hate crimes from mandatory arbitration clauses . . . and would prohibit contracts from requiring an individual to waive his or her legal rights, guaranteed under the Ralph Civil Rights Act, which provides protections for hate crime victims.

"Victims of hate crimes should never be forced into arbitration simply because they signed an employment or residential contract . . . that waives their right to seek justice in our courts," said Geoff Kors, executive director of Equality California.

Although California state and civil laws protect people from hate-related crimes, private contracts often require individuals to relinquish their fundamental rights and protections.

"Many employment contracts have a mandatory arbitration clause, which allows perpetuators of hate crimes to arbitrate and not go to court," said Assembly member Saldana. "This bill would make hate crimes an exemption if you sign one of these contracts."

(Source: Equality California 2010)

Discussion questions

1   California's recent passage of the Hate Crimes Protection Act reflects efforts to extend protections to victims of hate crime. How would those who are concerned with identity politics respond to this new law?

2   This new law permits hate crime victims to have the ability to file a civil law suit and sue for damages regarding their hate crime victimization. Are there any potential unanticipated consequences regarding hiring practices that could occur as a result of the Hate Crimes Protection Act?

3   Is it possible to over-legislate protection for hate crime victims?

Appendix

Local Law Enforcement Hate Crimes Prevention Act of 2009

HR 1913 RFS

111th CONGRESS
1st Session

H. R. 1913
IN THE SENATE OF THE UNITED STATES
April 30, 2009

Received; read twice and referred to the Committee on the Judiciary

---

AN ACT

To provide Federal assistance to States, local jurisdictions, and Indian tribes to prosecute hate crimes, and for other purposes.

Be it enacted by the Senate and House of Representatives of the United States of America in Congress assembled,

SECTION 1. SHORT TITLE.

This Act may be cited as the 'Local Law Enforcement Hate Crimes Prevention Act of 2009'.

SEC. 2. DEFINITION OF HATE CRIME.

In this Act—

1   the term 'crime of violence' has the meaning given that term in section 16, title 18, United States Code;

2   the term 'hate crime' has the meaning given such term in section 280003(a) of the Violent Crime Control and Law Enforcement Act of 1994 (28 U.S.C. 994 note); and

3   the term 'local' means a county, city, town, township, parish, village, or other general purpose political subdivision of a State.

SEC. 3. SUPPORT FOR CRIMINAL INVESTIGATIONS AND PROSECUTIONS BY STATE, LOCAL, AND TRIBAL LAW ENFORCEMENT OFFICIALS.

a   Assistance Other Than Financial Assistance—

1   IN GENERAL—At the request of a State, local, or tribal law enforcement agency, the Attorney General may provide technical, forensic, prosecutorial, or any other form of assistance in the criminal investigation or prosecution of any crime that—

A   constitutes a crime of violence;

B   constitutes a felony under the State, local, or tribal laws; and

C   is motivated by prejudice based on the actual or perceived race, color, religion, national origin, gender, sexual orientation, gender identity, or disability of the victim, or is a violation of the State, local, or tribal hate crime laws.

2   PRIORITY- In providing assistance under paragraph (1), the Attorney General shall give priority to crimes committed by offenders who have committed crimes in more than one State and to rural jurisdictions that have difficulty covering the extraordinary expenses relating to the investigation or prosecution of the crime.

(Source: www.govtrack.us/congress/bills/111/hr1913/text,
Accessed August 20, 2014)

Bibliography

Anti-Defamation League (ADL). (2012). *Hate Crimes Law: The ADL Approach*. Available from www.adl.org/assets/pdf/combating-hate/Hate-Crimes-Law-The-ADL-Approach.pdf [Accessed February 20, 2014].

Austin, C. A. & Wallace, P.S. (2005). *State Statutes Governing Hate Crimes*. CRS Report for Congress.

Black, N. (2009). Christians Say Hate Crimes Bill is Not What You Think. *Christian Post Reporter*. 26 June. Available from www.christianpost.com/article/20090626/christians-say-hate-crimes-bill-is-not-what-you-think/index.html [Accessed December 18, 2009].

Catholic Civil Rights League of Canada. (n.d.) Hate Speech. Available from https://ccrl.ca/?s=hate+speech [Accessed on March 8, 2015].

Cornell University Law School. (n.d.). Legal Information Institute. R.A.V. v. City of St. Paul. Available from https://www.law.cornell.edu/supremecourt/text/505/377#writing-USSC_CR_0505_0377_ZO [Accessed on March 8, 2015].

Cummings, Jr., M. C. & Wise, D. (1971). *Democracy Under Pressure*. New York: Harcourt Brace Jovanovich.

Dunbar, E. (1997). Race, Gender, and Sexual Orientation in Hate Crime Victimization. The Importance of Race and Gender Membership in Sexual Orientation Hate Crime Victimization and Reportage: Identity Politics or Identity Risk. Available from https://www.academia.edu/8332887/Running_Head_Race_Gender_and_Sexual_Orientation_in_Hate_Crime_Victimization_The_Importance_of_Race_and_Gender_Membership_ in_Sexual_Orientation_Hate_Crime_Victimization_and_Reportage_Identity_Poli-tics_or_Identity_Risk?login=carolyn.petrosino@gmail.com&email_was_taken=true [Accessed March 5, 2015].

Equality California. (2010). Press Release. California Assembly Passes New Hate Crimes Bill. EQCA-Sponsored Bill Would Strengthen Protections for Victims of Hate Crimes. Available from http://www.eqca.org/site/apps/nlnet/content2.aspx?c=kuLRJ9MRKrH&b=4869041&ct=8225923 [Accessed March 5, 2015].

Gerstenfeld, P. B. (2004). *Hate Crimes: Causes, Controls, and Controversies*. Thousand Oaks, CA: Sage Publications.

Griffing, J. (2009). Hate Crimes and the Sedition Act of 2009. *The American Thinker.* May 24. Available from www.americanthinker.com/2009/05/hate_crimes_and_the_sedition_a.html [Accessed December 19, 2009].

Hall, N. (2005). *Hate Crime*. Portland, OH: Willan Publishing.

Hambrick, G. (2009) South Carolina Baptists Resolve to "Avoid" LGBT Hate Crime. *Charleston City Paper*. Available from www.charlestoncitypaper.com/GayCharleston/archives/2009/11/16/south-carolina-baptists-resolve-to-avoid-lgbt-hate-crimes [Accessed December 19, 2009].

Herek, G.M., Gillis, J.R., Cogan, J.C. & Glunt, E.K. (1997). Hate Crime Victimization Among Lesbian, Gay, and Bisexual Adults: Prevalence, Psychological Correlates, and Methodological Issues. *Journal of Interpersonal Violence, 12*, 195–215.

Higginbotham, A.L. (1996). *Shades of Freedom: Racial Politics and Presumptions of the American Legal Process*. New York: Oxford University Press.

Jacobs, J. B. & Potter, K. (1998). *Hate Crimes: Criminal Law and Identity Politics*. New York: Oxford University Press.

Lawrence, F. M. (1999). *Punishing Hate: Bias Crimes Under American Law*. Cambridge, MA: Harvard University Press.

Leadership Conference on Civil Rights Education Fund (LCCREF). (2009). *Confronting the New Faces of Hate: Hate Crimes in America*. Washington, DC.

Leagle.com. (n.d.). Beauharnais v. Pittsburgh Courier Publishing Co. Available from http://www.leagle.com/decision/1957948243F2d705_1750.xml/BEAUHARNAIS%20v.%20PITTSBURGH%20COURIER%20PUBLISHING%20CO [Accessed February 7, 2015].

Leichson, A.J. (2009). Christian Attorneys Urge Senate to Vote Against "Hate Crimes" Bill. *Christian Post Reporter*. 1 May. Available from www.christianpost.com/article/20090501/christian-attorneys-urge-senate-to-vote-against-hate-crimes-bill/index.html [Accessed December 19, 2009].

Levin, B. (1999). Hate Crimes. Worse by Definition. *Journal of Contemporary Criminal Justice*, 15(1), 6–21.

Levin, B. (2002). From Slavery to Hate Crime Laws: The Emergence of Race and Status-Based Protection in American Criminal Law. *Journal of Social Issues*, 58(2), 227–45.

Levin, B. (2009). The Long Arc of Justice: Race, Violence, and the Emergence of Hate Crime Law. In B. Levin (ed.) *Hate Crimes. Volume 1: Understand and Defining Hate Crime*. Westport, CT: Praeger Publishers.

Levin, J. & McDevitt, J. (1993). *Hate Crimes: The Rising Tide of Bigotry and Bloodshed*. New York: Plenum Press.

Lieberson, S. & Silverman, A. (1965). The Precipitants and Underlying Conditions of Race Riots. *The American Sociological Review*, 30(6), 887–98.

Lofton, J. (2009). Hate Crime Bill Concerns Church Leaders. *Ada Evening News*. June 15. Available from www.adaeveningnews.com/local/local_story_166091705.html [Accessed December 19, 2009].

Minnesota Legislation Code, paragraph 292.02 (n.d.). Available from https://www.law.cornell.edu/supct/html/90-7675.ZO.html [Accessed on March 8, 2015].

Neiwert, D. (2009). Fox's Napolitano Fears Hate-Crimes Law Hurts Free Speech — But Ignores Explicit Language of Bill. Available from http://crooksandliars.com/david-neiwert/foxs-napolitano-fears-hate-crimes-la [Accessed December 19, 2009].

New York Times. (1994). Available from www.nytimes.com/1994/05/27/nyregion/new-jersey-bias-crimes- statutes-are-overturned.html [Accessed March 6, 2010].

National Public Radio (NPR). (2005). All Things Considered: Anti-Lynching Law in U.S. History—Interview of Prof. Harvard Sitkoff, University of New Hampshire, June 13. Available from www.npr.org/templates/story/story.php?storyId=4701576 [Accessed February 8, 2015].

Open Congress, S.909. (n.d.). Matthew Shepard Hate Crimes Prevention Act. Available from https://www.opencongress.org/bill/s909-111/text [Accessed on March 8, 2015].

State v. Miller, No. S90A1172, Supreme Court of Georgia, 260 Ga. 669; 398 S.E.2d 547; 1990 Ga. LEXIS 459; 59 U.S.L.W. 2374, December 5, 1990, Decided.

Swanson, J. L. (2002). Unholy Fire: Cross Burning, Symbolic Speech, and the First Amendment. *Virginia v. Black. Cato Supreme Court Review 2002–2003.* Washington, DC: Cato Institute.

Tuttle, W. M. (1996). *Race Riot: Chicago in the Red Summer of 1919.* Chicago, IL: University of Chicago Press.

US Code. (n.d.). Title 42. Chapter 21. Subchapter I. paragraph 1985. Conspiracy to Interfere with Civil Rights. .

US Department of Justice (DOJ). (2011). Justice News. Wednesday, August 10, 2011. Former TSA Employee Pleads Guilty to Federal Hate Crime for Assaulting Elderly Somali Man. Available from http://www.justice.gov/opa/pr/former-tsa-employee-pleads-guilty-federal-hate-crime-assaulting-elderly-somali-man [Accessed on March 8, 2015].

US Statutes at Large. (n.d.). Vol. XVIII, p. 335 ff. Available from http://chnm.gmu.edu/courses/122/recon/civilrightsact.html [Accessed March 2, 2010].

What Is Proposition 8? (n.d.). Available from www.whatisprop8.com [Accessed December 19, 2009].

Wisconsin State Legislature, paragraph 939.645. (n.d.). Penalty; crimes committed against certain people or property. Available from http://docs.legis.wisconsin.gov/statutes/statutes/939/IV/645 [Accessed on March 8, 2015].

Young, E. (2009). Ministry: "Hate Crimes" Law Will Fuel Hostility Toward Traditional Morality. *Christian Post Reporter.* May 17. Available from www.christianpost.com/article/20090517/ministry-hate-crimes-law-will-fuel-hostility-toward-traditional-morality/index.html [Accessed December 19, 2009].

4   The criminology of hate crime

Introduction

Public discourse on hate crimes and the laws intended to control them often reflects strong opinions. While most would prefer that these crimes did not occur at all, not everyone agrees with how to respond to them when they do occur. As we have learned in Chapter 3, some question the validity of hate crime laws, either seeing them as compromising constitutionally protected liberties or as laws that are potentially divisive—valuing the victimization of some over others. Still others see hate crime laws as legitimate tools that are necessary for the deterrence of these uniquely destructive acts.

Less common is discussion about *why* these behaviors occur. The criminology of hate crime, more specifically the study of the criminal behavior of hate crime perpetrators, is a growing body of scholarly literature. A variety of theoretical perspectives are represented including psychological, criminological, and even economic-based theories. Clearly it is beyond the scope of this work to include a comprehensive critique of each of these perspectives. This chapter reviews selected theories that are offered for the understanding of why hate crimes are perpetuated. Criminological theories are discussed primarily; however, we begin with acknowledging contributions from social psychology literature on the role of prejudiced attitudes in hate-motivated behavior. We then discuss several criminological theories including social disorganization theory, routine activities, social control, strain, and other potentially relevant theories.

Social psychology

There is a vast psychology literature brought to bear on the problem of bigotry and prejudice (i.e. sexism, heterosexism, racism, ethnocentrism, etc.) and subsequent behaviors. For our purposes, we limit our review to theoretical viewpoints discussed in social psychology.

Social psychology perspectives focus on how social environment, social construction of the "other," and psychological health work to shape attitudes and behaviors. Accordingly, prejudiced attitudes are explained as the product of underlying hostilities and invalid generalizations or negative stereotypes toward others (Allport, 1979). For example, Raphael Ezekiel's study of Klansmen and neo-Nazis (1995, 310–11) reports that "white racists . . . estimate that 80% of black people," are "cheaters," "violent robbers," who wish to "hurt whites." While members of extremist organizations are more likely to hold prejudiced attitudes, so are non-members. But individuals who are racially prejudiced do not necessarily engage in racist actions, let alone commit hate crimes. There are differences between those who harbor prejudice and those who act on their prejudice. Psychologist Gordon Allport addresses this important area and identifies a sort of social progression towards hate-motivated *criminal* behavior. He offers a five-point scale or typology of actions that illustrates that dynamic. The contributions of Allport to the field of psychology are well known. What is less recognized is the relevance of his work *for* the study of modern hate crime (see Table 4.1).

Allport further describes this progression that begins with prejudice and ends with what could qualify as hate crime actions (Allport, 1979, 57–58):

1   The negative stereotype of the victim group(s) is well recognized by the dominant culture.
2   The scapegoating of the targeted group has been well established.
3   There is a history of discrimination against the targeted group.
4   The dominant group experiences socioeconomic or political strain due to changing conditions.
5   Frustration and helplessness increases.
6   Some affected individuals choose to affiliate with extremist groups (Ku Klux Klan, neo-Nazi skinhead groups, Aryan Nation, or other such white supremacist groups).
7   These groups encourage the use of violence as justified.
8   An incident occurs (or is imagined) and is focused upon as a triggering event.
9   Like-minded individuals join together to commit violent and destructive acts against the targeted group.

What is implicit in this progression is that individuals observe, learn and understand broader social arrangements that provide members of the dominant culture with superior social positioning, social advantages, and expectations relative to members of minority cultures. These social arrangements and concomitant attitudes are internalized through socialization processes. The recognition and adoption of these norms also influences the social perception of *other* groups. The more *unlike* a minority group from the dominant group—the less well they are perceived, characterized and socially valued. Subsequently, some individuals reveal this attitude towards minority groups by indulging in antilocution only or perhaps in avoidance behavior. However, as Allport describes, the more *intense* and predominant these processes become in the life of individuals, the more susceptible they are to hate-motivated criminal behavior. Thus, some individuals journey well beyond antilocution toward physical attack. Allport also includes social strain as an aggravating feature or triggering agent in this process. We will see later a similar point of view expressed in criminological strain theory.

Table 4.1 Allport's scale of prejudice

Stages	Antilocution	Avoidance	Discrimination	Physical attack	Extermination
How the stage is manifested	Expressing prejudice among like-minded family and friends	Taking deliberate action to avoid the disliked group	Taking deliberate action to deny members of the disliked group civil rights or social equality	Participating in threats or assaults against the disliked group or their property	Taking actions that cause fatal injuries to members of the disliked group
How it is expressed by perpetrator	Less intense prejudice Less likely to result in hostile action	More intense prejudice More likely to result in hostile action	Increased prejudice Engages in negative action against disliked group	Intense prejudice Engages in violent action against disliked group	Participating in acts that cause life threatening or fatal injuries to members of the disliked group
How it is experienced by disliked group	Not aware	Less likely to be aware	Disliked group more likely to become aware of these actions	Greater certainty of awareness and why acts occur	Greater certainty of awareness and why acts occur
	+	++	+++	++++	+++++

Source: Adapted from Allport, 1979, 14–15

Social psychological perspectives shed light on why some prejudiced individuals may go on to commit hate-motivated crimes. While there is research to support the premise that the combination of personality factors, social learning, and developing social conditions together facilitate conditions prime for hate crime, there is less research to substantiate the stages of progression described by Allport in the lives of hate crime perpetrators. Other informative theories from social psychology include social learning theory and realistic group conflict theory.

Social learning theory

Social learning theory states that the acquisition of understanding the social world occurs through the processes of observation and imitation of the actions and values modeled by others. Just as essential to this fundamental dynamic is the reinforcement or shaping of the learners behavior through rewards (social approval) or punishment (social disapproval). This theory became better known through Bandura's famous Bobo doll experiments. The subjects were preschool-aged children who were divided into three groups. One group observed an adult playing aggressively with the Bobo doll (striking, kicking, etc.), the second group witnessed nonviolent play, and the third group served as the control group. As predicted, subjects who observed the aggressive modeling were more likely to imitate that behavior during their play time with the doll. The doll studies supported the theory that social learning involved: (1) a cognitive process that takes place in a social context; (2) observing a social behavior and the consequences of the behavior; (3) experiencing reinforcement and processing that information; and (4) making judgments about the observed behavior (Bandura, et al. 1961). But the idea of replicating social behavior or variations of that behavior is impacted by a variety of factors including how the observed behavior is introduced to the learner (direct observation), verbal representation or symbolic presentation (cultural depictions), and the cognitive abilities and learning style of the learner.

The theory of the authoritarian personality, an extension of social learning theories, was argued by Adorno and his associates in 1950. It describes a personality that defers to and strongly supports conventionalism as a result of a rigid and arrogant upbringing which facilitated what can be called an us versus them mentality. Authoritarian personalities follow social conventions that they perceive are condoned and demonstrated by the majority; that the purpose of their deference and submission is to be considered legitimate and acceptable, and that they are hostile against those who appear to deviate from or be contrary to conventionalism (Kessler & Cohrs, 2008). In fact, much has been written about the intolerance of various minority groups, especially anti-Semitic attitudes, demonstrated in the authoritarian personality (Solt, 2012). Moreover, authoritarians rationalize their hostility by pointing to social convention as justification.

How well does it account for hate crimes?

Social learning theory has real application for some hate crime offenders. There are several ethnographic works on participants in the hate movement which implicate the role of family in teaching (whether directly or indirectly) ideas of White superiority and concomitantly the inferiority of racial and other minorities (Ezekiel, 1995; Sims, 1978; Leyden, 2008, Simi & Futrell, 2010). Simi and Futrell's detailed description of Aryan homes is fraught with examples of the deliberate indoctrination of children into a mindset of racialism, anti-Semitism, heterosexism and the like. On a larger and perhaps more disturbing scale, main-stream culture itself contains values and norms that in addition to egalitarian themes, also implicitly support gendered, racialized, and ethnocentric social struc-tures. Thus, adhering to the dominant culture can also facilitate the learning of bigoted notions and ideals.

Wilkinson's 2004 article on hegemonic masculinity and anti-gay hostilities suggests that the authoritarian personality perspective provides a plausible expla-nation for discriminatory actions and perhaps hate crimes directed against gay men. Studies indicate that anti-gay attitudes are more endemic among men than women and that these attitudes are derived from gender norms in society that identify heterosexual males as not only the ideal representation of masculinity and manhood, but also that it is superior to all other masculinities, including homo-sexuality or any other sexual minority role preferred by men (see Herek, 1986; Kite & Whitley, 1998). The gender hierarchy constructed by society is reflected in the "gender belief system" (GBS) as discussed by Kite, 2001 and others. In GBS, heterosexual men reflect conventionality whereas gay men represent those who violate conventionality and deviate from the norm. In keeping with authoritar-ian personality theory, men who adhere to GBS would assume a hostile posture towards gay men that would condone the violent confrontation of gay men.

Altemeyer (1981) extended authoritarian theory through the testing and refinement of Adorno, et al.'s F-scale of authoritarianism. His construction of the Right-Wing Authoritarian (RWA) scale was designed to measure authoritarian aggression and conventionality. It is applicable in this discussion because it under-scores the desire of some to justify aggression towards others based on tradition and conventionalism that is manifested by the social construction of hegemonic power as demonstrated through dimensions of race, ethnicity, gender, religion, or sexual orientation. The idea is for dominant groups to maintain control over structural power by erecting and policing social boundaries. Altemeyer argues that individuals who score high on the RWA scale view the world as a place where those of inferior status pose a constant threat to the dominant group.

Realistic group conflict theory

Realistic group conflict theory (RGCT) seeks to explain the conditions that foment intergroup conflict and attitudes of prejudice (see Sherif, et al. 1954 The

Robber's Cave experiment). A fundamental tenet of RGCT is that competition for finite resources between and among groups can trigger feelings of threat, resentment, disagreement, and subsequently intergroup struggles in various forms. The theory also includes the acknowledgment of "out-groups" by "in-groups," meaning that those groups that are viewed as a threat are further demonized and alienated. There are several factors that help to situate a sort of us versus them perspective in RGCT. One of the most significant factors is the sense of entitlement and privilege that dominant groups have over minority groups. This reality creates a threat interpretation of competition which is viewed as a challenge to an advantage position and a zero sum perspective which heightens tension between groups. White privilege in particular has played a role in understanding the violent reaction of some Whites to school integration and school busing initiatives that occurred during the 1960s (Bobo, 1983). Another significant factor is concerned with perceived incompatibility or conflicting goals and other value systems between groups that create tensions. More recent RGCT studies focus on additional social conditions that may exacerbate intergroup tensions. For example, Filindra and Pearson-Merkowitz (2013) examine the impact of macroeconomic instability on out-group hostility represented by support of restrictive immigrant policy and found support for their hypothesis.

How well does it account for hate crimes?

Of course hate crime is not committed by groups, but by individuals. However, a common perspective espoused in the hate movement is the threat presented by out-groups, that is, racial minorities, Jews, homosexuals, and others. In general, one could use the rhetoric of hate to conclude that RGCT has some application when it comes to hate crime. There have been many instances when the first African-American or Hispanic family or the first same-sex couple moves into a neighborhood, they are met with hostility and attacked with hate graffiti, burning crosses, slashed tires, arson, or even physical attacks. Because of the threat caused by the presence of a representative of the out-group, a perpetrator seeks to "defend" against a changing life style, cultural values or even the market value of houses in a neighborhood. The defended neighborhood thesis tested with Chicago hate crime data, found that anti-Black hate crime occurred more frequently in homogenous white neighborhoods; the pattern for anti-White hate crimes was less discernable (Lyons, 2008).

Another reference to RGCT is Bobo's contention that a group may feel threatened if they perceive a shift in relative group status. Social policies like affirmative action, marriage equality, gay rights and women's rights may be viewed as real threats to the social location of straight white males and increase hostilities toward out-groups. Likewise, according to belief systems attributed to the hate movement, Jews continuously conspire to derail and to eventually destroy the status of White (Aryan) heterosexual, Christian males. Adherents of this and other similar views see the very existence of Jewish people as a threat to their group. The targeting of Jews by some hate crime perpetrators has included that motive.

Finally, this theory may also address the prospect of the increasing importance of aligning self-identity with that of the in-group. RGCT posits that when that occurs, the likelihood of intergroup conflict also increases, which further underscores the need to maintain in-group allegiance. This dynamic explains the attraction of some into a hate group as a way of providing a stronger sense of self, group solidarity, and group identity, which deepens emersion into the world of hate. A shortcoming of this theory is the order in which the in-group develops stereotyped attitudes toward the out-group. Classic RGCT asserts that this happens at the point of competition over resources and zero sum thinking. However, this order fails in addressing traditional prejudices and discriminatory practices of majority members on minorities even in the face of abject segregation and gross inequalities.

Criminological perspectives

Psychology involves the examination of human behavior as individuals engage in the social world from childhood until death. The human mind serves as the focus of study and is largely concerned with the individual, whereas criminology seeks to understand the nature of a specific human behavior—criminal behavior and the manner in which society responds to it. Social conditions, including those that exist along micro, meso and macro levels, play a critical role in the analyses of criminal behavior. Thus criminality involves a broader scope and seeks to explain phenomena that well extend beyond that of the individual offender. Criminological theories have exponentially increased our understanding of crime, criminals, and criminal behavior. But it is also recognized that there is no single theory that explains all criminal behavior. The same is true for hate crime. Now that we have acknowledged that, we turn to examine those criminological theories that may be useful in understanding hate crime.

Social disorganization

Social disorganization theory posits that when a community's socializing institutions become weakened and non-functional (becoming socially disorganized/dysfunctional), delinquent and/or criminal behavior is more likely to occur and continue as a matter of cultural transmission. Early studies characterized socially disorganized communities as primarily poor, heterogeneous urban neighborhoods with high mobility. Likewise, communities with stable and functioning social institutions are better protected against the development of criminogenic conditions. Such communities enjoy a vested interest in the community, social cohesiveness, informal social control mechanisms and collective efficacy.

For social disorganization to hold any promise in explaining hate crime, we would need to see a pattern of hate crimes occurring in socially disorganized neighborhoods. However, while hate crimes have occurred in such neighborhoods, many have not. These crimes occur in a variety of places from poor rural towns to Ivy League universities. In addition, there are some research findings that suggest anti-Black hate crime is more likely to occur in socially *organized* and more affluent communities (Lyons, 2007). This research suggests that these incidents are meant to defend such communities (i.e. the defended community perspective) against the entry of the undesired or targeted group. However, anti-White-motivated hate crimes may occur in more socially disorganized neighborhoods. Overall, social disorganization theory offers some assistance in explaining community level attributes where certain types of hate crimes may occur. But even more intriguing is the inverse view that the environment of socially *organized* communities tend to trigger racially motivated hate crime; that is majority versus minority incidents. The Department of Justice reported that in 2010, 31.4 percent of hate crime incidents occurred in or near residences. In fact, since 2005 this pattern has remained the same; one-third of all reported hate crimes occur in or near residential areas. These data, however, do not identify the socioeconomic characteristics of these residential areas. Clearly, more research is needed to test hypotheses like Lyons, as they relate to hate crimes.

Routine activities theory

This theory explains crime as the result of opportunities that arise from common daily activities. The attractiveness of the opportunity for offenders to commit crime is determined by three critical elements that must occur simultaneously: the presence of a motivated offender, a suitable target and the absence of a capable guardian or other preventative conditions. This approach presumes rationality; that offenders employ a real decision-making process that involves weighing the risks and benefits of committing an illegal act. If benefits (value of the target) outweigh potential risks (apprehension/arrest), the greater the likelihood the offender will commit the crime. Conversely, if the risks are perceived by the offender as too great, the crime is less likely to occur. As suggested by the theory's name, opportunities for crime are present in everyday routines and activities, that is, going to work, school, shopping, other leisure activities, and so on (Miller, et al. 2006; Lilly, et al. 2011). The focus in routine activities theory (RAT) is not on what causes someone to become criminal. It is on those basic elements that invite crime to occur. As such, the offender is concerned with the easy obtainment of instant gratification provided in the right opportunity. Marcus Felson and Lawrence Cohen, who proposed this theory in 1979, typically discuss property crimes rather than personal or violent crimes as they relate to RAT. However, are there some applications of this theory for hate crime? I believe so.

Utilizing the well-known offender typology offered by Levin and McDevitt (1993, 2002) we can consider the theoretical fit of RAT. Whether premeditated or spontaneous, hate crimes cannot occur without opportunity. Levin and McDevitts' typology of hate crime offenders (which also implies offense attributes) offers a rational discussion that supports aspects of RAT. For our purposes we will briefly analyze three of the four categories offered in the typology (thrill, defensive, and retaliatory) omitting mission, the rarest type of hate crime. In thrill hate crime, the predilection of hate crime offenders is to seek out their prey and randomly attack objects or persons once encountered. These offenders seek to experience a perverse thrill or excitement from hurting others and often seek their victims in locations where they are more expected to be found. They may or may not be deeply dedicated to hate ideology; but the end result is nevertheless the same. Victims are chosen because they are perceived by the offenders as suitable targets due to their supposed inferiority. This particular aspect causes members of sexual minorities to be particularly vulnerable to "thrill" attacks. Often members of the LGBTQ community will frequent gay friendly establishments which are also well known to those outside of that community. The RAT hate crime offender will take advantage of this practice—a routine activity—and victimize targets accordingly. What further exacerbates this vulnerability is the questionable support afforded this community by law enforcement. Thus, knowledge of the social gathering places of the LGBTQ community—which may be viewed as somewhat socially and politically isolated (Herek & Berrill, 1992)—provides an attractive target for thrill hate crime offenders. Similarly, due to racially segregated residential patterns throughout many communities, it is easy for these offenders to target African-Americans, Latinos and Asian-Americans as well.

Likewise, defensive hate crime occurs when offenders perceive that their world is being intruded upon, threatened or invaded by "undesirables." As a result they take actions to send a message to the so called invaders that they are not wanted in the community or workplace. We also find support for this category of hate crime with regard to RAT. A classic and historical illustration of defensive hate crime involves "move-in" violence. There are numerous instances where racially motivated crimes occurred when African-Americans first attempted to move into previously all-White communities (Lyons, 2007; Wexler & Marx, 1986; Green, et al. 1998). In these instances White perpetrators, who seek to prevent Black families from moving into their neighborhoods, commit various acts to thwart this occurrence. These acts, which fit the characteristics of defense hate crime, have ranged from the malicious damage or destruction of property and threatening bodily harm, to actual personal assaults. In keeping with RAT, these *newly available* suitable targets in the neighborhood as perceived by motivated offenders, also include the third element. With the history of strained relationships between law enforcement and racial minorities, at times law enforcement has been less than vigilant when it comes to protecting minorities under these circumstances. Such lax law enforcement helps to create the condition of the *absent capable guardian.* As described by Rothstein, 2012:

> State and local governments used force to preserve residential segregation in two ways: by failing to protect black families from violence (or, tacitly encouraging such violence) when these families have attempted to move to predominantly white neighborhoods; and by police harassment of black motorists or pedestrians who enter predominantly white neighborhoods.
>
> (14)

The absence of a capable guardian can take various forms beyond that of reluctant law enforcement. Likewise, expressions of territoriality and controlling one's turf extends beyond residential neighborhoods and also encompasses schools, the workplace, and other venues as well. In June 1949, the city of St. Louis, Missouri, opened the Fairground Swimming Pool, a public facility, to include Black residents for the first time. By the end of that first day, it was reported that hundreds of White residents came to the area, angry over the desegregation policy. To these individuals, the Fairground facility was their domain, their turf—and now it was being invaded. Violence did occur; its intent was to message to St. Louis' Black residents that they were not wanted at that facility (Jolly, 2006). Police, once again, were reluctant to play the role of capable guardians for Blacks (Wesley & Price, 1999).

A more recent incident occurred in 2009 at the Valley Club private swimming facility in Huntingdon Valley, Pennsylvania. Although no physically aggressive acts occurred that would constitute a defensive hate crime, several White club members actively engaged in an intense campaign to change the contract that permitted Black and Hispanic children from the Creative Steps Summer Camp to use the primarily White facility. The Valley Club owners denied any racial motivation in their decision to subsequently revoke the contract, but the Pennsylvania Human Relations Commission found that racial animus undeniably played a role in their decision (Grant, 2012). Even though the Human Relations Commission eventually acted in the role of capable guardian by speaking out against the acts of Creative Steps—"guardian-like" authorities were absent until that point.

Levin and McDevitt's third category, retaliatory hate crime, occurs when perpetrators believe that an attack of some sort has occurred on one of their own. Consequently, a retaliatory action is carried out. RAT is also applicable in this context because the motivation of the offender is clearly heightened as is the identification of a "suitable" target. What varies is the extent to which the offender is willing to risk the retaliation in light of the possible presence of preventative agents—capable guardians.

This notion of the presence of capable guardians requires additional consideration when it comes to hate crime. It is important to point out that the absence of a capable guardian could exist in different forms. There is the most concrete form—the physical—and then there is the more subtle form—the sociological or cultural form. For example, as mentioned earlier, the absence of a capable guardian can exist in the uncertainty of how law enforcement (and other potential guardians) might respond to the victimization of someone from the LGBTQ or other minority communities. There is a history of strained relationships between police and minority communities in general in the United States. Moreover, historically, society has signaled that the victimization of members of minority communities by members of the majority is viewed as less serious and did not trigger demands for justice (Perry, 2001; Petrosino, 1999). In this sense, there is a cultural mindset that implies a *symbolic absence of guardianship.*

There is much to consider in RAT for hate crimes. To the extent that hate crime is largely a function of opportunity with other necessary ingredients, we find offense elements that coincide with these ideas. However, it is also evident that RAT would suggest greater numbers of hate crime incidents. Clearly, each of the elements required in RAT, the motivated offender, suitable target and the absence of a capable guardian is particularly relevant in hate crimes. Given the persistence of intolerance and bigotry in society and the increasing availability of suitable targets due to population shifts and mobility, one would expect high numbers of hate crime. But these conditions do not *cause* hate crime. Still, the actual number of hate crimes is unknown because it is recognized that not all victims report to law enforcement for a variety of reasons. Notwithstanding, considering the general nature of hate crimes, RAT should not be dismissed as a contributing criminological theory for hate crime acts.

Social bonds theory

Hirschi's social control theory (also referred to as social bonds theory), presents the view that criminal behavior is not atypical but in fact is a common occurrence. A more significant question is what causes individuals *not* to commit crime. What are those social elements which hinder or restrain people from committing criminal acts? Hirschi's response is that social bonds or ties to conventional values, beliefs and practices are those elements that increase the likelihood of law abiding behavior. Individuals with strong social bonds are more likely to conform to society's mores and are therefore less likely to violate conventionality; whereas those with attenuated or weakened bonds are more likely to commit criminal behavior.

Central to the theory are four social bonds: attachment, involvement, commitment, and belief. Each reflects an individual's personal investment in pro-social beliefs, values, and practices. Attachment reflects the existence of significant and positive personal relationships (i.e. parent-child; relationship with peers; student-teacher, etc.). These relationships incentivize pro-social attitudes and behaviors. Involvement ties demonstrate engagement in conventional activities (i.e. volunteer to work in community projects, participating in sports programs for youth, etc.). These activities reflect support for traditional social customs and values. Commitment identifies investment in conventional goals and aspirations and the traditional means to obtain them (i.e. pursuit of vocational or academic training, financial plans to purchase a car or home, entrepreneurial pursuits, etc.). Again, such activities reflect agreement with societal prescriptions for success and accomplishment and show that we have "skin in the game" and thus much to lose should we risk it all for criminal pursuits. Finally, belief indicates agreement with the consensus perspective and the formal rules and regulations (laws) and authority structures that are employed to govern society. Individuals who agree with these mechanisms will seek to be in compliance with the same and would identify law breaking as undesirable and socially repugnant behavior.

If Hirschi's explanation for criminality is a valid explanation for hate crime, we should see its perpetrators with weak, minimal, or no social bonds as conspicuous among hate crime perpetrators. But is this the case?

Studies suggest at least two possible applications of social bonds theory for hate crimes: (1) social bonds has utility for some but not all hate crime offender types; and (2) strong social bonds to cultural values and practices which include embedded notions of bigotry *facilitates* hate crime. These viewpoints clearly assume different views on the role of conventional norms and the prevalence of prejudice.

The first application (social bonds as a prophylactic) acknowledges that there are hate crime offenders from troubled backgrounds that include dysfunctional, broken or non-existent relationships with parental figures, poor attachments and a life characterized by failure. To the extent that there is empirical evidence to support these dynamics, social bonds theory is plausible. Several studies indicate findings that could be construed as supportive of social bonds theory, noting perpetrators with poor adjustment to school; existing within the margins of society (Levin & McDevitt, 1993, 2002); possessing a history of delinquent and violent behavior and experiencing violence within the family (Ray, et al. 2004); multiple areas of dysfunction and deprivation, including substance abuse (Gadd, et al. 2005 reported in Chakraborti & Garland, 2009).

Hate crime offender and serial murderer, Joseph Paul Franklin, currently serving two life sentences, perhaps serves as a good example. Over a three-year period Franklin, acting as a sniper, shot and killed his many victims. It is reported that he was motivated by anti-Semitism and racism. Crime writer Charles Montaldo describes Franklin's background:

> Franklin . . . was born in . . . Alabama on April 13, 1950 . . . in a volatile impoverished home. As a child Franklin . . . turned to reading books, mostly fairy tales, as an escape from the domestic violence in the home. His sister has described the home as abusive, saying Franklin was the target of much of the abuse.
>
> (crime.about.com)

The second application (social bonds as criminogenic) situates successful socialization as paradoxical. Critical criminologists and sociologists contend that degrees of ethnocentrism, heterosexism, misogyny, racism, and other aspects of bigotry are *inherent* to the dominant culture. Therefore, it would follow that strong bonds to such social mores provides a greater capacity to commit hate crimes. Moreover, individuals who are reared *within racist or homophobic families*—will be more inclined to see bigoted attitudes and related behaviors as the norm. Therefore, given that context, such individuals would not view the animation of their bigotry as deviant, let alone criminal (Feagin, 2010; Sibbit, 1997; Perry, 2001; Leyden, 2008). Hamm's (1994) invaluable study of American neo-Nazi skinheads reveals that the majority of skinheads in his sample came from traditional working-class or white-collar households. In addition, those skinheads who were stronger adherents to Nazi ideology evidenced the achievement ideology (conventionalism) more so than their less committed peers. These findings are evidence of mainstream socialization and acceptance of normative ideals, goals, and social practices (strong social bonds).

Still, if it is accurate that embedded in the dominant cultural are various forms and degrees of bigotry—one might expect to see hate crime occurring at a much higher rate than what is currently reported. One might speculate, however, that educational efforts to construct multiculturalism as a strength rather than as a weakness in society may have created a hindering effect regarding the demonstration of racist or repugnant behaviors. Overall, it appears that Hirschi's social bonds theory provides, at best, a mixed "fit" in explaining hate crime.

Strain theory

Merton's strain theory focuses on the inadequacy of the social structure to articulate an array of conventional pathways or means to achieve economic (or other culturally defined) success. As a result, not all segments of society are able to easily access the means towards those ends. The anomic condition references the disjuncture caused by the lack of equal access to the means identified to achieve goals. Strain or frustration is routinely experienced by those individuals and groups that are unable to gain entrance to stipulated means.

Strain theory recognizes that socioeconomic class largely determines the likelihood of strain experiences. The United States in particular has a variety of class distinctions and is a socially stratified society. Thus the poor, racial and ethnic minorities and newer immigrant groups are more likely to experience strain and therefore are predicted to have a greater likelihood to commit crime. While Merton offers five adaptations to strain (conformists, ritualists, retreatists, innovators, rebels), some of the adaptations provide greater opportunities for criminal behavior. Specifically, *innovators* are those who continue to aspire to conventional goals, but replace the means to those goals with others that are not necessarily lawful or socially acceptable. *Retreatists* have given up on both the goals and means and adopt a lifestyle of abandonment and escape characterized by drug and alcohol addiction, transience, and homelessness. Finally, unlike the retreatists who give up on all, *rebels* desire to replace conventional goals and means with those that they value. These new goals and means lie outside of expected social norms and are more revolutionary and radical in nature; seeking to introduce a new social structure altogether. Of the three adaptations mentioned here, it is the rebel that best fits the vision of those who are strong adherents to the hate movement agenda.

But how well does strain theory predict hate crime? If strain theory has utility for hate crime, most of the perpetrators should be from those groups that are most likely to experience strain and frustration from economic and other emphasized goals of success. In other words the majority of perpetrators should be racial and ethnic minorities, immigrants, the poor, and those from other similarly situated groups. Moreover, if poverty serves as a proxy for strain likelihood—then hate crime perpetrators should be primarily drawn from racial minority groups. The 2010 US Census reports that 27 percent of Blacks and 26 percent of Hispanics live at the poverty level while that number is 9.9 percent for Whites. On a related note, in 2009 the dropout rate for White students was 5.2 percent, but it was almost twice that for Blacks (9.3 percent) while the rate for Hispanics was more than three times that of Whites (17.6 percent)

(US Department of Education, National Center for Education Statistics, 2011). Even more stark is the all-encompassing life expectancy statistic. A persistent outcome is that Blacks have a shorter life expectancy than Whites in the United States (Bharmal, et al. 2011). Clearly there are multiple factors that contribute to this disparity, but it is safe to assume that those factors, along with shortened life expectancy and conditions of poverty reflect problems with accessing legitimate means to achieve economic success.

According to this theory, such conditions should ensure that hate crime perpetrators are racial minorities. However, this expectation is not borne out. Federal hate crime statistics indicate that since 2004 nearly six out of ten *known* hate crime offenders were White. In fact, it appears that White males as perpetrators have remained a constant since these data have been compiled. Taken together, these factors suggest that strain is not sufficient in explaining hate crime phenomena.

Social learning and cultural transmission theories

Social learning theory explains crime as a result of observing and learning from intimate social groups (family members/peers) and then practicing criminal mores. Our social environments and who we interact with on a regular basis (our socio-cultural network) provides a continuous classroom of sorts. The social interactions, norms, values, and messages communicated, both implicit and explicit, are either supportive of law-abiding or law-violating behavior. When law-violating behavior is viewed as more acceptable, in fact normal, the likelihood of criminal behavior increases. Differential Association, a social learning theory, contends that the type of criminal behavior that emerges is determined by particular criminal habits taught and subsequently learned (Miller, et al. 2006). Thus, if social interactions condone law breaking in a particular form or direction—the resulting criminal behavior will reflect that pattern.

If these theories are valid explanations for hate crime, the following patterns should be evident: that families that are unabashedly bigoted produce more hate crime offenders; that territorial White ethnic neighborhoods that have demonstrated resentment toward "outsiders" moving into their areas, would see more hate crime incidents and; that areas in the country where the cultural values are antithetical and resistant to the notion of racial or social equality, would produce more hate crime offenders and/or see more incidents of hate crime.

Ezekiel's (1995) study of neo-Nazi and Klan members appear to support the racist family influence perspective. Most of his subjects described either a parent or grandparent as having strong negative views on Jews and Blacks in particular. One of his participants stated:

> my grandfather always spoke highly of Adolf Hitler. He said the only mistake Hitler made was not getting rid . . . of all the Jewish people . . . My grandfather's the one who told me, read Mein Kampf.

(260)

A female subject's background was described in the following way:

> Rosandra's mother, who lived in a small town in northern Michigan, was heavily involved with the Klan ... Rosandra Said ... (that) her mother would (only) let her associate with Klan or NS (National Socialist).
>
> (265)

Many of the families of Ezekiel's subjects were Whites who were trapped in urban neighborhoods that had changed over to be predominately African-American. He characterized them as isolated, with some joining hate groups out of fear and hatred of Blacks. As a result, they primarily fraternized with fellow members of the group and family.

Ethnic neighborhoods resisting "others"

One of the most highly publicized hate crimes in the United States occurred in 1989 in Bensonhurst, New York. Bensonhurst was primarily a White, working-class, mostly Italian neighborhood. Many of its young male residents were highly territorial and apparantly suspicious toward other groups. Four black teenagers, including Yusuf Hawkins, came into Bensonhurst for the purpose of inspecting a used car advertised in the newspaper. Shortly after they arrived, they were brutally attacked by a mob of bat-wielding White youths, which tragically ended in the shooting death of sixteen-year-old Hawkins. Unfortunately, this sort of incident (anti-Black violence as a result of their sheer presence) has a long history in the United States. Stephen Meyer's (2001) work, *As Long As They Don't Move Next Door* documents the efforts of Whites to thwart—often violently—racial integration of White neighborhoods. He states, "According to Rose Helper, when whites even see African Americans in their neighborhoods, they often feel 'concerned,' ... 'jittery, disturbed'" (Meyer, 11).

Differential Association theory states that everything allied with crime is learned—even the very reasons used to rationalize committing crime. Continuing with the Bensonhurst incident, while not all residents participated in the attack on Hawkins, many of the residents held similar attitudes as the attackers. The following was reported in the *New York Times*, August 22, 1999:

> Mr. Hawkins's family who marched through Bensonhurst after the shooting were cursed by residents, hit with pieces of food and spat upon. They were taunted with chants of "useless, useless," a play on the name "Yusuf."
>
> (Sachs, 1999, paragraph 5)

Following the Bensonhurst incident, several large-scale protest marches took place in the community. Many residents resented the marchers along with the corresponding media coverage. Anger and frustration were clearly felt by many residents, but the manner of that expression was often steeped in a racially repugnant manner and may be somewhat reflective of cultural values found in the Bensonhurst community. The notion of particular geographical areas with unique cultural beliefs and traditions also include attitudes toward others and is relevant to note for this discussion. For example, the history of the US includes the existence of "sundown towns" (Loewen, 2005). The official practice of these towns was to blatantly exclude African-Americans and other racial minorities from even visiting in the area *past sun down*—hence the name. This was accomplished through restrictive covenants, official law enforcement practices or by threat from citizen groups or racist organizations like the Ku Klux Klan. Loewen estimates that there were literally thousands of sun down towns in the US, peaking in the 1970s.

To the extent that bigoted ideas, discriminatory and even hostile acts toward "the other" are normative within families, neighborhoods and even in geographical areas, social learning theory could further the understanding of hate crime.

Techniques of neutralization and drift theory

Similar to social control and social learning theories, techniques of neutralization and drift theories are aimed at explaining the behavior of juveniles. This does not diminish application in hate crime as many of its offenders are young—including teenagers and young adults. Techniques of neutralization explains how individuals who normally uphold conventional social norms, beliefs, and values are able to *suspend* them during periods of delinquent or criminal activity, only to return to them afterward. According to Matza and Sykes (1961), these individuals have learned to employ rationalizations for their involvement in crime. There are five rationalizations or techniques of neutralization described: (1) denial of responsibility; (2) denial of injury; (3) denial of the victim; (4) condemnation of the condemners; and (5) appeal to higher loyalties. While the rationalizations are employed in a variety of delinquent and criminal scenarios, they are particularly useful in hate crime indulgences.

Denial of responsibility is used to project blame to some external cause to explain the involvement in delinquent or criminal behavior. For the hate crime offender who is motivated by hate ideology, he or she projects blame on "dangerous" Blacks and Hispanics, "repulsive" and "diseased" gays, and or the "pollution of illegal aliens," and so on, and says that these things caused his or her criminal behavior. This stance corresponds well with Levin and McDevitt's category of defensive hate crime. These are hate crimes committed in response to the *intrusion* of enemy groups into the community, the school campus, or the workplace.

Because racists, ethno-centrists, or heterosexists by definition see the "other" as inferior or even as a subspecies—the denial of injury and the denial of the victim rationalizations are probably easiest to use. Evidence of the objectification of the other is easily viewed in the culture of hate. The other is referred to in derogatory terms (spics, niggers, bitches, dirty Jews, etc.); hate crimes often involve brutal attacks causing serious physical injury to the victim. The nature of the attacks indicates the offender's complete disregard of the victim. On August 8, 2011, James Anderson, a 49-year-old auto plant worker was murdered in

Jackson, Mississippi because he was Black. The language and behavior of his killer, 18-year-old Deryl Dedmon, Jr, reveals the disdain he had for his victim and illustrates the denial of injury mindset. The following are excerpts from an article published October 24, 2011 by Scott Bronstein and Drew Griffin, CNN correspondents regarding the Jackson hate crime:

> Dedmon announced, "Let's go fuck with some niggers," . . . the teens beat Anderson repeatedly . . . used racial slurs . . . As Anderson staggered towards the truck's headlights, the . . . driver . . . (Dedmon) slammed on the gas, aimed . . . at Anderson, and ran him down . . . Dedmon boasted . . . about the killing . . . "I ran that nigger over," Dedmon . . . said in a phone conversation . . . he was laughing . . . about the killing.
>
> (CNN)

"Condemnation of the condemners" is also relatively easy to engage in for the hate crime offender who has adopted the common beliefs of the hate movement. Those who would condemn his or her hate crime act are categorized as race traitors or those under the influence of the Zionists who have control of the US government. These individuals are the enemy of the Aryan race; their authority is not recognized. In fact, their very existence justifies the hate crime acts committed by the offender. Finally, "appeal to higher loyalties" is also relied upon by hate crime offenders—particularly those who are seriously committed to the movement. For them, loyalty to the White race supersedes local ordinances, state and federal law, democratic values, or even traditional religious teachings.

Overall, drift theory and techniques of neutralization may have some application for hate crime offenders who have not yet embraced the goal of total revolution and the overthrow of the government. For such individuals, there is no desire to invest in conventional mores to any degree because they are repugnant to him or her. Moreover, to observe conventionality but periodically suspend their controlling effects in order to justify committing a hate crime would not occur. But for the occasional hate crime offender, drift and techniques of neutralization may have some validity.

The preceding discussion focuses on the adequacy of some criminological theories to address hate crime dynamics. What we see is that each theory reviewed may have at best *some* utility in its application. None of them is able to stand alone and sufficiently address the broad contours of this crime. Why is hate crime such a difficult challenge to theoreticians? Its complexity hinders the ability to adequately situate the who, what, where, how and why elements in a logical and coherent fashion. For example, hate crime offenders greatly range in their investment in hate ideology thus the degree and depth of bias varies; hate crimes can involve the simple defacement of property or a horrific premeditated murder that is nightmarish. These offenders may have extremely dysfunctional backgrounds, having witnessed continual domestic abuse, neglect, and violence while others come from privileged backgrounds with stable parents and addresses in exclusive communities. Victims may be randomly chosen or specifically targeted because of some supposed infraction they committed. Hate crime can occur because of the public observance of Jewish holidays or can be unplanned and done on a spur of the moment. Finally, while the overwhelming majority of hate crime offenders are White males, others are racial minorities.

What may be more helpful is to pivot away from traditional criminological theories and to consider constructs involving power and privilege that are utilized in critical criminological frameworks. The political aspect of hate crime is included in these perspectives. In a way, hate crime offenders strive to divert victims from enjoying their fair share of civil liberties, freedoms, and entitlements. As stated in the famous clause in the Declaration of Independence:

> We hold these truths to be self-evident, that all men are created equal, that they are endowed by their Creator with certain unalienable Rights, that among these are Life, Liberty and the pursuit of Happiness.—That to secure these rights, Governments are instituted among Men, deriving their just powers from the consent of the governed . . .
>
> (Declaration of Independence, July 4, 1776)

Hate crime offenders seek to send a message to victims that would cause them to think better of their pursuit of happiness and in effect limit their freedoms. This message is coupled with a threat of violence and therefore has political consequences particularly in a democracy. This undermines a fundamental element of the state and would cause significant negative implications if hate crimes were permitted to go unchecked. But how does this approach help us better summarize hate crime phenomena? Instead of relying on critical criminological perspectives, let's consider the idea of relative deprivation, a sociopolitical theory, which may provide a better fit for understanding hate crime.

Relative deprivation

Ted Robert Gurr (1970) discusses relative deprivation as a means to understand political violence including rebellion. He contends that tension and subsequently levels of aggression and frustration intensify in societies where individuals or groups perceive a growing gap between expectations for social status and accomplishment and their capacity to achieve that end. Gurr notes that this perception may be experienced even by those deemed successful if they perceive a sense of inequality or deprivation when compared to others. One individual's condition of success is another's insufficiency; it is a *relative* condition a sense of *relative* deprivation brought on by the comparison of one's overall welfare with that of another's (Stouffer, et al. 1949). Other scholars have used the concept of relative deprivation to specifically investigate the motive to commit terrorist acts (Moghaddam, 2005; Richardson, 2011).

Given these basic theoretical elements, it can be argued that relative deprivation may be effective in explaining the complex nature of hate crime. While the concept of relative deprivation is often discussed in the context of material gains, I would extend its application of well-being to that of the maintenance of hegemony. Gurr emphasizes that some are of the belief that they *deserve* a certain quality of life. In the US, there is little question that the social group that holds the greatest amount of social capital, power, privilege, and influence are White Protestant heterosexual males. The social place of this bloc remained undisturbed until the gains of the Black Civil Rights Movement, the Women's movement and the most recent gains made by LGBTQ community.

For a significant number of White males, the gains made by these groups are perceived as a clear threat to their dominance—their expectation of social status and welfare. Sociologist Joe Feagin describes the persistent problem of racism and the expectation of White privilege in the following way:

> Racist thinking is more than rationalizing oppression . . . it also represents a defensive response, a fear of losing power to Americans of color. In recent years many advocates of white superiority have directed their attacks at the values or cultures of new immigrants of color coming to the U.S., as well as at black Americans. In one recent interview study elite numerous white men openly expressed some fear of the growth of Americans of color in the U.S., seeing Western civilization as under threat.
>
> (Feagin, 2001, 101)

Therefore, with the advent of affirmative action, women's rights, equal-opportunity initiatives, political correctness, and multiculturalism, many White males interpret these developments as signaling a destabilization of their social place. Despite the fact that White males continue to outpace all other social groups in the metrics that measure quality of life standards, some feel a sense of social injustice and inequality. As a result, of this perceived condition of relative "deprivation" some Whites respond with insecurity, fear, anger, frustration, and subsequently aggression (Turpin-Petrosino, 2002; Gurr, 1970). A cursory review of social history in the US suggests periodic surges in hate-motivated crimes (majority on minority) and hate-group activity when social and legal gains were made by marginalized groups. A more recent example of this trend is illustrated with the election and reelection of Barak Obama, the first African-American President of the United States. Various watch group organizations, such as the Southern Poverty Law Center reported increases in the number of hate groups; for example, there was a 48 percent increase in the number of groups between 2000 and 2007 (Beirich & Potok, 2009).

Therefore, according to relative deprivation theory, White males perceive themselves as unfairly disadvantaged in comparison to all other "undeserving" social groups who are making social and other gains. This dynamic helps to explain why this frustration, discontent and anger felt by some is expressed by dis-criminatory practices (Feagin, 2001), hate-motivated acts or even the subsequent affiliation with extremist groups (Turpin-Petrosino, 2002; Richardson, 2011). So while this may be a collective experience felt at different levels for some White males in particular (or even by Whites in general), it is expressed on the individual level by committing hate crime or as a social movement—the modern hate movement. The perceived destabilization of the White male hegemonic bloc and other social developments that are intensifying and converging could be the trip wire that would cause some to commit hate crimes.

Research is needed to test the validity and utility of relative deprivation theory in the context of perceived threat to White privilege for hate crime events. This proposal extends the application of the theory beyond that conceptualized by Gurr and Richardson. If it provides some supportive findings, its application is tested by minority on minority and minority on majority hate-motivated acts. Still, it offers some theoretical promise that should be investigated.

Conclusion

This chapter reviews several criminological theories to examine their effectiveness for explaining hate crime phenomena. Most students of criminology understand that there are many theories offered to explain crime and criminal behavior because the scope of crime and the variation among criminals is quite broad. There is no single theory in existence that is powerful enough to explain all aspects of criminality. We find no different outcome when it comes to hate crime. In fact, it is far easier to determine why theories are inadequate in explaining hate crime than it is to argue why they work. At any rate, it is hoped that reviewing aspects of social psychology as well as some of the conventional criminological theories, such as social control and strain has been constructive. I am most intrigued with the review of routine activities theory as it sheds light on the nature of hate crime more so than the doing of it. In addition, the approach offered by relative deprivation theory is interesting and has some theoretical potential. The criminological study of hate crime continues to be nascent and hopefully will be the focus of many scholars over the next several decades.

Chapter summary

- There are several theoretical perspectives that may offer some understanding of why hate crimes are committed. This chapter reviews the relevancy of social psychological perspectives as well as criminological theories.
- Social psychology perspectives focus on how social environment, social construction of the "other" and psychological health work to shape attitudes and behaviors. Accordingly, prejudiced attitudes are explained as the product of underlying hostilities and invalid generalizations or negative stereotypes toward others (Allport, 1979).
- While most hate crime offenders are motivated by prejudiced attitudes, not all prejudiced persons commit hate crimes.
- Allport addresses this distinction and identifies a sort of social progression towards hate-motivated *criminal* behavior. He offers a five-point scale or typology of actions that illustrates that progression: antilocution, avoidance, discrimination, physical attack, and extermination.

- Social learning theory and realistic group conflict theory may provide some limited insight into those dynamics that facilitate propensity towards committing a hate crime.
- Social disorganization theory posits that when a community's socializing institutions become weakened and non-functional, delinquent and/or criminal behavior is more likely to occur and continue as a matter of cultural transmission. For social disorganization to explain hate crime, we would see hate crimes occurring in socially disorganized neighborhoods. However, while hate crimes have occurred in such neighborhoods, many have not. There is research that suggests that anti-Black hate crime is more likely to occur in socially *organized* and more affluent communities.
- Routine activities theory (RAT) explains crime as the result of opportunities that arise from common daily activities. To the extent that hate crime is a function of opportunity, we find elements that coincide with RAT. Given the persistence of bigotry in society and the availability of suitable targets due to population shifts and mobility, RAT would predict high numbers of hate crime. But these conditions do not *cause* hate crime.
- Social bonds theory states that individuals with strong social bonds are more likely to conform to society's mores and are therefore less likely to violate them; whereas those with weakened bonds are more likely to commit criminal behavior. But this theory provides a mixed "fit" in explaining hate crime. There are offenders from turbulent backgrounds and limited ties to society and others who are well rooted, from stable families and who aspire to the classic work ethic.
- Strain theory recognizes that socioeconomic class largely determines the likelihood of strain experiences. If strain theory has utility for hate crime, most of the perpetrators should be from those groups that are most likely to experience strain and frustration from their attempts to attain the economic goals of success. In other words, the majority of perpetrators should be racial and ethnic minorities, immigrants, the poor and those from other similarly situated groups. However, the majority of perpetrators are White males, and not always from the underclass. This suggests that strain does not easily apply to hate crime.
- Social learning and differential association explains crime as a result of observing and learning from intimate social groups (family members/peers) and then practising criminal mores. To the extent that bigoted ideas and habits are normative within families, neighborhoods, and even in geographical areas, social learning theory could further the understanding of hate crime.
- Techniques of neutralization and drift theory explains how individuals who normally uphold conventional social norms, beliefs, and values are able to *suspend* them during periods of delinquent or criminal activity only to return to them afterward. There are five rationalizations used to mitigate delinquent/criminal acts: (1) denial of responsibility; (2) denial of injury; (3) denial of the victim; (4) condemnation of the condemners; and (5) appeal to higher loyalties. Each can be employed by hate crime offenders as justification.

- Relative deprivation holds that aggression and frustration may increase in societies where individuals or groups perceive a growing gap between expectations for social status and the capacity to achieve that end; this may be experienced more by those deemed successful if they perceive a sense of inequality or deprivation when compared to others. For a number of White males, the gains made by women, racial minorities and other "marginalized" groups are perceived as a threat to their dominance.
- There is no single theory adequate enough to explain all aspects of hate crime. At any rate, it is hoped that reviewing aspects of various theories has been constructive. The criminological study of hate crime is nascent and will be the focus of many scholars over the next several decades.

Case study 4.1 White supremacist sentenced to life for deadly 2009 rampage

No one has the ability to know with certainty what was in the mind of Keith Luke on January 21, 2009. What is known are the actions that he took that day and his explanation for why he did them.

On that day Luke killed a 20-year-old woman, Selma Concalves, who walked in on the rape and sodomy of her handcuffed sister by Luke. He shot Selma three times to stop her from getting help. After the sexual assault, he shot his victim who survived the horrendous attack. While fleeing, Luke came upon 79-year-old Arlindo Depina Concalves, a homeless man; who he subsequently shot to death.

Those were his actions. The explanation he gave to Brockton police was that he was tired of being a virgin and that he wanted to kill all non-Whites. In fact, he was on a mission to kill non-Whites and Jews and that he expected to be killed in the process.

The fact that he committed his crimes shortly after the inauguration of Barak Obama, the first African-American President may be very relevant. Luke identified himself as a neo-Nazi who believed that the White race was on the verge of becoming extinct. This was the constant warning of hate groups on the Internet. Luke was a consumer of this rhetoric. All three of his victims were Cape Verdean racial minorities.

He apologized for firing upon police, because the officers were Caucasian. But he stated he did not regret killing and raping his victims because he hated all non-Whites. Luke was subsequently placed on trial and found guilty of several charges, including attempted murder, rape, kidnapping, armed home invasion and two counts of murder. He was convicted and sentenced to two consecutive life sentences, with no possibility of parole.

Keith Luke was merely 22 years old when he committed these crimes. What was his background? He was described as having a history of mental illness, after all he did carve a swastika into the skin of his own forehead.

He saw all non-Whites (and Jews) as his personal problems and told police that he intended to target the local synagogue next. His mother described his early childhood as a happy one but that he later became isolated with few friends, became truant and periodically received mental health treatment. She also said that he made it a habit to sleep on cinderblocks arranged in the shape of a cross.

Luke attempted suicide several times during incarceration and eventually succeeded May 12, 2014.

(Source: SPLC, 2013)

Discussion questions

1   Which of the crime theories reviewed could accommodate the use of the Internet as an tool that could influence an individual to commit a hate crime, as described in the above case?
2   Keith Luke committed murder and rape. Are there any crime theories that would appear to address violent hate crime more easily than nonviolent hate crime?
3   Although not discussed in the chapter, would consideration of the offender's gender suggest that one or more of the the criminological theories are more appropriate than others?

Bibliography

Altemeyer, B. (1981). *Right-Wing Authoritaranism.* Winnipeg, MB: University of Manitoba Press.
Allport, G. W. (1979). *The Nature of Prejudice.* Reading, MA: Perseus Books.
American-Arab Anti-Discrimination Committee. (2003). Report on Hate Crimes and Discrimination Against Arab Americans: The Post-September 11 Backlash September 11, 2001–October 11, 2002. Washington, DC.
Bandura, A., Ross, D., & Ross, S. A. (1961). Transmission of Aggression Through Imitation of Aggressive Models. *Journal of Abnormal and Social Psychology*, 63, 575–82.
Beirich, H. & Potok, M. (2009). USA: Hate Groups, Radical-Right Violence, on the Rise. *Policing: A Journal of Policy and Practice*, 3(3), 255–63.
Bharmal N., Tseng, C. H., Kaplan, R., & Wong, M. (2011). *State-Level Variations in Racial Disparities in Life Expectancy.* Washington, DC: Health Research and Educational Trust.
Bobo, L. (1983). Whites' Opposition to Busing: Symbolic Racism or Realistic Group Conflict? *Journal of Personality and Social Psychology*, 45(6), 1196–1210.
Bronstein, S. & Griffin, D. (2011). *Teen Murder Suspect Carried "Backpack of Hatred".* Available from http://www.cnn.com/2011/10/22/us/mississippi-hate-crime-teens/ [Accessed May 15, 2011].
Bureau of Justice Statistics. (2006). *Prisoners in 2006.* Washington, DC: US Department of Justice.

Chakraborti, N. & Garland, J. (2009). *Hate Crime: Impact, Causes and Responses.* London: Sage.

CNN Special Investigations Unit (October 24, 2011). Available from www.cnn.com/2011/10/22/us/mississippi-hate-crime-teens/index.html [Accessed May 15, 2011].

Crime.about.com. (n.d.) Available from http://crime.about.com/od/hatecrimecriminalcases/a/josephfranklin.htm [Accessed March 5, 2015].

Dunbar, E. (2006). Race, Gender, and Sexual Orientation in Hate Crime Victimization: Identity Politics or Identity Risk? *Violence and Victims*, 21, 323–37.

Ezekiel, Raphael S. (1995). *The Racist Mind: Portraits of American Neo-Nazis and Klansmen.* New York: Penguin Books.

Feagin, J. R. (2001). *Racist America: Roots, Current Realities, and Future Reparations.* New York: Routledge.

Feagin, J. R. (2010). *Racist America: Roots, Current Realities, and Future Reparations* (2nd ed.). New York: Routledge.

Filindra, A. & Pearson-Merkowitz, S. (2013). Together in Good Times and Bad? How Economic Triggers Condition the Effects of Intergroup Threat. *Social Science Quarterly*, 94(5). Doi: 10.1111/ssqu.12028.

Gadd, D., Dixon, B., & Jefferson, T. (2005). *Why Do They Do It: Racial Harassment in North Staffordshire.* Keele: University of Keele, Centre for Criminological Research. Reported in Chakraborti & Garland, 2009.

Gaines, S. O. & Reed, E. S. (1995). Prejudice: From Allport to DuBois. *American Psychologist*, 50(2), 69–103.

Grant, J. K. (2012). The Valley Swim Club of Huntington Valley Discrimination Controversy: The Racial, Economic, and Legal Implications for African-Americans and Latinos. *Widener Journal of Law, Economics and Race.* Available from http://blogs.law.widener.edu/wjler/archive/special-projects/controversey-swim-club-of-huntingdon-valley/grant/ [Accessed January 9, 2012].

Green, D. P., Glaser, J., & Rich, A. (1998). From Lynching to Gay Bashing: The Elusive Connection Between Economic Conditions and Hate Crime. *Journal of Personality and Social Psychology*, 75(l), 177–93.

Green, D. P., Strolovitch, D. Z., & Wong, J. S. (1998). Defended Neighborhoods, Integration and Racially Motivated Crime. *American Journal of Sociology*, 104(2), 372–403.

Gurr, T. R. (1970). *Why Men Rebel.* Princeton, NJ: Princeton University Press.

Hamm, M. S. (1994). *American Skinheads: The Criminology and Control of Hate Crime.* Westport, CT: Praeger.

Herek, G.M. (1986). The Social Psychology of Homophobia: Toward a Practical Theory. *Review of Law and Social Change*, 14 (4), 923–934.

Herek, G. & Berrill, K. (1992). *Primary and Secondary Victimization in Anti-Gay Hate Crimes: Official Response and Public Policy in Hate Crimes Confronting Violence Against Lesbians and Gay Men.* Newbury Park, CA: Sage.

Herek, G. M. (2009). Hate Crimes and Stigma-Related Experiences Among Sexual Minority Adults in the United States: Prevalence Estimates from a National Probability Sample. *Journal of Interpersonal Violence*, 24, 54–74.

Jackson, J. W. (1993). Realistic Group Conflict Theory: A Review and Evaluation of the Theoretical and Empirical. *Psychological Record*, 43(3), 395–413.

Jolly, K. S. (2006). *Black Liberation in the Midwest: The Struggle in St. Louis, Missouri, 1964–1970.* New York: Routledge.

Kessler, T. & Cohrs, J. C. (2008). The Evolution of Authoritarian Processes: Fostering Cooperation in Large-Scale Groups. *Group Dynamics: Theory, Research, and Practice*, 12(1), 73–84.

Kite, M. E. & Whitley, B. E., Jr. (1996). Sex Differences in Attitudes Toward Homosexual Persons, Behavior, and Civil Rights: A Metaanalysis. *Personality and Social Psychology Bulletin,* 22, 336–353.

Lawrence, Frederick M. (1999). *Punishing Hate: Bias Crimes under American Law.* Cambridge, MA: Harvard University Press.

Levin J. & McDevitt, J. (1993). *Hate Crimes: The Rising Tide of Bigotry and Bloodshed.* New York: Plenum Press.

Levin J. & McDevitt, J. (2002). *Hate Crimes Revisited: America's War on Those Who Are Different.* Boulder, CO: Westview Press.

Leyden, T. J. [with Cook, M. B.] (2008). *Skinhead Confessions.* Springville, UT: Sweetwater Books.

Lilly, J. R., Cullen, F. T., & Ball, R. A. (2011). *Criminological Theory* (5th ed.). Los Angeles, CA: Sage.

Loewen, J. W. (2005). *Sundown Towns: A Hidden Dimension of American Racism.* New York: New Press.

Lyons, C. J. (2007). Community (Dis)organization and Racially Motivated Hate Crime. *American Journal of Sociology*, 113(3), 815–63.

Lyons, C. J. (2008). Defending Turf: Racial Demographics and Hate Crime Against Blacks and Whites. *Social Forces*, 87(1), 357–85. Doi: 10.1353/sof.0.0071.

Matza, D. & Sykes, G. (1961). Juvenile Delinquency and Subterranean Values. *American Sociological Review*, 26(5), 712–19.

Merton, R. K. (1994). Social Structure and Anomie. In Joseph E. Jacoby (ed.) *Classics of Criminology* (2nd ed.) (pp. 178–87). Prospect Heights, IL: Waveland Press.

Meyer, S. (2001). *As Long As They Don't Move Next Door: Segregation and Racial Conflict in American Neighborhoods.* New York: Rowman & Littlefield Publishers.

Miller, J. M., Schreck, C. J., & Tewksbury, R. A. (2006). *Criminological Theory: A Brief Introduction.* New York: Pearson/Allyn & Bacon.

Moghaddam, F. M. (2005). The Staircase to Terrorism: A Psychological Exploration. *American Psychologist*, Vol. 60(2), 161–169.

Montaldo, C. (n.d.). Profile of Serial Killer Joseph Paul Franklin. Serial Extremist Killer. Available from http://crime.about.com/od/hatecrimecriminalcases/a/josephfranklin.htm [Accessed January 12, 2012].

Morgan, G. S., Wisneski, D. C., & Skitka, L. J. (2011). The Expulsion from Disneyland: The Social Psychological Impact of 9/11. *American Psychologist*, 66(6), 447–54.

Parrott, D. J., Peterson, J. L., & Bakeman, R. (2011). Determinants of Aggression Toward Sexual Minorities in a Community Sample. *Psychology of Violence*, 1(1), 41–52.

Partners Against Hate. (n.d.). Available from www.partnersagainstate.org. A Collaborative Project of the Anti-Defamation League, The Leadership Conference Education Fund and The Center for Preventing Hate [Accessed March 6, 2015].

Perry, Barbara. (2001). *In the Name of Hate.* New York: Routledge.

Petrosino, C. (1999). Connecting the Past to the Future: Hate Crime in America. *Journal of Contemporary Criminal Justice*, 15(1), 22–47.

Ray, L., Smith, D., & Wastell, L. (2004). Shame, Rage and Racist Violence. *The British Journal of Criminology*, 44(3), 350–68.

Richardson, C. (2011). Relative Deprivation Theory in Terrorism: A Study of Higher Education and Unemployment as Predictors of Terrorism. Available from http://politics.as.nyu.edu/docs/IO/4600/Clare_Richardson_terrorism.pdf [Accessed May 16, 2012].

Rothstein, R. (2012). Racial Segregation and Black Student Achievement. In D. Allen and R. Reich (eds.) *Education, Justice, and Democracy.* Chicago, IL: University of Chicago Press.

Sachs, S. (1999). Recalling Yusuf Hawkins and Hate That Killed Him. *New York Times*, August 22. Available from www.nytimes.com/1999/08/22/nyregion/recalling-yusuf-hawkins-and-hate-that-killed-him.html?ref=yusufkhawkins [Accessed May 14, 2012].

Sears, David O. & Henry, P. J. (2003). The Origins of Symbolic Racism. *Journal of Personality and Social Psychology*, 85(2), 259–75.

Sherif, M., Harvey, O. J., White, B. J., Hood, W. R. & Sherif, C. W. (1954). Intergroup Conflict and Cooperation: The Robbers Cave Experiment. Available from http://m.friend feed-media.com/d9487a89bebe9e28b3edc16f4dea8e54d7fbd568 [Accessed March 5, 2015].

Sibbitt, R. (1997). The Perpetrators of Racial Harassment and Racial Violence. Home Office Research Study 176. London: Home Office.

Simi, P. & Futrell, R. (2010). *American Swastika: Inside the White Power Movement's Hidden Spaces of Hate*. Lanham, MD: Rowman & Littlefield.

Sims, P. (1978). *The Klan* (2nd ed.). Lexington, KY: The University Press of Kentucky.

Solt, F. (2012). The Social Origins of Authoritarianism. *Political Research Quarterly*, 65(4), 703–13.

Southern Poverty Law Center (SPLC). (2010). Idaho Community Commemorates SPLC's Aryan Nations Victory, paragraph 10. Available from www.splcenter.org/get-informed/news/idaho-community-celebrates-10th-anniversary-of-splcs-aryan-nations-victory [Accessed February 8, 2015].

Southern Poverty Law Center (SPLC). (2013). White Supremacist Sentenced to Life for Deadly 2009 Rampage. Hate Watch. Available from http://www.splcenter.org/blog/2013/05/31/white-supremacist-sentenced-to-life-for-deadly-2009-rampage/? [Accessed March 5, 2015].

Stouffer, S. A., Suchman, E. A., DeVinney, L. C., Star, S. A., & Williams, Jr., R. M. (1949). *The American Soldier: Adjustment During Army Life*. Princeton, NJ: Princeton University Press.

Turpin-Petrosino, C. (2002). Hateful Sirens . . . Who Hears Their Song? An Examination of Student Attitudes Toward Hate Groups and Affiliation Potential. *Journal of Social Issues*, 58(2), 281–301.

University of Massachusetts Amherst. (March 5, 1995). *Hate Groups in America*, paragraph 5. Available from www.umass.edu/jewish/programs/hate_95/ [Accessed February 8, 2105].

US Department of Education, National Center for Education Statistics. (2011). Trends in High School Dropout and Completion Rates in the United States: 1972–2009. Available from http://nces.ed.gov/pubs2012/2012006.pdf [Accessed on March 5, 2015].

Utsey, Shawn O., McCarthy, Eileen, Eubanks, Robin, & Adrian, Genaro. (2002). White Racism and Suboptimal Psychological Functioning Among White Americans: Implications for Counseling and Prejudice Prevention. *Journal of Multicultural Counseling & Development*, 30(2), 81–95.

Wesley, D. A. & Price, W. (1999). *Lift Every Voice and Sing: St. Louis African-Americans in the Twentieth Century*. Columbia, MO: University of Missouri Press.

Wexler, C. & Marx, G. T. (1986). When Law and Order Works—Boston's Innovative Approach to the Problem of Racial Violence. *Crime and Delinquency*, 32(2), 205–23.

Wilkinson, W. W. (2004). Authoritarian Hegemony, Dimensions of Masculinity, and Male Antigay Attitudes. *Psychology of Men & Masculinity*, 5(2), 121–31.

5 Perpetrators

What do we know about them?

Introduction

Just as the types of hate crimes vary greatly, so do perpetrators. Hate crime offenders differ in age, education, and family background in addition to the underlying causes of their acts and the type of hate motive expressed. Differences also lie in whether he or she is a serial offender who is strongly committed to the ideological beliefs advocated by the hate movement or an individual who, under the right set of circumstances, commits a hate crime.

Serious hate crimes receive media attention and public officials respond accordingly. As a result, we often see the hate crime offender as a distinct type of individual; one that is unlike ordinary citizens. However, this could very well be the wrong assumption. Clearly there are individuals who've committed hate crime with particularly troublesome and dysfunctional backgrounds with a history of violence and violent behavior directed towards ethnic and other minorities. But there are also those offenders who have unremarkable backgrounds; backgrounds that are perhaps indistinguishable from law-abiding citizens. In fact, hate crimes are often committed by ordinary members of the public (Ray, et al. 2004). It is an unsettling reality that even the "guy or girl next door" is capable of harming another because of their bias toward another's social identity. A more attractive notion is that individuals who are capable of hate-motivated crime are throw-backs from a distant past, who march around with robes and hoods and burn crosses or scream "Heil Hitler"—those who are not exactly like ordinary folk. But there is no simple profile of the hate crime perpetrator.

This chapter is a survey of what is known about people who commit hate crimes—the hate crime offender. We begin by reviewing three media accounts of hate crime offenders where we begin to obtain a preliminary sense of the offender. Official hate crime data also adds to the image of the perpetrator so we review some of these sources. Hate groups are sometimes viewed as ground zero for hate crimes. So we turn our attention to the relevance of hate groups for understanding more about these offenders. Following this discussion, we look briefly at women in the hate movement and at minorities as hate crime perpetrators. We then turn to recruitment strategies and ideological beliefs extolled in the hate movement. Being aware of the rationale of some offenders—the belief system—enables better understanding of the acts and motives of perpetrators so we begin to wind down the chapter by reviewing a sample of hate crime acts. The chapter ends with the observation that the distinctions viewed among hate crime offenders means little relative to those found in the general population.

Contemporary profiles of perpetrators: media depictions

First news story: "Bellmore teen faces hate crime charge in attack"

. . . police arrested a Bellmore teen on hate crime charges who was part of a knife-wielding duo yelling anti-gay slurs that chased down a man on the street. The duo began shouting . . . slurs, then got out of the car to chase the victim . . . The victim escaped uninjured . . .

(Chayes, 2009)

Second news story: "Elderly man admits to charges of hate crime"

A 73-year-old Port Jefferson man has pleaded guilty to splashing motor oil onto the front door of the Kingdom Hall of Jehovah's Witnesses in Mount Sinai, William Frank Kelley was arrested after members of the congregation discovered the damage and found video evidence implicating him, Mr. Kelley . . . pleaded guilty to a charge of felony criminal mischief as a hate crime Mr. Kelley had contact with members of the house of worship at a March 30 service . . . He allegedly questioned the congregation's beliefs and was asked to leave, Mr. Kelley returned in the early morning hours when the hall was closed and poured two quarts of motor oil onto an exit door. He told investigators that he intentionally did the damage "believing that he was doing God's work," police said. "He selected them because of their beliefs. And that is what makes it a hate crime."

(*North Shore Sun*, 2010)

Third news story: "DOJ probes discriminatory policing in New York county"

In MA . . . boys aged 11–14 were charged . . . with severely beating a Guatemalan immigrant with bricks, bottles and rocks . . . The victim . . . was hospitalized for a month with head injuries. . . . Police said the boys targeted (the victim) because of his ethnicity." . . . investigators were looking into "the possibility . . . the attack was not the first . . . by these youths."

(*Intelligence Report*, 2009)

Each of these accounts is typical among hate crimes reported in the media and yet we find that the offenders involved are remarkably different in several ways. In the first account, the offender is a sixteen-year-old teen who, despite his age, acted in a very deliberate and predatory way. He appeared to be on a hunt; seeking a homosexual (or perhaps another acceptable target) to victimize. It was not enough to scream epithets once finding the victim. The sixteen-year-old attempted to chase the victim as well. This is a very aggressive and personal attack on the victim. Even more disturbing is the fact that this young man had previous contact with the criminal justice system. He was about to be sentenced on a prior conviction—which clearly had no deterrent impact on him in any way.

The second account describes a 73-year-old "senior citizen," who claimed that his actions, which were meant to damage or destroy the church, were motivated by religious reasons. He reportedly disagreed with the teachings of this church and thus saw his illegal act as obedience to God. He acted alone and believed he was answering a higher calling. He also wanted to avoid harming the congregants (as he committed the act after the building was closed and in the early morning hours), focusing solely on the building.

Ironically, the third account involving the youngest offenders is also the most violent. Bricks were used to viciously attack an adult—causing life threatening injuries. Even more disturbing is the intentionality of these young offenders to physically attack another based on the perceived ethnicity of the victim. This is an ideologically driven motive in full bloom and committed at such a young age.

While these acts were all reckless and also reflect a violent nature, the offenders could not be more different in the manner in which they carried out their crimes and in the implied rationales represented by their actions.

These contrasts show the range in offender types and also suggest why identifying universal characteristics of hate crime offenders is challenging. However, what more do we know about these offenders? Hate crime data provides us with some additional information.

The National Crime Victimization Survey (NCVS) is comprised of crime data generated by the surveys of a representative sample of US households. These data capture crime events which may not have been reported to police and therefore not included in the annual uniform crime reports. The questions are designed to determine the likelihood of crime victimization based on residential (or nearby) area characteristics, socioeconomic data, type of crimes experienced in the household (from property to violent crimes), frequency of crimes—how many times did it occur? What time of the day? The nature of the relationship between the perpetrator and the victim and other elements. The NCVS also includes inquiries about hate crime victimization experiences ("do you suspect that the offender targeted you because of race, religion, ethnicity, disability, gender, sexual orientation, etc."). To address the need for more in-depth information regarding crimes reported to police, an expanded data collection system was constructed. The National Incident-Based Reporting System (NIBRS) provides for the recording of multiple contextual and other specific factors on single crime events included in Group A offenses. It also has provided substantive data on hate crimes.

These two data sources sketch out a rough outline of hate crime perpetrators. The NIBRS data referenced here is from incidents reported between 1995 through 2000 and the NCVS data is based on victimizations that occurred from 2003–09.

In observing these reports from 1995–2009, we identify some characteristics of hate crime offenders. For example, it appears that racial bias is a predominate motive among perpetrators. Offenders are also more likely to be young (18 years and younger) white and male. The likelihood that the perpetrator targets a stranger is also apparent. So looking at these two important datasets, we continue to see that the profile of the typical offender is a young white male who is more likely to be racially motivated. Two of the more substantive official crime data sources seem to agree on the general attributes of perpetrators.

Several researchers have constructed profiles of hate crime offenders. Levin and McDevitt (1993, 2002) provide one of the earliest descriptions. Included in their characterization is the dysfunctional background of these offenders. A troublesome childhood, problems in the home and difficulty in school is evident among some offenders, according to Levin and McDevitt. Yet they often lack criminal histories (at least formally recorded ones) due to their younger age range. An important component of the social psychology of youth is the need for peer approval and acceptance. The desire to fulfill these needs often results in a young person participating in a hate crime to garner acceptance and to enjoy camaraderie with others. Levin and McDevitt acknowledge this dynamic in their description of "thrill" hate crimes. As a result of this motivation, hate crimes are frequently committed by groups of young males.

To assist the efforts of criminal prosecutions of hate crimes, Levin and McDevitt (2002) developed an offender typology, describing four levels of crime participation or roles and the corresponding degrees of culpability for offenders involved in group attacks. The four levels include: leader, fellow traveler, unwilling participant, and hero. The "leader" role is self-evident and describes the principal party who ignites, shapes, and directs the attack. The "fellow traveler" is the offender who joins in with the others once the attack begins. Levin and McDevitt describe the "unwilling participant" as the offender who does "not condone the act, nor participates, but is present during the attack and does no intervening" (Levin & McDevitt, 2002, 198). Lastly, "the heroes" are those individuals who attempt to thwart the attack from occurring. Similar to this is Willems's (1995) categorization of racially motivated perpetrators, which is also illuminating. Willem classifies these offenders according to how entrenched they are in hate ideology: "sympathizers" is similar to the fellow traveler-reluctant participants who wish not to disappoint their peers (and are not sympathetic to the victim); "criminal adolescents or thugs" are youth who are already problematic and have established destructive patterns of behavior, which is akin to the "leader" role. Willems's last two categories are the most committed: the "ethnocentric or xenophobe" and the "extreme right-wingers," who are most comparable to Levin and McDevitt's "leader" role.

Each of these classifications provide insights into the nature of hate crime perpetrators and warrant discussion here. The following one includes information regarding the social environment or residential community of potential perpetrators. Rae Sibbit (1997) examined the characteristics of perpetrators of racially motivated hate crime in two London suburbs. One of the most compelling findings reported is that the hostile attitudes of the attackers towards ethnic minorities were likewise held by the residents of those communities. It was also found that the community did not condemn these acts but "actively reinforced" that behavior, (Sibbit, 1997, vii). This suggests that there may not be that much difference between the hate crime offenders' and ordinary citizens' attitudes toward minority communities. What is key here is that community attitudes created an environment that facilitated (even nurtured) racial hatred, discriminatory acts, and hate crime. Sibbit's "pensioners" were residents who witnessed changes in the community such as economic strains, new social problems, and an increasing number of immigrants. In their opinion, their communities and the nation itself were being "invaded" by the problematic *other*. The "people next door" category are those who grew up in households parented by the pensioners. They routinely hear that racial minorities and immigrants are to be feared, blamed, and resented for a whole host of reasons. This group is more likely to commit racist acts towards others. Those characterized by the term "problem family" represents households especially beset with problems (e.g. poverty, unemployment, truancy, mental health problems, and poor health in general). Children are more likely to be abused in such families and, in turn, these children victimize others. This category represents those who are likely to set out and deliberately victimize minorities. Sibbit analyzed the racist tendencies of community youth according to age and found that the youngest group (ages 4–10) has the greatest chance of becoming dangerous racists who will act accordingly. This group is most exposed to prejudiced ideas, as they are surrounded by older siblings, parents, grandparents, and other authority figures who are inclined to hold racist worldviews and xenophobic notions. They also have the greatest potential to be isolated and to start careers as racist thugs at an earlier age than the other age groups.

While Sibbit, Levin, and McDevitt, and others provide profiles of offenders from struggling socioeconomic classes, their offerings are less applicable to offenders from wealthier subgroups. Not all hate crime offenders, sympathizers with the hate movement or even members of hate groups are dysfunctional failure-prone uneducated individuals who exist in the margins of American society (see Table 5.1). William L. Pierce, founder of the National Alliance, a virulent neo-Nazi organization, earned a PhD in physics and was a University of Oregon professor. Former Florida State Legislator, Ben Klassen, founded the Church of the Creator, a race-based theological doctrine and church. David Duke, former National Director of the Knights of the Ku Klux Klan, graduated from Louisiana State University and served in the Louisiana State Legislature. Matt Hale, onetime leader of the World Church of the Creator (previously known as the Church of the Creator)—later renamed the Creativity Movement, earned a BA from Bradley University, and a JD degree from Southern Illinois University Carbondale, Southern Illinois University. Don Black, former Klansmen and architect of the hate website Stormfront, attended the University of Alabama. The educated and the middle class are represented in the hate movement, which shows the ability of these ideas to attract those from diverse backgrounds, perspectives, and experiences (Hamm, 1993; Petrosino, 1999).

The preceding section brings to bear news items found in print media, government statistics, and academic research to describe portrayals of the hate crime perpetrator. This individual's most common attributes are pretty static but other aspects vary, such as socioeconomic background, educational obtainment, and degree of commitment to hate-filled ideology or the type of hate crimes committed. In addition, affiliation with a hate group is not part of the documented profile of most hate crime offenders although some offenders are members or affiliated with a hate group or are inspired by hate groups. Thus a discussion about hate crime perpetrators should include an examination of hate groups.

Hate groups

What exactly constitutes a hate group? Is it determined by the number of members or the appropriateness of its agenda? Is the existence of a hate movement the same type of organism as a hate group? The former may be understood as a rudimentary social movement comprised of a "loose coalition of groups and

Table 5.1 Education/occupation of past and present leaders in the United States hate movement

	Affiliation	*Education/achievements*
Richard Barret	Nationalist Movement	Attended Rutgers University and Memphis State University. Earned Law degree. Argued before US Supreme Court
Stephen D. Black	Knights of the KKK*	Graduate of University of Alabama
Richard Butler	Aryan Nations	Lockheed Aircraft Engineer
Willis A. Carto	Liberty Lobby	Graduate of Denison University
Harold Covington	National Socialist White People's Party	Ran in the 1980 Republican primary for Attorney General of North Carolina and received 43 percent of the vote
George Dietz	Liberty Bell Publications	Farm Broker and Commercial Printer
David Duke	NAAWP**	Graduate of Louisiana State University
Dan Gayman	Church of Israel	Former High School Principal
Kirk Lyons	CAUSE	Defense Attorney
Theodore Winston	National Prayer Network	Graduate of Portland University
Mark Weber	Institute for Historical Review	Graduate of Indiana University. Earned Master's degree
Matt Hale	World Church of the Creator	Southern Illinois University Law School at Carbondale

Source: ADL, 1996

Notes: *KKK = Ku Klux Klan **NAAWP = National Assoc. for the Adv. of White People organizations" (Kollman, 2011), that expresses interest in achieving some commonly held goals. In hate crime literature, one will see references to the term "hate movement" as sometimes representative of extremist *groupthink* (e.g. pan-Aryanism or RAHOWA); and one will also see references to hate groups connoting the same concept. One of the most straightforward and clear definitions of a hate group states, "a hate group (which is comprised of at least two or more individuals) has beliefs or practices that attack or malign an entire class of people, typically for their immutable characteristics" (SPLC, 2012a). This definition identifies the most salient feature of a hate group that distinguishes it from other social groups—that its primary purpose for existing revolves around its hostility toward particular social groups based on definitive traits demonized by the hate group. Hate groups made their first appearance as far back as 1866 in the United States with the founding of the Ku Klux Klan in Pulaski, Tennessee. Now, 145 years later, there are 939 active hate groups in the United States, as of 2013, according to the Southern Poverty Law Center (SPLC, 2012b). This civil rights organization has monitored hate groups in the US since the 1980s and makes that information available to the public and to law enforcement through various publications and online reports.

Today, every state has one or more hate groups which up until very recently was not the case. The states with the largest numbers of active hate groups are: California (77), Florida (58), Texas (57), Georgia (50), New Jersey (44), New York (42), and Pennsylvania (41). These numbers are fluid—as these groups wax and wane over time and sometimes morph into new groups with new nametags (e.g. The World Church of the Creator to The Creativity Movement). Also, actual membership numbers are only rough estimates at best. In this netherworld of loosely aligned hate groups, individuals may enjoy multiple memberships in several organizations or groups, concurrently. In addition, with the added dimension of the Internet, it is unknown how mere psychological affiliation is represented in *membership* codification—if at all.

The SPLC and the Anti-Defamation League (ADL) as well as other watchdog groups report that the number of hate groups had increased since the 1990s until recently. There are several observations offered to explain the surge: (1) a too-slow economic recovery and the lack of jobs; (2) increasing awareness of the numbers of immigrant and non-White racial and ethnic groups residing in the US; (3) the election of the first African-American President—Barack Obama; (4) it is projected that the US will no longer be a predominately White nation by 2050, (US Census); and (5) the sociopolitical but slow destabilization of the hegemonic bloc of White Protestant Heterosexual Males (SPLC, 2012b).

An added level of complexity involves the variation among hate groups. They all have the common element of animus towards other group(s) (e.g. gays, Blacks, immigrants, the government), but there are real differences in group structure, organization, leadership, level of sophistication, group philosophy, types of members, and adopted strategies. So while racist skinhead groups are primed to seek violent confrontation on the streets with targeted victims; other groups like the Nationalist Coalition's Arizona chapter hold family "spaghetti night" meet and greets in order to draw more persons from mainstream America (Conant, 2009). Still others hold weekend retreats, combining KKK rallies with readings from the Bible "decorated with confederated flags" (Conant, 2009).

How does the existence of hate groups impact the occurrence of hate crime? As early as 1993, Levin and McDevitt reported "only about 15% of all hate crimes are perpetrated by organized groups" (104). Since then, the FBI has estimated that racist skinheads were responsible for at least 63 percent of the violent acts attributed to White nationalist extremists from January 2007 through September 30, 2008, including 65 percent of assaults and 71 percent of murders (FBI, 2010). So unlike Levin and McDevitt who looked at all hate crimes, the FBI focused on a subcategory of hate crime acts—those committed by the extreme elements in the hate movement, and found that racist skinheads (who are group affiliated) were mostly responsible. Researchers Matt E. Ryan and Peter T. Leeson (2011) evaluated the relationship between hate groups and hate crime and found "little evidence that hate groups are connected to hate crime in the United States" (3). However, the long view of this question may provide a different result. Recent research on the life course of White supremacist groups indicates that group longevity and sphere of influence explains their relationship to hate crime rather than the sheer existence or growth of a hate group (Freilich, et al. 2009).

Much more research is needed to answer the question regarding the influence of hate groups on hate crime. Here are a few essential questions that should be considered to this end:

1   Not all hate groups have the same agenda—so there needs to be a closer scrutiny regarding: Whether or how the *type* of hate group differentially impacts hate crime?
2   Does a hate group's geographic location impact the nature of hate crimes committed in that area?
3   Neo-Nazi skinhead groups seem to be in the forefront of violent physical confrontation and assaultive behavior as a matter of strategy. Assuming that there is some validity in this observation, is there more reported hate crime (violent or nonviolent) where neo-Nazi skinhead groups are located?
4   What are the differences between hate groups that have essentially an Internet presence and those with a brick and mortar presence regarding crime?

While it is important to better understand the role of hate groups when it comes to hate crime occurrence, it must still be recognized that ordinary persons, those unaffiliated with hate groups, commit the lion's share of hate crimes (Chakraborti & Garland, 2009).

Even though hate-group involvement in hate crimes is not typically found, these groups still play an important role in this overall dynamic and in the incitement of violence in particular.

Several scholars have emphasized the culture of hatred, antagonism, and irrational violence that is nurtured within hate groups (Hamm, 1993; Simi & Futrell, 2010; Levin & McDevitt, 1993; Blee, 2002). The objects of their loathing (gays, Jews, Blacks, Hispanics, and others) are consistently presented in the most contemptible light. Vicious rants are a significant part of the social bonding of hate-group members (Simi & Futrell, 2010). Jews are often presented as the actual off spring of Satan or are depicted as vermin, a pestilence—deserving destruction; Blacks are subhuman or animals and most other minorities are inferior "mud people." Constant references of this nature results in dehumanization, which permits members of hate groups to develop tolerance and even comfort with physically brutalizing or killing the "enemy." In order to reinforce and maintain these perspectives, hate-group culture includes "totalism" which requires the practice of separatism. Similar to the separatism viewed in various religious cults, hate-group members minimize and eventually eschew social interactions with non-hate-group members (Lifton, 1989 cited in Woolf & Hulsizer, 2004). The result is increasing social isolation and constant exposure to the echoing of violent diatribes deemed necessary to respond to imaginary threats. In addition to the violent culture of hate groups and the absorption of this ideology, mounting pressure is placed on newer members to show their commitment to the cause by participating in violent attacks. As extreme and as reprehensible the ideology and agenda of hate groups might appear to ordinary citizens, the roots of their beliefs stem from mainstream social institutions, cultural biases, and systemic bigoted and racist practices that are part of the past and extant social conditions in the United States and elsewhere.

But that is only half of the conditions necessary for the proclivity of hate group members to commit more violent hate crimes. Hate groups in and of themselves provide the encouragement, rationalizations, and incentives for their members to indulge in violence. But to offset attrition, these groups must be replenished with new members. Are there certain types of individuals who are drawn to hate groups? Are there types of individuals who are more likely to embrace the violent messages that are spewed from these groups? Is there a difference between ordinary citizens who commit hate crime and those individuals who join hate groups and subsequently commit hate crime?

Contemporary hate-group members are frequently described as youth who are academically unsuccessful, have poor family relationships, feel insecure, alienated, impotent, and angry (Levin & McDevitt, 1993; Lang, 1990; Kronenwetter, 1992; Zia, 1991; Sears, 1989; Came, 1989; Ezekiel, 1995). Studies have also indicated that backgrounds of family violence, child, and substance abuse are not uncommon (Levin & McDevitt, 1993; Aho, 1994; Hamm, 1993). Law-breaking behavior is not uncommon (Sims, 1996; Wooden, 1995), although criminal records tend to be minimal in younger hate-group members (Levin & McDevitt, 1993). The desire for power, acceptance, economic gain, and support for particular views have been included as reasons for joining hate groups and other deviant collectives (Jankowski, 1990 as cited in Sheldon, et al. 1997). Christensen's (1994, 13) study of Portland, Oregon skinheads noted: "excitement of gang activity, peer pressure, attention, respect, sense of family and survival" as motives for joining. The survey research and content analysis of California Youth Authority case files conducted by Wooden (1995) found similar reasons for joining among racist skins, that is, the lure of excitement and the need for one's own ideological community.

Individuals who enter into hate groups don't arrive at the doorstep with an agenda that exactly mirrors that of the group. In fact, the requisite attitude of racist, anti-Semitic, homophobic or other prejudiced attitudes are not even necessarily harbored by new recruits. Blee (2002) describes in her research "conversion by near death stories" whereby individuals experience personal crises and emotional traumas leaving them seeking security, stability, and a justification of their victimization (cited in Woolf & Hulsizer, 2004, 46). Hate groups are an attractive option. What is more evident is that these are individuals with significant unmet needs that they may not even be aware exist. They are in search of having their needs addressed and hate groups are ready to offer them a means to obtain satisfaction that includes scapegoating, demonizing others, and feeding a sense of entitlement via a relentless blustering of the superiority of in-groups and the need to control and diminish out-groups. It is during this process of seeking self-fulfillment, security, and acceptance that indoctrination and the internalization of hate ideology occurs.

Those individuals who are from stable family backgrounds may still develop a sense of uncertainty on the broader world stage as they face an increasingly multicultural and multiracial world. I have examined high-school and university students' potential attraction toward hate groups and their messages. Results indicated that while high-school respondents more often held beliefs that were similar to those in the hate movement and expressed more interested in hate groups, there was still a portion of university students who did as well. College-educated youth have been and continue to be drawn to hate groups, even in the absence of traditional risk factors. I argue for a "middle-class" application of deprivation theory; neo-deprivation theory. According to some social scientists, the family is the first line of defense against externally derived destabilizing factors (e.g. Kanter, 1972). Society itself is a type of family: a macro family structure, particularly for middle- and upper-class White youth. It provides a sturdy network of support in the form of acceptance, presumptions and affirmations culturally, politically, educationally, and economically. However, with the advent of affirmative action, equal opportunity initiatives, political correctness, and multiculturalism, many White males interpreted these and similar developments as signaling a breakdown of their macro family structure. As a result, some White youth are insecure, uncertain of their future, resentful, and feel less powerful, *despite the benefits of higher education and aggregate upward mobility.* Therein lies the "new" deprivation: a perceived disturbance of White privilege—a class, race, and gender deprivation. Thus, some middle-class educated White youth become attracted to an ideology that argues for the "reinstatement" of White entitlement and privilege.

Are those who join hate groups more inclined to commit violent hate crimes?

Many hate groups disseminate a good deal of odious hate-filled rhetoric, leaflets, and other publications, in addition to the numerous hate web sites that serve to inspire, transmit, and support similar messages. There are examples where organized hate groups inspired hate crimes committed by others. The 1988 murder of Mulugeta Seraw by skinheads in Portland, Seattle was encouraged by the hate group White Aryan Resistance (WAR), as determined in a wrongful death civil suit (*Berhanu v. Metzger case #* A8911-07007). Nevertheless, these types of linked events happen infrequently, in comparison to the more common hate crimes.

What might be more insidious than recognized hate groups are the appearance of so-called *advocacy* groups which hold the same worldview and objectives of traditional hate groups, but have modified their approaches to become more palatable and in fact resonate with voices heard in mainstream sociopolitical discourse. The Leadership Conference on Civil and Human Rights published a report that implies a connection between the recent increase in attacks against Hispanics in the US, anti-immigrant advocacy groups that indulge in demonizing Spanish-speaking illegal immigrants, and the political and media outlets that give such groups a platform and thus legitimize them. Their online publication, *The State of Hate: Escalating Hate Violence Against Immigrants*, paragraph 4, states:

> Some groups opposing immigration reform, such as the Federation for American Immigration Reform (FAIR), the Center for Immigration Studies (CIS), and Numbers USA, have portrayed immigrants as responsible for numerous societal ills, often using stereotypes and outright bigotry. While these groups, and other similar organizations, have strived to position themselves as legitimate, mainstream advocates against illegal immigration in America, a closer look at the public record reveals that some of these organizations have disturbing links to . . . extremists in the anti-Immigration movement. These seemingly "legitimate" advocates against illegal immigration are frequently quoted in the mainstream media, have been called to testify before Congress, and often hold meetings with lawmakers and other public figures.
>
> (LCCREF, 2009)

The LCCREF (2009) reported that Keystone United (formally known as the Keystone State Skinheads—a white supremacist group) has used the immigration issue to draw new recruits. The report noted the following, "Ann Van Dyke of the Pennsylvania Human Relations Commission said of Keystone United: 'It appears they are tapping into and fanning the flames of mainstream America's fear of immigrants. They are increasingly using the language of Main Street, things like, "We want safe communities to raise our children" ' " (19). Therefore, as mainstream news reports and legitimate political discourse focuses on serious social issues, such as immigration reform; these issues are then socially constructed as racial and ethnic problems which concomitantly feed the paranoia of pseudo advocacy groups (FAIR) as well as traditional hate groups (Keystone United).

Individuals who join hate groups may pay a serious price for getting out. Not unlike the violent subculture of many street gangs, recruits of hate groups are commonly expected to show loyalty. A primary test of allegiance is observing the "blood in, blood out" oath. One is expected to spill blood of the enemy to become a trustworthy and loyal member. But leaving the group (blood out) means that it will cost the member his own blood (perhaps life) to leave. There are several compelling published testimonies of former hate group members that attest to this custom. Thomas T.J. Leyden, a former national leader and recruiter for racist neo-Nazi skinhead groups like American Firm, Western Hammerskins, and Hammerskin Nation, became disillusioned with the movement and eventually left. But when he did, he became a marked man. On April 26, 1996 he left the movement. After his first public speaking engagement warning youth about hate groups: "The next day . . . (less than twenty-four hours later), there was an entire website devoted to my demise. . . . Western Hammerskins wrote advice to others in the Movement to 'terminate [me] on sight'" (Leyden & Cook, 2008, 153). Bryon Widner, former co-founder of the Vinlanders Social Club and known leader in the racist skinhead movement, reported a similar experience. Once he left the movement, death threats were made against him by his former brothers.

There is the "neither-nor" reality of those individuals who are not directly affiliated with an actual hate group but who strongly identify with the hate movement. Gruenewald (2011) conducted a comparative analysis of hate crime offenders classified as *far-right extremist perpetrators* (FREP) who committed homicides with the homicides of ordinary offenders. Using open-source data, FREP homicides were identified as homicide acts where at least one of the perpetrators was affiliated with the far-right extremist movement. Gruenewald expected to find that: (1) far-right extremist perpetrators will be older than the average homicide offender; (2) they are more inclined to target strangers than the average homicide offender; (3) these offenders disproportionately commit non-firearm-related homicides and; (4) FREP homicides involve more offenders than the average homicide. Results indicated that murders committed by far-right extremist perpetrators differed. The majority of FREP homicides (52.5 percent) were committed with a firearm. There was also greater use of blunt objects, knives, and other weapons used in killings (47.5 percent to 31.7 percent). It was anticipated that FREP offenders would be older and they did fit more often in the upper age categories (19–28 years and 29–38 years). The involvement of multiple offenders was also found more often in this group, as was the lack of a relationship with the victim. Far-right homicides are most often committed by White males. When race is identified, FREP homicides are primarily inter-racial, while typical homicides tend to be intra-racial. An unforeseen finding was the percentage of FREP homicides that actually involved a profit-seeking element. Homicides committed by far-right extremist are typically represented in the literature as ideologically driven. But Gruenewald reports that as much as 24 percent of FREP homicides included a profit motive as well. Finally, criminals who identify with the hate movement involve themselves with ordinary crimes along with those that are hate-motivated.

Recruitment strategies of hate groups

Today's hate groups do not replicate the recruitment methods of the past. Early Klan groups were very secretive and favored clandestine meetings and ritualized ceremonies. Now they use strategies that even groups with non-sinister objectives employ to reach a targeted population. The modernization of recruitment strategies is illustrated by the British white power band *Skrewdriver* and its late founder Ian Stuart Donaldson. Using music as the primary mechanism, Donaldson packaged the attraction of free rock concerts with the dissemination of literature espousing his worldview of nationalism, racial superiority, xenophobia, and the use of violence to achieve these ends. This strategy mastered by Donaldson was replicated in early racist skinhead groups in the US, since then recruitment tactics evidenced by hate groups have been extraordinary.

Klan groups, the Aryan Youth Movement, and the Canadian Heritage Front have distributed racist flyers and related publications outside of high schools, encouraging membership (McDonald, 1995). The Nizkor Project provides information to the public on how hate groups target youth. Understanding the psychology of youth, members of these groups look for alienated youth to befriend and offer them the guise of social acceptance, support, and friendship. Introduction to hate doctrine comes later:

How Hate Groups Recruit –

* They always lie to new members, never telling them of their true agenda of hatred and violence before it is too late.
* Young people are brainwashed through rituals, rallies, training camps and the dissemination of hate propaganda, until they give up their independent identity, join the cause and become hatemongers themselves.

(The Nizkor Project)

Hate groups have used local newspapers to identify student leaders, honor roll inductees or local star athletes for recruitment purposes. Geographic location plays a practical role in recruitment activities. Campuses in close proximity to headquarters of hate groups receive consistent attention. Ohio State, the University of Ohio, and the University of Cincinnati experienced recruitment activity when skinhead groups formed in nearby communities (Anti-Defamation League, 1989). The University of Massachusetts Lowell received attention by a local Ku Klux Klan group with the distribution of their flyers, shortly after establishment of the cell in the area (Wills, 1999).

The Internet has also become an effective recruitment tool for hate groups. With the explosion of computers and consequently access to the Internet, many are exposed to these groups and their destructive messages. Far more insidious is the ability for many to psychologically affiliate with hate groups without physically joining and attending formal meetings and so on. The Leadership Conference on Civil Rights Education Fund (LCCREF) 2009 reported the potential impact of the Internet on furthering the agenda of hate groups (8):

Whereas hate mongers once had to stand on street corners and hand out mimeographed leaflets to passersby, extremists now use mainstream social networking sites such as MySpace or Facebook to access a potential audience of millions . . . Daniel Cowart . . . and Paul Schlesselman . . . arrested in the fall of 2008 for plotting an assassination attempt on Barack Obama followed by a plan to engage in a multi-state racist shooting spree, were reportedly introduced to each other by a mutual friend on a social networking website.

Pollock (2010) reports on the world of Internet newsgroups and websites as online spaces that encourage bigots in the maintenance of their hate-filled ideas and encourage deeper connections with the hate movement. "E-powered small haters" (Pollock's term) are individuals or small groups who use the Internet to solicit and disseminate hateful speech via newsgroups. These individuals are independent of hate groups, but the views they espouse frequently coincide and encourage hate-group affiliation.

Pollock examines three newsgroups, (which function like discussion forums) in particular—alt.flame.niggers, alt.politics.white-power, and alt.skinheads—and describes how these "alternative" groups are structured, how they operate, and whether they encourage others to commit hate-motivated crimes. The name of the newsgroup identifies its general area of interest. For example, alt.flame. niggers makes the following claim: "the newsgroup is a: ' . . . wonderful place where members of non-nigger races can join together to discuss typical nigger behaviour.'"

Ads are also found on these forums that promote extremist ideas, goods, and services. For example, White power merchandisers ply their wares such as Nazi flags, jewelry, newsletters and books on these newsgroups. Owners of White supremacist music stations advertise in these venues and provide information on rallies, concerts, and other promoted events. An announcement found on Alt. flame.niggers:

> IF YOU ARE SICK OF NIGGERS TAKING OVER DUBUQUE PLEASE COME TO OUR MEETING OF NIGGER HATERS OF AMERICA, MON-DAY AT 7PM AT 264 E 14TH IN DUBUQUE. COME AS YOU ARE. WE ONLY ASK THAT YOU ARE WHITE. ANY BLACKS WILL GET THEIR ASS KICKED ON SITE.
>
> (Pollock, 2010, 145)

These communications have the potential to attract sympathizers and encourage involvement in the hate movement or even specific hate groups. Pollock cautions us to note that these newsgroups have grown in number and in popularity in recent years.

All in all, hate groups are developing wide-ranging methods to draw new members into their ranks and/or to develop a larger audience of sympathizers to the cause. What we have yet to learn is: (1) how effective hate web sites (and chat rooms/forums) are in growing the membership of local hate groups and; (2) whether the former question is even relevant in light of the shift in strategy to small cell groups or lone wolf scenarios.

Women in the hate movement

Cultural beliefs that support White privilege and maintaining the hegemony of White Protestant heterosexual males also support a gender hierarchy. In this social arrangement, males are placed in an advantaged social location over that of females. The critical view that mainstream cultural practices include gendered arrangements that provide males social, political, and economic advantages and females disadvantages seems to repeat itself in the hate underworld.

Nevertheless, it is also true that the role of women may be expanding in some hate groups. Thomas (T. J.) Leyden, former leader in the neo-Nazi skinhead group American Firm, states that women have become a major recruitment tool. Leyden states "White separatists are not immune to the fact that sex sells—most particularly to their targeted audience of young, impressionable white males" (Leyden & Cook, 2008, 181). Thus, a specific strategy involves the use of women—to get them into the movement and have them take on an active role in recruiting males. This use of female White separatists still involves using them as sexual objects and does not reflect the progress of women within the movement.

Perhaps even more destructive than racist male skinheads looking for violence, are young White mothers who are adherents to hate ideology, raising and training their children from birth—to understand and adopt this malevolent worldview. "Most Aryan families homeschool (sic) their children to preserve them from 'mongrel ideas'" (Leyden & Cook, 2008, 182). Leyden goes on to describe the typical life of an Aryan woman affiliated with a racist skinhead group. She is instrumental in setting up a household that reflects the ideology of the movement. Not only is the home decorated with iconic hate images, but she also adorns herself with these symbols (jewelry, tattoos, etc.). As a mother, she homeschools, which furthers the isolating aspects of her social life. For some groups, the women strategize to take advantage of public assistance programs including welfare, food stamps, and health care. Yet she is also increasingly involved with the reality of both violent and non-violent attacks upon others.

The National Incident-Based Reporting System's (NIBRS) 1997–99 hate crime data shows that 17 percent of known offenders were female. Seventeen percent of violent and 18 percent of non-violent incidents was committed by female offenders. The 2003–09 National Crime Victimization Survey (NCVS) reports a similar statistic; 19 percent of violent incidents were committed by female offenders.

It may be disturbing to some to consider that while hate culture primarily supports traditional gender roles of women as homemakers, child rearing, and supporters of their male partners, it also invites them to engage in violent acts. For example, on March 23, 2003 Tristain Frye, a female White supremacist, along with her three male peers, bludgeoned with bats and stomped to death Randy Townsend, a homeless man—so that she could earn her red shoelaces (*Intelligence Report*, 2004).

But this dual and somewhat counterintuitive role is not a new phenomenon. Blee (2002) provides a historical and sociological perspective on the evolution of the role of women in the Ku Klux Klan. In it, she contends that their level of participation corresponded with the increasing opportunities for women in general. As the Klan devised various tactics to hinder Black equality, women were effective in employing these tools sometimes used by surrogate groups for the Klan, to create economic and political threats and obstacles and to leading local chapters for women. They also participated in the most horrific violence, both witnessing and celebrating the gruesome lynching of Blacks.

Today, there are hate groups which make a concerted effort to recruit women for a variety of reasons (appear more mainstream, add a stabilizing factor and thus increase membership longevity, draw more male members via women, broaden strategies, etc.). Blee (2002) notes that women are less likely to participate in terrorist activities aimed at state institutions and more likely to be involved in street violence. Women continue to engage in traditional roles and increasing involvement in hate crimes and other illegal activities.

Unexpected offenders: minorities against minorities

The Los Angeles County Commission on Human Relations (LACCHR) collects, screens, and then publishes annual reports on hate crime for the region. The Commission's 2012 hate crime report found that Latinos committed 68 percent of the anti-Black racially motivated attacks in the county, while African-Americans were suspects in 58 percent of the anti-Latino attacks. There is a clear pattern of racially motivated violence being committed by Blacks and Latinos. This pattern remains unchanged according to the most recent Commission reports.

The NCVS 2003–09 dataset indicated that 43 percent of violent hate crimes were committed by White offenders and 29 percent by Black offenders. The 2009 Hate Crime Statistics Report shows 62.4 percent of all hate crimes (violent and nonviolent) were committed by White offenders and 18.5 percent of these crimes were committed by Black offenders. Less focused upon is when both the offender and the victim are members of minority groups. Minority on minority hate crime is, in many ways, even more disturbing and more of an anomaly particularly for this type of crime.

Whereas the traditional hate crime involves a perpetrator from the dominant group victimizing someone from a minority group, when both actors are members of minority groups, what motivates these actions? Are they somehow distinct from traditional hate crime dynamics? What do we know about minority-on-minority hate crime?

Some have argued that this type of hate crime is primarily reflective of group conflict and the struggle for power, control, and desirable resources (Perry, 2001; Levin & McDevitt, 1993). With minority groups contending over successive places of decreasing power, there is considerable pressure to outmaneuver multiple racial and ethnic minority groups in the United States. It seems simpler for the dominant group (Whites). In that context, it is Whites against non-Whites—simple and straightforward. For minorities, multiple groups are in second, third, and other "subordinate" social positions. But the racist and bigoted notions expressed in traditional hate crimes are also found in minority-on-minority hate crimes.

Perry contends that minority groups also vie for social dominance and to assert their own self-identities and therefore use the tools perfected by dominant groups; that of marginalization, subordination, and subsequent oppression of the "other." This is the sociopolitical dynamic and function of hate crime itself (Perry, 2001).

Even more disturbing are organized efforts by some minority groups to threaten, intimidate, and attack others; even forming their own versions of racist hate groups. The following newspaper article describes these reported events:

> Four Hispanic teenagers were charged with a hate crime Thursday, (June 9, 2011) after allegedly attacking two black teens in Moline, Ill. Moline police were called about 9:30 p.m. Wednesday after a large group of men were spotted "beating up on a black kid" with baseball bats, bricks, sticks and large pieces of wood near the 100 block of Fourth Avenue. When officers arrived, they found the victims, a 19-year-old male and a 17-year-old female, surrounded by a number of individuals who had come out of their homes, witnessed the attack and chased away the attackers. Police (stated) . . . that the teens were yelling racial slurs and stole property from the victims.
>
> (*HuffPost Chicago*, 2011)

The ugly spate of racial violence between Blacks and Latinos is further complicated by the persistent problem of gang violence. The gangs in the Los Angeles mostly break down along racial lines. The Los Angeles County Commission's 2012 report refers to the perpetrators of racially motivated crimes as gang members and that some of the motivation involves turf issues over drug territories. Currently, the Latino gangs have been very aggressive in targeting Blacks for the purpose of forcing them to leave particular neighborhoods. The Commission's 2005 report states the following (12):

> The large number of anti-black and anti-Latino crimes can be attributed to a number of factors. Racialized gang violence continued to play a significant role in communities, public schools, and the County jails and juvenile detention facilities . . . In 2005, there were 56 cases of gang-involved racial hate crime, involving 69 victims and 130 suspects. In other words, 11 percent of all victims were targeted by gang members, similar to last year.
>
> As in previous years, the overwhelming majority of these were cases in which Latino gang members' targeted African-American victims. The data show that 54 (78 percent) of racial crimes committed by gang members were anti-black, and only 8 (12 percent) targeted Latinos. Very few reports indicated that these racial crimes were committed by gang members against rival gang members; most were against victims who were not identified as gang members.
>
> US Attorney Thomas P. O'Brien brought indictments against members of the Varrio Hawaiian Gardens gang in 2009 for multiple charges, including kidnapping, murder, illegal guns and narcotics. This Latino street gang

is reported to take pride "in their racism and often refer to themselves as the 'Hate Gang'". Furthermore, "VHG gang members have expressed a desire to rid the city of Hawaiian Gardens of all African-Americans and have engaged in a systematic effort to achieve that result by perpetrating crimes against African-Americans."

(*The Huffington Post*, May 23, 2009)

Some community residents refer to these crimes as a form of "ethnic cleansing" that is occurring right in Los Angeles County (*Intelligence Report*, 2007, paragraph 1). Inter-minority racism is when minorities practice multiracial White supremacy, sometimes in attitude only, other times in actions (Lum, 2011). Dr. Nitasha Sharma, scholar of African-American and Asian-American studies observes the example of race-based distrust and negative stereotyping becoming more demonstrative among some Asian Indians and African-Americans. Levin and McDevitt (2002) explain minority-on-minority hate crime as an artifact of living in a society where dominant views support a racial hierarchy. Minorities may internalize these views and with sufficient provocation—real or imagined—these views may be expressed in ugly racist acts. In addition, racial minorities as political interest groups may periodically compete for available, but limited, resources. This awareness may also fuel feelings of resentment and hostility that is expressed through racial conflict—and possibly as hate crime.

Belief systems in the hate movement

There are several beliefs espoused in the hate movement. Many of these views are popular and well established throughout the hate movement, but it is important to recognize that not every participant embraces all of these outlooks. For example, Christian Identity theology is not adopted by those who are followers of Odinism or by those who do not adhere to any religious teachings. On the other hand, some of these views overlap with others (e.g. white supremacy and the denigration of racial minorities) and there is little contradiction among them.

White supremacy

White supremacy is the belief that White racial and ethnic groups are superior biologically, psychologically, intellectually, and morally to their counterparts of color. This mindset coincides with a sense of White entitlement and privilege. These are the attitudes that support and facilitate ethnocentrism, discrimination, and racism. Unfortunately, notions of White supremacy/superiority or privilege do not exist only in the hate movement. These perspectives are deeply entrenched in American culture and were the toxic zeitgeist of its past and to some degree, to its present. The remnants of a sociopolitical and economic system that maintained Black slavery, apartheid, and White dominance for more than 300 years continues to thrive today. Institutionalization of White and male privilege remains part of society's social structure. Although significant progress has occurred in addressing the myriad forms of institutionalized and cultural racism, research continues to show that many Whites continue to hold negative opinions of Blacks, Jews, and other minorities and women in less esteem.

Perverted Christian precepts to justify White supremacy

When theology is mentioned as part of hate ideology, it is almost always discussed in reference to Christian Identity, which is discussed later in this section. Christian Identity theology is a gross distortion of traditional biblical teachings in Christianity. But it may be feasible to some due to a longstanding misinterpreted biblical teaching within traditional Christianity that was used to justify Black inferiority.

In Genesis 9:19–27, the scripture tells of an incident involving Noah (of Noah's Ark) and his youngest son, Ham. Ham committed an immoral act that involved Noah, who had become drunk. The exact nature of the act has been highly debated, but it appears to be of a sexual nature. Subsequently Noah cursed Ham's son, Canaan, to a life of servitude.

Advocates of African slavery during the antebellum period helped to promote the idea that Canaan was the progenitor of the Black race. As such, Black slavery is *legitimized* by scripture and is in essence God's will for Blacks. Thus the social construction of Blacks as an evil, uncivil race with rapacious sexual tendencies that needed to be restrained and controlled via the institution of slavery became socially and politically advantageous (Wineburg, 2001; Haynes, 2002). This interpretation was more commonly adopted among southern White Christians, where the advocacy of Black slavery was most keenly expressed (Lee, 2003).

Heterosexism and anti-gay sentiments

Members of the LGBTQ community are persistently targeted by hate crime perpetrators. Gay men are more often attacked than lesbians, who are generally viewed as less threatening to notions of proper masculinity; but transgendered individuals are often targeted for vicious attacks. There are a variety of explanations regarding the vilification of homosexuality in the hate movement. First, the image of the ideal Aryan male does not include a homosexual orientation, particularly among young men in the movement who are finding their footing regarding their own sexuality. The National Socialist Movement's homepage includes the eligibility requirements for membership. It states the following:

> Party Membership is open to non-Semitic heterosexuals of European Descent. If you really care for your heritage and for the future of your family, race and nation, fill out a Membership Application today.
>
> (National Socialist Movement)

In addition, there is the idea that Jews—who are the alleged enemies of White civilization, share in the blame for AIDS due to their advocacy of homosexuality. Some believe that AIDS is God's punishment for homosexuality. Except for a very small contingent of neo-Nazis who are also homosexual, the dominant view in the hate movement supports heterosexism and condemns homosexuality.

Denigration of racial minorities, immigrants, and anti-Semitism

For some White supremacists, the ultimate ascendancy of the White race is directly linked to an all-out war which primarily targets Blacks, Jews, other racial minorities and Whites who oppose this agenda. The idea of a cataclysmic event ushering in a race war is referred to in the hate movement as RAHOWA or Racial Holy War. Founder of the Creativity Movement (or Church of the Creator), Ben Klassen, first coined the term in his writings on the struggle of the white race. The following excerpts are taken from Klassen's (1987) book 'RAHOWA' – *Rahowa This Planet is All Ours* (4):

> There is now a new consciousness bestirring the White Race in America, in South Africa and even in Europe. It is a realization of what the Church of the Creator has been preaching for 15 years, namely (a) That we are embroiled in a racial war for survival on this Planet Earth, (b) All mud races are our enemies in this fight for survival. (c) The Jews are leading and orchestrating this war against us; and (d) The Christian churches are their most ardent ally and most potent weapon.
>
> (Paragraph 12)

> It is all spelled out in the Creativity creed and program. It is further polarized in the more recent fighting word of the White Race—RAHOWA! In this one word we sum up the total goal and program of not only the Church of the Creator, but of the total White Race, and it is this: We take up the challenge. We gird for total war against the Jews and the rest of the goddamned mud races of the world.
>
> (Paragraph 13)

Racially motivated violence against minorities is also reflected in the persistency of this category of hate crime. Writer Loretta Ross (2010) stated in an article written for Political Research Associates: "FBI statistics report that 65 percent of America's hate crimes are committed by whites against Blacks. Some of the haters, living on the United States' borders, are petrified at the thought that brown hordes of Mexicans, Chinese, or Haitians may swarm over them (paragraph 13; paragraph 14).

In their efforts to appeal to mainstream Whites, some White supremacist websites deny that they are racist. Instead, they argue that they are seeking to emphasize their love for the White race. But further exploration of these websites quickly reveals the worst type of racism imaginable. For example, should one visit various White power websites, you would likely see ugly racist depictions of President Barak Obama. A Klan site depicts President Obama in the minstrel tradition: blackened skin, wildly exaggerated facial features, large lips usually painted red and so on. Equally absurd and repulsive was a caption under the image indicating comments in classic poor grammar while the character eats the stereotypical diet of watermelon and fried chicken.

Anti-Semitism continues to anchor most of the beliefs found in the hate movement. For adherents, Jews are the archetypal enemy of Whites. This anti-Semitism appears as obsessive within the hate movement. Jews are the driving force for all things negative and detrimental to Whites on the planet. Included in these ideas is the existence of a Jewish cabal plotting to destroy White civilization: Jews are the architects for all of the evils of liberalism; they are in control of the US government; referred to as ZOG (Zionist Occupied Government), the banking institutions, and the media industry.

Negative attitudes towards immigrants existed in the 1800s in the US (and probably earlier) among some in the general populace. Fear of various groups bringing unfamiliar cultures, practices and values disrupting the status quo prompted political responses. Hence the Nativist movement and its progeny sought to restrain the number of Catholics and Chinese immigrants, for example. In the hate movement, the fear of immigrants has been racialized. Immigrants, especially those with brown complexions, are viewed as representing a multifaceted threat to Whites and the American way of life (Perry, 2001). Spanish-speaking immigrants (both legal and illegal) are currently most feared. They are depicted in highly negative terms by right-wing extremists. The following quote, reported by the Anti-Defamation League reflects the racist rhetoric directed toward Latinos:

> One member of an Aryan Nations faction, "Pastor" Jay Faber of Pennsylvania, claimed on April 10 on the Aryan Nations Internet forum that "I already know they will not throw one of these stumpy little brown beasts out of here, so for the amount of guats in my area, I have at least 10 rounds of ammunition for each of them."
>
> (ADL, 2006)

The US Border Guard, an Arizona-based militia group with ties to neo-Nazi national socialist groups, appointed itself to the task of patrolling the Mexican Arizona border. The group's founder once advocated using deadly force including constructing a minefield to stop illegal immigration (Castellanos, 2012).

Christian Identity theology

Christian Identity theology is not to be confused with traditional Christianity—which strongly supports the nation of Israel. Rather it is linked to the theory of *British Israelism*, which argues that the ten lost tribes of Israel migrated to Britain from Canaan. As a result, God's chosen people are not the Jews of Israel, but the British people. Further developed during the mid-1940s, by former Methodist minister and Klansmen, Wesley Swift, he later founded the Church of Jesus Christ Christian, a Christian Identity-based church.

Swift developed a racist and anti-Semitic *two-seed theory* to explain the origin of the races. Essentially, the Black race is seen as pre-Adamic and referred to as "mud people." In this doctrine, they are described as soulless and not fully human. Later God "corrected" this first failure and created Adam and Eve. But the serpent (the Devil) would seduce Eve, who subsequently gives birth to Cain who becomes the father of the Jewish nation. Hence the Jews are the literal spawn of Satan—and are therefore evil. This theology goes on to state that Abel is the offspring of Adam and Eve and becomes the father of the Aryan race—the Chosen people of God (true Israelites). Christian Identity was adopted by Richard Butler, the founder of Aryan Nations and it became an ideological pillar in the hate movement. Essentially, Christian Identity theology justifies racism, anti-Semitism, xenophobia, disrespect of governmental authorities, and endorses the use of violence.

Political ideology and strategies

Anti-statism is the general position that the government is not to be trusted and is a detrimental institution, therefore hostility towards the government is commonly expressed. Given that it is believed that the government is a Zionist occupied entity—its overthrow is most desired. Moreover, anti-statism supports the contention that government is the tool to be used for the destruction of White civilization—the ultimate goal of Jews. Federal policies concerning civil rights and social welfare initiatives (e.g. affirmative action, the Voting Rights Act), gun control laws, and more recently universal health care are viewed as efforts to somehow disempower Whites (Duffy, 2003). Social movements inspired by anti-statism views include Posse Comitatus and the militia movement. Posse Comitatus groups do not acknowledge governing authorities beyond the county level. They deny the legitimacy of federal and state authorities and the laws generated at those levels. Militia groups also formed as a result of suspicion and hostility towards the federal government. The focus of militia groups centers on advocating guns and other weapons along with survivalist training in anticipation of violent confrontation with federal and state law enforcement agents.

For those factions in the hate movement preparing for RAHOWA, there appear to be at least two possible outcomes from this violent struggle: the physical separation of racial groups by assigned territories or the annihilation of non-Whites. The following was found on an Aryan Nation website:

> We believe that the Aryan . . . deserve . . . a sovereign existence and racial self-determination within a territorial area characterized by our own . . . culture. . . . This is in line with the "Blood and Soil" concept of Third Reich-era National Socialists and follows the logic that for a people to survive . . . they must have their own land. . . .
>
> (Aryan Nations, paragraph 12)

The creation of racial territories is advocated within the Aryan Nations, however other factions seem to prefer the more violent option. *The Turner Diaries* is a fictional account of a violent revolution led by an army of White revolutionaries. Written by the co-founder of the National Alliance, William Pierce, under the pseudonym Andrew MacDonald, the novel describes the systematic murder of Jews, Blacks, other racial minorities and any group who stands in the way of the establishment of "the dream of a White world" (MacDonald, 1978, 210). This novel articulates a vision that is shared by many in the hate movement. It does not support the mutual existence of the races even in distinct geographical territories, but the genocide of all, save the White race.

What distinguishes hate crimes from other crimes is that the offender's action of targeting the victim is prompted by prejudiced attitudes. It is not the attitude or belief that is criminalized, but the action of the offender that stems from the attitude or belief. Now that we've surveyed the array of beliefs found among hate groups and in the hate movement itself, we turn our attention to the nature of acts produced by these beliefs.

A sample of hate crime acts—when, how, who, and why

Hate crime acts vary by target, degree of intended harm, hate motive, level of criminal sophistication demonstrated by the offender, and the nature of the injury sustained by the victim. The following is a sample of acts identified as a hate-motivated offense in online news websites. The belief underlying these acts are easily discernible.

Attempted bombing targeting Martin Luther King, Jr. Unity Parade attendees

Spokane, Wash.—The man who confessed to leaving a pipe bomb inside of a backpack on the Martin Luther King, Jr, Unity March . . . was sentenced to 32 years in prison Tuesday. Kevin Harpham, 37, was given the maximum sentence from U.S. District Court Judge Justin Quackenbush. . . . In September, Harpham plead guilty to attempted use of a weapon of mass destruction as well as the hate crime of placing the bomb in an effort to target minorities. . . . the FBI said Harpham placed a bomb loaded with lead fishing weights and coated in rat poison, an anti-coagulant.

(khq.com, 2011)

Some hate crimes are purposely committed around specific holidays such as Martin Luther King Day or Chanukah. The US Department of Justice references the significance of *when* a hate incident occurs in data collection guidelines created for law enforcement. An incident that occurs during a "significant ethnic holiday is a possible indicator of hate crime: 'The incident coincided with a holiday or a date of particular significance relating to a race, religion, disability, sexual orientation, or ethnicity/national origin, e.g., Martin Luther King Day, Rosh Hashanah'" (US Department of Justice, 1999, 5). Other countries also note an ethnic holiday or observance may prompt hate-motivated crimes. The Organization for Security and Co-operation in Europe (OSCE), an international organization that provides a forum for conflict prevention, crisis management and problem-solving initiatives published a report in 2007 on the problem of hate crime in the OSCE region (ODIHR, 2008). Stated in the Executive Summary, 4: "This year's ODIHR report on hate crime . . . finds a continued pattern of brutal attacks on visibly identifiable groups . . . Many of the attacks coincided with religious holidays and/or prayer times. Another alarming development was the emergence of the Holocaust as a rhetorical means to threaten . . . Jews, underlined by frequent damage to Holocaust memorials."

Milton man faces hate crimes charges

A black man walking on a Milton street was attacked . . . and hit . . . with a metal pipe after . . . a group of white males yelled a racial slur at him, police said. Authorities later recovered a metal pipe with blood on it. A 24-year-old Milton man has been ordered held . . . on hate crime charges.

(The Patriot Ledger, 2009)

Hate crime perpetrators sometimes act in groups as described in the preceding case. In 2014, the Bureau of Justice Statistics reported the percentage of violent hate crimes that were committed by two or more persons: 2004: 27 percent; 2011: 42 percent; and 2012: 34 percent. Thus, on average, one out of every three violent hate crimes is committed by a group of two or more offenders. A weapon was used in about 23 percent of hate crimes committed throughout the nine year reporting period and injuries were sustained in 20 percent of the violent hate crime victimizations that occurred in 2012 alone (Bureau of Justice Statistics, 2014).

Man charged with Provincetown hate crime

Provincetown, MA.—A Massachusetts man has been charged with a hate crime after police say he beat up a woman while screaming anti-homosexual language on a crowded street in Provincetown. Twenty-year-old Eric Patten of Winthrop was arrested shortly after 1 a.m. Saturday. Police say Patten approached two women in front of a cafe on Commercial Street, called one of them an offensive name referring to gay men and pushed one of them into a cafe window, which broke. Authorities say Patten was drunk and thought the two women were gay men. Police say both women were treated at a hospital for minor injuries. Patten faces several charges, including assault and battery under the state hate-crime law.

(capecodonline.com, 2009)

Victimization rates of sexual minorities are at best imprecise estimates. These crimes are not consistently reported to police for several reasons. Police relations with the LGBTQ community historically have been strained, with crime victims being unsure of police response. Other complexities include whether the victim is prepared to have his or her sexual orientation made public or even the fear of reprisal. Although the victims of the Provincetown incident described were lesbians—the perpetrator perceived them as gay men. In reality, gay men are generally victimized at a higher rate than lesbians or other members of the LGBTQ community. The National Coalition of Anti-Violence Programs (2010) recently reported the following statistics on hate crime victimization of the LGBTQ community (8): "People who identified as gay, predominantly non-transgender men, made up nearly half of 2010's reports to NCAVP (48.4 percent), followed by people who identified as lesbian (26 percent), heterosexual (10.4 percent) and bisexual (8.9 percent)."

Teen beaten for "enslaving our people"

The victim . . . told police he was walking . . . home . . . when he saw two men [an Asian and a Black]. As he got closer, they surrounded him . . . burned him with a cigarette . . . and urinated on him. . . . both suspects made comments like, "the white man . . . kept us down, this is for enslaving our people".

(SeattlePi.com, 2010)

Here is an example of racial minority offenders targeting a Caucasian victim in part for racial reasons. Though the importance of *Wisconsin v. Mitchell* is that it affirmed the constitutionality of hate crime laws, it also involved African-American offenders and a White victim. But what is more evident in hate crime is the inverse. It is more common that White males are the offenders who commit anti-Black hate crimes. Still, this does not preclude minorities being the aggressors in hate crime.

Waukesha teens appear in court for hate crime

Police said Kurtis Hickey, Dylan Barnett, and Thor Eggum burned a swastika and the letters KKK into a Waukesha basketball court. Police said the three didn't like African Americans playing on the courts. The teens are charged with arson with a hate crime enhancer. That means if convicted, the hate crime charge could increase each sentence by five years. Police say in the criminal complaint that Hickey started the fire "due to his hate for blacks." "He goes on to say he knew the 'KKK' and swastika would 'bring about a bad feeling when black people saw these symbols.'" The complaint also reveals that Hickey and Eggum admitted to being racist.

(R.E.A.L. Organization, 2009)

In this instance, the perpetrators damaged property as a result of their racially motivated bias. An offense in the form of a crime against property—motivated by the perpetrator's bias against a religion, sexual orientation, ethnicity, or as in this case, race, is also impactful to victims. In the 2012 Hate Crimes Statistics report, 38 percent of all reported hate crimes were crimes against property. Of these, approximately 75 percent were acts of property destruction and/or vandalism.

Evidence of bias in these crimes is manifested by the messaging left by the perpetrator. The most common written symbols indicating hate include "KKK" and the swastika, which are placed on the targeted property to be highly visible— as noted in the Waukesha case. Another hate symbol that is sometimes left on property is a hangman's noose (either in a drawing or an actual noose). These symbols are chosen by the perpetrator to intimidate and harass victims as they have special meaning to the minority communities and others. The Jena Six case brought national attention to the repulsiveness of the noose to the African-American community. On or about September 1, 2006, two or three hangman's nooses were found hanging from a tree on the grounds of Jena High School in Jena, Louisiana. Four months later, a White student was severely assaulted by several Black students at the high school. These students were subsequently arrested and five of them were charged with attempted murder. These incidents triggered public rallies and many public forums about race and the criminal justice system and the triggering event began with a hate symbol (democracynow.org, 2007).

These are but a small sample of hate crime acts that are committed by offenders, yet they show the range of these crimes and the beliefs that animate these actions. Regardless of the particular form that these crimes take, each seeks to communicate a powerful unwelcoming message to the intended victim and his or her community.

Conclusion

People are not born bigoted or ethnocentric but learn these attitudes and adopt these views over time. Hate crime perpetrators emerge from these populations. Despite the fact that hate crimes are relatively rare events, their occurrence is no longer surprising. Society is perhaps becoming more accustomed to these ugly acts, not recognizing their potential danger, or feel unaffected by them. Similarly, there is nothing that really distinguishes the hate crime offender from others (see Figure 5.1). These offenders are individuals from troubled backgrounds and dysfunctional families, with problematic school experiences, psychological or emotional difficulties, and poor job histories. They are also from middle- and upper-middle-class communities and stable families that practice conventional lifestyles and hold pro-social values. Some of these offenders even possess college degrees and have noteworthy skills, talents, and abilities. Regardless of their backgrounds, at some point these individuals consciously chose to take steps that moved them further along the ideological continuum toward extremism and hatred. What may start out as familiar stereotypes and bigoted cultural norms and mores became increasingly dogmatic, irrational, paranoiac, and in some instances fanatical. While it may be unsatisfying to note that, thus far, it is not possible to predict who will commit these crimes—it is perhaps more disturbing to accept that little differentiates the hate crime offender from the ordinary citizen.

Chapter summary

- The nature of the acts committed by hate crime offenders possess the common strain of animus, but outside of that, the vagaries found among offenders are significant. This reality partially explains why identifying universal characteristics of hate crime offenders is challenging.

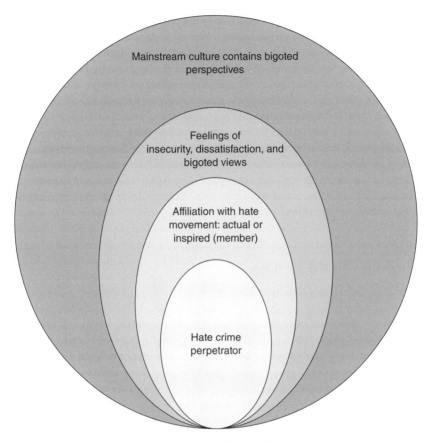

Figure 5.1 Hate crime perpetrators are not alien species

Note: Proximate social distance between the hate crime perpetrator and the ordinary citizen

- Examination of NIBRS and NCVS data regarding hate crime perpetrators suggests that
- Racial bias is a predominate motive; offenders are more likely to be young (18 years and younger), white and male.
- There are several offender typologies offered to shed light on the roles and social environments of these offenders. But each has limited utility in further uncovering who these individuals are rather than what role they play in a crime.
- Not all hate crime offenders are dysfunctional failure-prone individuals. There are also well-educated and middle-class people who are participants in the hate movement.
- A hate group is comprised of at least two or more individuals who hold beliefs or practices that attack or malign an entire class of people, typically for their immutable characteristics.

- As of 2013, there are 939 active hate groups in the United States. However, only a small percentage of all hate crimes are perpetrated by organized groups.
- Individuals who enter into hate groups may do so in search of fulfilling unmet needs. Hate groups are an attractive option for them and offer a means to obtain satisfaction that includes scapegoating, feeding a sense of entitlement, and the need to control and diminish inferior groups.
- The role of women in hate groups continues to be subordinate to men; but women have become an important recruitment tool.
- There are instances in which hate crimes are perpetrated upon minorities by minorities. Some believe that such acts merely reflect group conflict and the struggle for control over resources. It is also argued that minorities have internalized the racist, sexist, and homophobic perspectives and attitudes found in mainstream culture and in turn act on them resulting in the targeting of minorities by minorities.

Case study 5.1 On the inside

Bob's upbringing and overall childhood appears to be quite ordinary. He grew up in southern Ohio in a white working-class neighborhood. One of his closest friends, Gene, according to him, was African-American. Gene would've never predicted that Bob would eventually grow up and join the Knights of the Ku Klux Klan. But he did. In fact, Bob became a close confidant to a dangerous Klansman in the group; one targeted by federal authorities.

In January 2014 all thirteen chapters of the Knights of the KKK were ordered to disband by the imperial wizard. This was brought on by the conviction of one of its members on federal weapons charges—specifically the illegal sale of guns to a convicted felon.

The federal investigation and subsequent conviction was possible because of the cooperation of an informant on the inside of the KKK. The informant was Bob. With his help, federal authorities were able to interrupt the activity of the renegade Klan member to support a violent splinter group committed to targeting Blacks and Hispanics.

Although Bob's childhood appeared typical, he did begin to get into real trouble by age 13. His level of offending caused him to be in and out of the juvenile justice system. But his law breaking continued into adulthood. During one of his stints in prison, he met a Klan Grand Dragon who attempted to introduce him to extremist views. But Bob declined joining the group at that time despite becoming somewhat intrigued. The idea of the plight of the white man was attractive; but more than ideology, Bob had the desire to be part of something. He felt estranged from his family during this period of his life and was adrift.

Years later, in 2010, Bob joined the Ku Klux Klan following his meeting with another member of the group near his home in Virginia. It became official at a ceremony in Ellijay, Georgia.

So it is clear that two things happened that Bob could attest to; first, he became a member of a notorious racist organization and second, he helped to take down the same. Bob does not understand fully why he joined to begin with. But acknowledges that there must be some psychological reason for his actions. Still his wife states that the ideas held by the Klan are also supported widely by their neighbors and their larger community. Racist views concerning minorities are common. She states that even local church leaders support notions of racial separation and white superiority. What is clear is that no one forced Bob to join the Klan.

(Source: www.splcenter.org. *Intelligence Report*, Summer 2014, 154)

Discussion questions

1   In what ways was Bob's background ordinary? In what ways was it atypical?
2   Bob eventually joined the Ku Klux Klan. Given the explanation he provides, do you see similarities in any of the typologies offered by Levin & McDevitt, Sibitts, or Willems?
3   Bob states that he turned informant, voluntarily, as he feared the potential threat posed by Fullmore. How do you interpret this in light of Bob's embrace of racist ideology?

Bibliography

Aho, J. A. (1994). *This Thing of Darkness: A Sociology of the Enemy.* Seattle, WA: University of Washington Press.

Anti-Defamation League (ADL). (1989). *Skinheads Target the Schools.* New York: Author.

Anti-Defamation League (ADL). (1996). *Danger: Extremism. The Major Vehicles and Voices on America's Far-Right Fringe.* New York: Author.

Anti-Defamation League (ADL). (2006). *Extremists Declare "Open Season" on Immigrants: Hispanics Target of Incitement and Violence.* Available from www.adl.org/NR/exeres/D7BECD3A-D17C-48ED-9BA6-5A109D1125FA,DB7611A2-02CD-43AF-8147-649E26813571,frameless.htm [Accessed June 2, 2012].

Aryan Nations. (n.d.). The History of AN. Available from http://aryan-nations.org/history [Accessed May 23, 2012].

Blee, Kathleen. (2002). Women and Organized Racial Terrorism. *Studies in Conflict & Terrorism*, 28, 421–33.

Bureau of Justice Services. (2001). Hate Crimes Report in NIBRS, 1997–1999. Published by the Bureau of Justice Services. Office of Justice Programs. By Kevin J. Strom, PhD. Published September 2001. NCJ 186765.

Bureau of Justice Services. (2005). Hate Crime Reported by Victims and Police. Published by the Bureau of Justice Services. National Criminal Victimization Survey and Uniform Crime Reporting. By Caroline Wolf Harlow, PhD. Published November 2005. NCJ 209911.

Bureau of Justice Services (BJS). (2011). Hate Crime 2003–2009. Published by the Bureau of Justice Services. Lynn Langton and Michael Planty. Published June 2011. NCJ

234085. Available from www.bjs.gov/index.cfm?ty=pbdetail&iid=1760 [Accessed June 3, 2012].

Bureau of Justice Statistics (BJS). (2014). Hate Crime Victimization, 2004–2012—Statistical Tables. Available from www.bjs.gov/content/pub/pdf/hcv0412st.pdf [Accessed June 3, 2014].

Came, B. (1989). A Growing Menace: Violent Skinheads Are Raising Urban Fears. *Macleans*, January 23, 43–44.

capecodonline.com. (2009). Winthrop Man Charged with Hate Crime in Province-Town Beating. May 24. Available from www.capecodonline.com/apps/pbcs.dll/article?AID=/20090524/NEWS/905240326/ [Accessed February 8, 2015].

Castellanos, D. (2012). Border Militia Founder Reportedly Shot Dead in Arizona. *Los Angeles Times*, May 3. Available from http://articles.latimes.com/2012/may/03/nation/la-na-arizona-shootings-20120503 [Accessed May 22, 2012].

Chakraborti, N. & Garland, J. (2009). *Hate Crime: Impact, Causes and Responses*. London: Sage.

Chayes, M. (2009). Bellmore Teen Faces Hate Crime Charge in Attack. Available from www.newsday.com [Accessed August 10, 2011].

Christensen, L. (1994). *Skinhead Street Gangs*. Boulder, CO: Paladin Press.

Conant, E. (2009). Rebranding Hate in the Age of Obama. *Newsweek*, April 25. Available from www.newsweek.com/id/195085 [Accessed December 20, 2009].

democracynow.org. (2007). The Case of the Jena Six: Black High School Students Charged With Attempted Murder for Schoolyard Fight After Nooses Are Hung from Tree. Available from www.democracynow.org/2007/7/10/the_case_of_the_jena_six [Accessed June 2, 2012].

Duffy, M. E. (2003). Web of Hate: A Fantasy Theme Analysis of the Rhetorical Vision of Hate Groups Online. *Journal of Communication Inquiry*, 27(3), 291–312.

Ezekiel, R. S. (1995). *The Racist Mind: Portraits of American Neo-Nazis and Klansmen*. New York: Penguin Books.

Federal Bureau of Investigation. (2010). *Rage and Racism: Skinhead Violence on the Far Right*. FBI Counterterrorism Division. Available from http://publicintelligence.net/fbi-rage-and-racism-skinhead-violence-on-the-far-right/ [Accessed May 29, 2012].

Federal Bureau of Investigation. (2010). Hate Crime Statistics 2009. US Department of Justice. Criminal Justice Services Information Division. Available from www2.fbi.gov/ucr/hc2009/index.html [Accessed June 3, 2012].

Freilich, J. D., Chermak, S. M., & Caspi, D. (2009). Critical Events in the Life Trajectories of Domestic Extremist White Supremacist Groups. *Criminology & Public Policy*, 8(3), 497–530.

Gruenewald, J. (2011). A Comparative Examination of Homicides Perpetrated by Far-Right Extremists. *Homicide Studies*, 15(2), 177–203.

Hamm, M. S. (1993). *American Skinheads*. Westport, CT: Praeger.

Haynes, S. R. (2002). *Original Dishonor: Noah's Curse: The Biblical Justification of American Slavery*. New York: Oxford University Press.

Huffington Post, The. (2009). 147 Gang Members Indicted in California. May 23. Available from www.huffingtonpost.com/2009/05/21/147-gang-members-indicted_n_206594.html [Accessed December 20, 2009].

HuffPost Chicago. (2011). Moline Hate Crime: Four Teens Accused Of Attack On Black Youths. June 12. Available from www.huffingtonpost.com/2011/06/10/four-teens-charged-with-q_n_875115.html [Accessed August 13, 2011].

Intelligence Report. (1995). The Dynamics of Youth, Hate and Violence. Southern Poverty Law Center, October, 11–15.

Intelligence Report. (1998). Hate Crime Alarms College Campuses. Southern Poverty Law Center, Fall, Issue 92.

Intelligence Report. (2000). Hate Goes to School. Southern Poverty Law Center, Spring, Issue 98. Available from www.SPLCENTER.org [Accessed February 8, 2015].

Intelligence Report. (2004). Kurtis Monschke and Other Racists Commit Violent Killing. Southern Poverty Law Center. Summer, Issue 114. Available from www.splcenter.org/get-informed/intelligence-report/browse-all-issues/2004/summer/two-faces-of-volks-front [Accessed June 3, 2012].

Intelligence Report. (2007). More "Ethnic Cleansing" Violence Hits Los Angeles. Southern Poverty Law Center. Spring, Issue 125.

Intelligence Report. (2009). DOJ Probes Discriminatory Policing in New York County. Southern Poverty Law Center. Winter, Issue 136.

Intelligence Report. (2012). Hate and Extremism. Southern Poverty Law Center, Spring, Issue 98. Available from www.splcenter.org/what-we-do/hate-and-extremism [Accessed June 2, 2012].

Jankowski, M. S. (1990). Islands in the Street: Gangs and American Urban Society. Cited in R. G. Sheldon, S. K. Tracy, and W. B. Brown (1997). *Youth Gangs in American Society.* New York: Wadsworth Publishing Company.

Kanter, R. M. (1972). *Commitment and Community: Communes and Utopias in Sociological Perspective.* Cambridge, MA: Harvard University Press.

khq.com. (2011). In-Depth Coverage: Backpack Bomber Kevin Harpham Sentenced. Posted December 20, 2011. Available from www.khq.com/story/16366575/in-depth-coverage-the-harpham-sentencing [Accessed February 8, 2015].

Klassen, B. (1987). *Rahowa! This Planet Is All Ours.* Otto, NC: Creativity Book Publisher.

Kollman, K. (2011). *The American Political System.* New York: W.W. Norton & Company.

Kronenwetter, M. (1992). *United They Hate: White Supremacist Groups in America.* New York: Walker Publishing Company Inc.

Lang, S. S. (1990). *Extremist Groups in America.* New York: Franklin Watts.

Leadership Conference on Civil and Human Rights (LCCHR). (2009). *The State of Hate: Escalating Hate Violence Against Immigrants.* Available from www.civilrights.org/publications/hatecrimes/ [Accessed May 29, 2012].

Leadership Conference on Civil Rights Education Fund (LCCREF). (2009). *Confronting the New Faces of Hate: Hate Crimes in America.* Available from www.civilrights.org/publications/hatecrimes/ [Accessed May 29, 2012].

Lee, F. R. (2003). From Noah's Curse to Slavery's Rationale. *New York Times*, November 1. Available from www.nytimes.com/2003/11/01/arts/from-noah-s-curse-to-slavery-s-rationale.html?pagewanted=all&src=pm [Accessed May 21, 2012].

Levin, J. & McDevitt, J. (1993). *Hate Crimes: The Rising Tide of Bigotry and Bloodshed.* New York: Plenum Press.

Levin, J. & McDevitt, J. (2002). *Hate Crimes: America's War on Those Who Are Different.* Boulder, CO: Westview Press.

Leyden, T. J. & Cook, M. B. (2008). *Skinhead Confessions.* Springville, UT: Sweetwater Books.

Lifton, R. J. (1989). Thought Reform and the Psychology of Totalism. Cited in L. M. Woolf & M. R. Hulsizer (2004). Hate Groups for Dummies: How to Build a Successful Hate Group. *Humanity and Society*, 28(1), 40–62.

Los Angeles County Commission on Human Relations. (1989). Intergroup conflict in Los Angeles County schools. Los Angeles, CA: Author.

Los Angeles County Commission on Human Relations. (2005). 2005 Hate Crime Report. Los Angeles: Author. Available from www.lahumanrelations.org/hatecrime/reports/2005_hateCrimeReport.pdf [Accessed June 3, 2012].

Los Angeles County Commission on Human Relations. (2007). 2007 Hate Crime Report. Los Angeles: Author. Available from www.lahumanrelations.org/hatecrime/reports/2007_hateCrimeReport.pdf [Accessed June 3, 2012].

Los Angeles County Commission on Human Relations. (2009). 2009 Hate Crime Report. Los Angeles: Author. Available from www.lahumanrelations.org/hatecrime/reports/2009_hateCrimeReport.pdf [Accessed June 3, 2012].

Los Angeles County Commission on Human Relations. (2012). 2005 Hate Crime Report. Los Angeles: Author. Available from www.lahumanrelations.org/hatecrime/reports/2012_hateCrimeReport.pdf [Accessed June 2, 2014].

Loyal White Knights of the Ku Klux Klan. (n.d.) Racist Jokes & Pictures. Available from www.kkkknights.com/racist_jokes__pictures [Accessed June 2, 2012].

Lum, L. (2011). NCORE Conference: Scholar Offers Perspectives on Inter-Minority Racism. Diverse. *Issues in Higher Education*. June 6. Available from http://diverseeducation.com/article/15778c2/ncore-conference-scholar-offers-perspectives-on-inter-minority-racism.html [Accessed June 1, 2012].

Macdonald, A. (1978). *The Turner Diaries*. Hillsboro, WV: National Vanguard Books.

McDonald, M. (1995). The Enemy Within: The Far Right's Racist War Against Society is Opening New Fronts Across Canada. *Macleans*, 108(19), 34–35.

National Socialist Movement. (n.d.). National Socialist Movement—Snapshot. Available from www.nsm88.org/ [Accessed June 2, 2014].

Nizkor Project. (n.d.). Available from www.nizkor.org/hweb/orgs/canadian/league-for-human-rights/target-recruit.htm (Accessed March 6, 2015).

Nizkor Project. (n.d.). Is Your Child a Target? A Pamphlet for Parents and Teachers on the Dangers of Hate Group Recruitment in Canada. Available from www.nizkor.org/hweb/orgs/canadian/league-for-human-rights/target-recruit.html [Accessed June 2, 2012].

North Shore Sun. (2010). Elderly Man Admits to Charges of Hate Crime. July 9. Available from http://northshoresun.timesreview.com/2010/07/877/elderly-man-admits-to-charges-of-hate-crime/ [Accessed August 10, 2011].

National Coalition of Anti-Violence Programs. (2010). Hate Violence against Lesbian, Gay, Bisexual, Transgender, Queer and HIV-Infected Communities in the United States in 2010. Available from http://www.avp.org/storage/documents/Reports/2011_NCAVP_HV_Reports.pdf [Accessed March 6, 2015].

Office for Democratic Institutions and Human Rights (ODIHR). (2008). Hate Crimes in the OSCE Region – Incidents and Responses. Annual Report for 2007. Executive Summary. Available from http://www.osce.org/odihr/33989?download=true [Accessed on March 6, 2015].

Patriot Ledger, The. (2009). Milton Man Faces Hate Crimes Charges. July 21. Available from www.patriotledger.com/news/cops_and_courts/x1114024530/Man-faces-hate-crime-charges [Accessed December 21, 2009].

Perry, B. (2001). *In the Name of Hate*. New York: Routledge.

Petrosino, C. (1999). Connecting the Past to the Future: Hate Crime in America. *Journal of Contemporary Criminal Justice*, 15(1), 22–47.

Pollock, E. T. (2010). Understanding and Contextualising Racial Hatred on the Internet: A Study of Newsgroups and Websites. *Internet Journal of Criminology*. Available from http://www.internetjournalofcriminology.com/pollock_racial_hatred_on_the_internet.pdf [Accessed February 8, 2015].

Ray, L., Smith, D., & Wastell, L. (2004). Shame, Rage and Racist Violence. *British Journal of Criminology*, 44(3), 350–68.

R.E.A.L. Organization. (2009). Wisconsin: Waukesha Teens Appear in Court For Hate Crime. October 13. Available from www.realcourage.org/2009/10/wisconsin-waukesha-teens-appear-in-court-for-hate-crime/ [Accessed May 24, 2012].

Ross, L. (2010). *White Supremacy in the 1990s*. Political Research Associates. Available from www.publiceye.org/eyes/whitsup.html [Accessed May 22, 2012].

Ryan, M. E. & Leeson, P. T. (2011). Hate Groups and Hate Crime. *International Review of Law and Economics*, 31(4), 256–62.

Sears, E. (May 24, 1989). Skinheads: A New Generation of Hate-Mongers. *USA Today*, 24–26.

SeattlePi.com. (2010). Teen Beaten "for Enslaving Our People," Police Say. September 21. Available from www.seattlepi.com/local/articles/teen-beaten-for-enslaving [Accessed June 3, 2014].

Sheldon, R. G., Tracy, S. K., & Brown, W. B. (1997). *Youth Gangs in American Society*. New York: Wadsworth Publishing Company.

Sibbit, R. (1997). The Perpetrators of Racial Harassment and Racial Violence. Home Office Research Study 176, Research and Statistics Directorate. London: Home Office.

Simi, P. & Futrell, R. (2010) *American Swastika: Inside the White Power Movement's Hidden Spaces of Hate*. Lanham, MD: Rowman & Littlefield Publishers.

Sims, P. (1996). *The Klan* (2nd ed.). Lexington, KY: University Press of Kentucky.

Southern Poverty Law Center (SPLC). (2012a). Active U.S. Hate Groups. Available from www.splcenter.org/get-informed/hate-map [Accessed June 2, 2012].

Southern Poverty Law Center (SPLC). (2012b). Hate and Extremism. Available from www.splcenter.org/what-we-do/hate-and-extremism [Accessed June 2, 2012].

US Department of Education. (1998). *Preventing Youth Hate Crime: A Manual for Schools and Communities*. Office of Elementary and Secondary Education. Safe and Drug-Free Schools Program. Washington, DC: Author.

US Department of Education. (1999). *Protecting Students from Harassment and Hate Crimes. A Guide for Schools*. Washington, DC: Author.

US Department of Justice. (1999). *Hate Crime Data Collection Guidelines*. Federal Bureau of Investigation. Criminal Justice Information Services. Washington, DC: Author.

US Department of Justice. (2001). Special Report. Hate Crimes Reported in NIBRS, 1997–99. Office of Justice Programs Bureau of Justice Statistics. September 2001, NCJ 186765. Available from http://bjs.ojp.usdoj.gov/content/pub/ascii/hcrn99.txt [Accessed May 24, 2012].

US Department of Justice. (2010). Hate Crimes Statistics 2010. Federal Bureau of Investigation. Available from www.fbi.gov/about-us/cjis/ucr/hate-crime/2010/narratives/hate-crime-2010-incidents-and-offenses [Accessed June 2, 2012].

Willems, H. (1995). Right-Wing Extremism, Racism or Youth Violence? Explaining Violence against Foreigners in Germany. *New Community*, 21(4), 501–23.

Wills, J. (1999). Ku Klux Klan Solicit in Lowell. *Connector*, 30(11), 2.

Wineburg, S. S. (2001). *Historical Thinking and Other Unnatural Acts: Charting the Future of Teaching the Past*. Philadelphia, PA: Temple University Press.

Wooden, W. A. (1995). *Renegade Kids, Suburban Outlaws*. Belmont, CA: Wadsworth Publishing.

Woolf, L. M. & Hulsizer, M. R. (2004). Hate Groups for Dummies: How to Build a Successful Hate Group. *Humanity and Society*, 28(1), 40–62.

Zia, H. (1991). Women in Hate Groups. Who Are They? And Why Are They There? *Ms.*, 1(5), 20–7.

6 Victims

Who are they?

Introduction

The criminal justice system is more effective in responding to crime than preventing it. The heavy emphasis on reacting to crime also prioritizes punishing the offender more than understanding the experience of crime victims. But the impacts of crime victimization must be better understood for several reasons. First, the immediate and long-term effects of crime victimization require the availability of appropriate supportive social services. Second, better appreciation of the harms caused by crime is necessary to more accurately gauge proper levels of punishment. Finally, understanding the scope of the trauma caused by the crime provides a view of the mindset of the perpetrator.

These concerns should be heightened for victims of hate crime because the impacts from these crimes are arguably *more* traumatic than those from non-hate equivalents. It is not a situation of having a *random* chance of being targeted for crime but that the perpetrator *preferred* him or her as a target over others due to *personal* characteristics.

This chapter discusses the victims of hate crime, how they are targeted and the impacts of their victimization experience. Also reviewed is the perspective of *communities-as-victims* and how communities respond to local hate crime events.

A distinctive victimization

All crime victimizations are deplorable and potentially scarring to crime victims. But there are study findings which indicate that the impact of hate crime victimization exceeds that of ordinary crime victimization (Garcia & McDevitt, 1999; Herek, et al. 2002). The sobering realization that one was targeted for harm because of immutable or prominent *personal* characteristics weakens feelings of safety and security. No installation of a sophisticated home security system, self-defense instructions, or parking only in well-lit areas change the *characteristics* of individuals targeted for hate crime. Thus, there is a unique sense of *vulnerability* and *exposure* that these victims are likely to experience. Non-hate crime victims also feel vulnerable, but there are substantive differences about hate crimes themselves that may exacerbate the victim's sense of vulnerability. These crimes distinguish themselves in two critical areas: (1) there is a *historical* continuity of hate-motivated victimization of racial minorities, Jews, and homo-sexuals; and (2) a continuing complicity of social institutions and mainstream culture in the targeting of victim groups (Petrosino, 1999; Perry, 2001). Given these added components, the harm factor in hate crime victimization is distinctive and significantly impactful in comparison to non-hate crime.

Some victims of hate crime endure serial attacks, which must compound feelings of impotence and defenselessness. Bowling described the following racially motivated events experienced *repeatedly* in the borough of Newham, a suburb of London (as found in Hall, 2005, 65):

> During the year January 1987 to January 1988, 53 incidents targeted against seven families in two streets were recorded by the police . . . The overwhelming majority of the incidents consisted of verbal abuse and harassment, egg throwing, damage to property, and door knocking. Conceived of as individual instances of offensive or threatening behavior, and employing any kind of hierarchy of seriousness using legal categories, many of these incidents would be regarded as minor. However, in the context of the life of any individual family . . . in the life of a locality the repeated incidence of harassment is bound to have a cumulative effect.
>
> (Bowling, 1999, 189)

Since 1973, the Department of Justice has reported national crime victimization statistics. It was not until the year 2000 that the data collection process documented hate crime victimizations. The NCVS reported that there was an average of 210,000 victimizations and 191,000 hate crime incidents per year from July 2000 through December 2003 (Bureau of Justice Services, 2005). Several elements in this report were striking: the overwhelming majority of these crimes (84 percent) were violent and a weapon was involved in a third of the crimes. Despite the violent nature of these crimes, less than half of the victims (44 percent) reported them to police. A number of reasons were given for this behavior: (a) victims preferred to report to advocacy organizations; (b) they believed the crime was not important enough to report or; (c) it was not clear to them that they were the intended target. Victims identified racial bias most frequently as the offender's motive (56 percent), ethnic bias was second (27.9 percent); sexual orientation (17.9 percent); religious bias (12.4 percent) and then disability (10.5 percent).

The most recent NCVS report (2013) shows that from 2007–11 the average number of hate crime victimizations was 259,700. This number shows a slight increase since the 2000–03 period. Likewise, the average number of hate crime incidents was 194,390, which is slightly up from the 2000–03 estimate of 191,000. There is some consistency in victim perceptions of offender bias (see Figure 6.1).

There were slight increases in each of the categories shown above with the exception of two areas. Perceived racial bias shows a decrease in 2007–11 (63 percent to 54 percent), but religion has more than doubled (10 percent to 21 percent) for the same time period. A particularly unsettling change noted in this report is the increase in the percentage of violent victimizations. 92 percent of the victimizations were

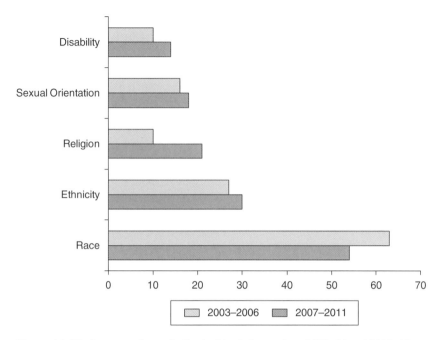

Figure 6.1 Victim perceptions of offender bias in hate crime, 2003–06 and 2007–11

Source: Adapted from Bureau of Justice Services, Hate Crime Victimization, 2003–11. Special Report. March 2013. Sandholtz, N. Langton, L., and Planty, M. US Department of Justice. NCJ 241291

identified as violent, which is up 8 percent from the earlier period. In fact, the report indicates that the increase in hate crime victimizations in general was due to the apparent escalation in violent rather than non-violent hate crimes. Yet despite this growth in serious hate crime victimizations, reports to the police decreased to 35 percent. After noting these changes in trends, two obvious questions present themselves. Why is there an increase in victim perception of anti-religion incidents? And why are victims even less inclined to report their ill-treatment to law enforcement? Clearly self-report measurement is imperfect because its accuracy is dependent upon the recall of individuals after the fact. However, if the 21 percent is reflective of a true increase, then *more perpetrators* are committing these crimes or the increase represents *more reporting* of this bias behavior. The decrease in reporting is unexpected in light of media and other campaigns aimed at the public to educate about hate crime and the efforts of law enforcement to better facilitate reporting.

Victim groups and their experiences

Blacks and African-Americans (anti-Black animus)

The FBI's annual Hate Crime reports have consistently shown racial bias as the most frequently reported bias motivation category. Of the racial categories included (anti-White, anti-Black, anti-American Indian/Alaskan Native, anti-Asian/Pacific Islander, and anti-Multiple Races, Group) anti-Black incidents are usually several times that of the other racial categories *combined* (see Table 6.1).

These data indicate that nearly 29,000 reported anti-Black-motivated hate crimes occurred from 2000–10; averaging 2,400 incidents per year. But if the true annual average of hate crimes is estimated to be nearly twenty-three times that of what is reported, according to the NCVS (2005), then the number of anti-Black hate crimes is likely much larger—possibly approaching 55,200 per year.

Some of the most highly publicized hate crimes have targeted Blacks. They include Howard Beach, New York (Michael Griffith); Bensonhurst, New York (Yusef Hawkins); Fayetteville, North Carolina (Jackie Burden and Michael James); and Jasper, Texas (James Byrd, Jr.). Following are brief synopses of three of these cases:

- *Fayetteville, North Carolina, December 7, 1995*—Jackie Burden and Michael James, two African-Americans, were shot to death on the streets of Fayetteville by two White Fort Bragg soldiers, who were also neo-Nazi skinheads. Witness statements indicated that the codefendants sought a "dimly lit place where, they could victimize blacks" (*New York Times*, "Ex-G.I . . . ," 1997, paragraph 15). Court testimony indicated that some skinhead groups use a spider-web tattoo to signify that the wearer has murdered a black person. One of the soldiers involved in the killings, Private James Burmeister, remarked that he might be "earning his spider web tattoo" that very night (*New York Times*, "Ex-G.I . . . ," paragraph 14). He achieved his objective and qualified for the tattoo. Burmeister and Private Malcolm Wright shot six bullets into the heads of the victims that they happened upon as they entered a Black neighborhood in Fayetteville.

Table 6.1 Reported anti-Black motivated incident 2000–10

Year	% racially motivated of all bias categories	% anti-Black of all racial categories	Reported incidents
2010	47.3	69.8	2,201
2009	48.5	71.4	2,284
2008	51.3	72.6	2,876
2007	50.8	69.3	2,658
2006	51.8	66.2	2,640
2005	54.7	68.2	2,630
2004	52.9	67.5	2,731
2003	51.3	66.2	2,548
2002	48.8	68.2	2,486
2001	44.9	66.3	2,899
2000	53.8	66.4	2,884

Source: DOJ, FBI Hate Crime Statistics 2000–10

- *Jasper, Texas, June 7, 1998* — James Byrd Jr. fell victim to one of the most horrendous racially motivated murders in recent US history. Prosecutors believed the killers sought to use the Byrd murder to spark new membership in their nascent hate group, the *Texas Rebel Soldiers.* Byrd was beaten, and some accounts state that his face was also sprayed with black paint. He was then chained about the ankles to the back of a truck and dragged until his body tore into pieces (*San Francisco Chronicle in Education*, "A Murder . . . ," 2007, paragraph 2; Babineck, 2004). All three defendants—John William King, Lawrence Brewer, and Sean Berry—were found guilty of murder. King and Brewer received death sentences, and Berry received a life sentence. The Byrd murder received enormous media attention. Many were repulsed over the violence of this crime; but not everyone was outraged. Two white men, Joshua Talley and John Fowler, were arrested and charged with desecrating the grave of James Byrd, Jr. (Barnes, 2004).

- *Chicago, Illinois, March, 1997* — It was early evening on March 21, and thirteen-year-old Lenard Clark, Jr. had just finished playing basketball with two other kids at Armour Square Park bordering Chicago's Bridgeport neighborhood. As the teens left the park, they decided to check out the nearby Chicago White Sox stadium, which was undergoing preparation for opening day. It was just a few blocks away. They never made it. According to witnesses, Lenard and the other two youths were attacked by a gang of whites, who were angry that two Black and one Latino youth were in "their neighborhood." The three teenagers split up in order to get away. Two escaped. Lenard didn't. Shouting racist insults, the group of Whites knocked Lenard off of his bike. They smashed his head into a wall. They beat and kicked him into unconsciousness, causing permanent brain damage. It was reported that they later boasted about how they had, "taken care of the n*ggers in the neighborhood."

(RW ONLINE, 1997, paragraph 1–3)

There are several theories that address racially motivated crimes including the "power threat" hypothesis and the "power differential" hypothesis. The power threat hypothesis predicts the likelihood of attacks on minorities when Whites believe that incoming minority groups threaten their economic, social, and political security (Blalock, 1973; Eitle, et al. 2002; Tolnay, et al. 1989). The flash point—that is, when Whites feel sufficiently threatened and begin to target minorities (primarily Blacks) for harassment, intimidation, or worse—can occur at different points during the community-change process (Bobo, et al. 1986; Horowitz, 1985). Power differential hypothesis asserts that when Whites dominate a given neighborhood by sheer numbers and control its political institutions, they are less constrained from committing racially motivated acts (Green, et al. 1998; Levin & McDevitt, 1993). These theories suggest that localized anti-black hate crime may be a product of conflict dynamics in which hate crime perpetrators act to protect White hegemony.

The scope and characteristics of anti-Black hate crime

The Southern Poverty Law Center's *Intelligence Report* and the Journal of Blacks in Higher Educations' *The Race Relations Reporter* (hereafter referred to as *The Reporter*) are periodicals that report hate crime incidents obtained from media sources. *The Reporter* (currently inactive) maintained a record of race-related incidents as reported in a variety of US newspapers. Newspaper accounts of crime events are not without error and do not necessarily include all of the relevant facts, but research of newspaper articles is a fairly common data collection method in the social sciences. Archival research of *The Reporter* is used as a source of information on the nature of anti-Black hate crime. Every issue of *The Reporter* published from 1994–2002 was examined by the author for anti-Black incidents (Turpin-Petrosino, 2009). The types of crimes that appeared most frequently were selected in order to discern common features. The following highlights the most consistent factors in the 88 case studies.

Attacks occurred in or around the residence of the victim

Forty-four percent of the sample incidents (39 of 88) took place in or around the victim's home—the largest category for offense location. Even though anti-Black hate crime is often triggered when African-Americans move into predominately White neighborhoods (Bell, 2002; Crump, 2004), there is less awareness that they are also targeted in predominately Black neighborhoods. Levin and McDevitt (1993) contend that some hate crime perpetrators enter the environs of the targeted group to carry out attacks. Such attacks may have greater ramifications for victims who could lose their sense of security and protection even in their own neighborhoods.

Anti-Black hate crimes occur in every geographic region of the United States

As previously mentioned, these crimes are a large percentage of the racially motivated hate crimes that occur across the country, even in states where few African-Americans reside. In 2010, Black Americans numbered 38.9 million, or roughly 13 percent of the population. The majority of African-Americans live in the South (55 percent), 17 percent live in the Northeast, and another 18 percent live in the Midwest. The area with the lowest percentage of African-Americans is the West, at 10 percent (US Census Bureau, 2010). States with disproportionately low numbers of Black citizens but still see anti-Black hate crimes underscore the *insistent* nature of this crime. From 1992 through 2006, Arizona reported a total of 50 racially motivated hate crimes; 37 (74 percent) were anti-Black incidents.

However, Blacks make up only about 3.6 percent of the population in Arizona (US Census 2000 Bureau). A state with similar data is Idaho. There were a total of 10 racially motivated hate crimes recorded in 2003; six (60 percent) of them were anti-Black, yet Blacks are only 0.6 percent of Idaho's population (US Census Bureau, 2000). The *Reporter* sample included incidents that occurred throughout the United States (e.g. Maine, Florida, Michigan, Colorado, Kentucky, and California), but a disproportionately high rate of anti-Black hate crime appears to be constant, *regardless of geographical region*. When racially motivated crime occurs, the likelihood is that a Black person, or one who is perceived to be Black, is the target.

Destructive acts alone are not sufficient: racist branding is consistently included

Regardless of whether the act targeted an individual or property (Bell, 2002), the application of *racial branding*—the use of racist symbols and/or slurs—is part of the harmful act. So that the point is not lost on the victim, attackers harm them by destroying their property, causing them bodily injury and incorporating racist branding—the use of ugly slurs that are meant to hurt and demean. Attackers readily use symbols that originated with hate organizations, even though most hate crimes are committed by unaffiliated individuals. The power of such symbols and their effect on victims should not be underestimated.

Perpetrators do not refrain from victimizing Black children

The following incident appeared in *The Reporter* (1994): A complaint was filed by the Colorado Civil Rights Commission that alleges racial harassment against a Black family residing in Aurora. The complaint alleges that two men grabbed one of the children by the back of the collar and shouted racial slurs at him. Reportedly, the verbal abuse by the two men against the Black family continued for several days. Another incident highlighting the targeting of Black children: "Racial slurs have been directed at a mixed race child by neighbors in Sanford, Maine, according to the child's mother. Neighbors referred to the child as 'nigger,' 'black dog,' 'brown dog,' and 'brown spot on the road'" (*The Reporter,* 1995, 4). Because Black families are sometimes targeted in their homes, there is greater likelihood that children will witness and experience the attack. Cross burnings, acts of arson, racist graffiti, and racial epithets painted on homes along with verbal or physical threats, can have extraordinary effects on children. In the *Reporter* sample, 13 of the cases (15 percent) indicate that children were present during the incident. 11 of these cases are incidents that targeted children 17 years of age and younger. In addition to children, Black women are also victimized. In the sample, 8 cases (9 percent) specifically targeted women. In these instances, perpetrators harmed Black children or women who were present during attacks.

Sample analyses also identify offense characteristics that may be unique to anti-Black hate crimes; I make the following observations:

- Anti-Black hate crime is both historical and contemporary. Racism as well as other attitudes of intolerance is rooted in American culture and helps to explain why anti-Black incidents *continue* to persist. With this history and the ongoing racialization of social problems in the United States, it is no surprise that anti-Black hate crime outpaces all other categories of racially motivated hate crime and that it occurs in every quadrant of the United States.

- Anti-Black hate crimes have an omnipresent quality and a depravity reflected in the willingness to identify Black children (and women) as legitimate targets that are as threatening as Black males. What adds to the malicious nature of these crimes is the absolute need to racially debase the victim, in addition to committing the base crime (i.e. malicious damage, aggravated assault, etc.). For example, one incident described in the *Reporter* sample—an assault with a deadly weapon—involved the shooting of a Black male as the perpetrator screamed racial epithets. Another incident involved perpetrators destroying the Black victim's car, urinating on it, and then writing racial slurs on the vehicle. The omnipresent quality of anti-Black hate crime is reflected in the diversity of locations in which Blacks have been victimized including their homes, workplaces, schools, and churches.

- The viewpoint that minorities and the poor are responsible for the social ills of society is found in the dominant culture as well as the hate movement. "With the national racial order firmly in place, most white Americans, from childhood on, come to adopt the views, assumptions, and proclivities of previous generations and established white authorities. In this manner the system of racism is reproduced from one generation of whites to the next" (Feagin, 2001; 90). Recognizing this common area, ideological convergence between mainstream cultural beliefs and the views of the radical right may embolden hate crime perpetrators. Anti-Black hate crime enforces a racial hierarchy and ensures white hegemony.

Asian-Americans (anti-Asian animus)

The murders of Matthew Shepard and James Byrd, Jr. are well known tragedies marking the vulnerability of the LGBTQ and African-American communities to hate crime attacks. The Asian community can also contribute a name to this list— Vincent Chin.

On June 19, 1982 Vincent Chin, a young Chinese-American man, was in the midst of enjoying his bachelor's party in a Detroit lounge when he encountered White males Ronald Ebens and Michael Nitz. The two were autoworkers angered by the US auto industry losing ground to foreign imports. For Ebens and Nitz, the Japanese were to blame. Assuming that Chin was Japanese, Ebens and Nitz began making insulting remarks. "Ebens began making racial and obscene remarks toward Chin calling him a 'Chink' and a 'Nip' and making remarks about foreign car imports" (Ho, paragraph 5). "It's because of you little m—f—s that we're out of work," as well as other anti-Asian racial epithets" (Ho, paragraph 5). A brief fight occurs in the lounge between the two parties. Later both leave.

But minutes later, Ebens and Nitz find Chin and Ebens, being the aggressor, beat Chin in the head and on his upper body with a bat. Chin died from his injuries a few days later.

This racially motivated attack revealed several things about the targeting of Asian-Americans for hate-motivated crimes: the relative economic success of Asian-Americans brings the resentment of some (e.g. "Asian Americans are now the best-educated, highest-income, fastest-growing racial group in the country," according to the Pew Research Center, 2014b); the Chin perpetrators failed to appreciate multiculturalism among those of Asian descent, seeing all Asians as the same; and regardless of the fact that many Asian-Americans were born in the US they are often viewed by some as perpetual "foreigners." We will come back to this point a bit later.

According to the 2010 Census from 2000–10, the Asian-American population grew faster than any other racial group in the US. Residents who self-identify as Asian now constitute 4.8 percent (14.7 million) of the total US population. The majority of Asian-Americans (46 percent) reside in western states, including Arizona, California, Colorado, Hawaii, Idaho, Montana, Nevada, New Mexico, Oregon, and Utah. It is interesting that despite the fact that the Asian population has outpaced other racial minority groups in growth—their rate of hate crime victimization has not shown a correlating increase (see Table 6.2). If the group threat hypothesis has any validity, it seems to have little utility in this particular case. Dunbar and Nikolova (2004) used census data and hate crime reports for Los Angeles and observed interesting patterns of victimization that corresponded with race and ethnicity. The risk of victimization for Asians was at a much lower threshold. In other words, their targeting occurred in those census tracts where these groups constituted no more than 20 percent of the residents. Dunbar and Nikolova explain this by noting that where Asians and Blacks are fewer in number among a dominant racial group (Whites) they are more visible, more targetable, and thus more vulnerable to victimization.

Table 6.2 Reported anti-Asian/Pacific Islander motivated incidents 2000–10

Year	% racially motivated of all bias categories	% anti-Asian of all racial categories	Reported incidents
2010	47.3	.047	150
2009	48.5	.039	126
2008	51.3	.034	137
2007	50.8	.048	188
2006	51.8	.045	181
2005	54.7	.050	199
2004	52.9	.053	217
2003	51.3	.060	231
2002	48.8	.059	217
2001	44.9	.064	280
2000	53.8	.064	281

Source: DOJ, FBI Hate Crime Statistics 2000–10

Much of the rationale exhibited by Chin's attackers fuels attacks of Asians and Pacific Americans in general: racism, anti-immigrant sentiment, xenophobia, and ignorance. What may be a unique aspect to Asian victimization was brought to light in a recent report published by the Leadership Conference on Civil Rights Education Fund (LCCREF) in 2009. The report describes how Asian youth are singled out for racial harassment and worse (LCCREF, paragraph 3; 5):

> In 2005, while waiting on a subway platform in Brooklyn, New York, 18 year-old Chen Tsu was accosted by four high school classmates who demanded his money. . . . they assaulted him, taking turns beating his face. At his school, Lafayette High in Brooklyn, Chinese immigrant students like him are harassed and bullied so routinely that school officials . . . agreed to a Department of Justice consent decree to curb alleged "severe and pervasive harassment directed at Asian-American students by their classmates."
>
> (paragraph 3)

> In Fresno, California at Edison High School, Hmong students had been taunted and had food thrown at them during lunch. On February 25, 2005, the taunts escalated into fights involving at least 30 students, resulting in numerous injuries, suspensions, and expulsions. Eight students were convicted of misdemeanor assault.
>
> (paragraph 5)

These types of attacks more easily happen in school settings for a variety of reasons. The school campus brings together hundreds of young people from different backgrounds sharing a central location for a time period of some duration; the vulnerability of targeted students is exacerbated by real number differentials (majority versus minority); Asian students are racial minorities that are highly visible; if these students are also immigrants—they are at a cultural disadvantage. In addition, faculty and school officials often are unaware of harassment behaviors in general (or fail to intervene appropriately) and schools fail to implement effective and common-sense policies to deal with these occurrences.

Other Asian-Americans have experienced more deadly hate crimes. Postal worker Joseph Ileto and Indiana University graduate student Won-Joon Yoon were both murdered by White supremacists. On August 10, 1999, avowed racist Buford O. Furrow, Jr. walked into the lobby of the North Valley Jewish Community Center in Granada Hills, California and opened fire with a semiautomatic weapon, wounding five people. Shortly thereafter, Furrow murdered Joseph Santos Ileto, a few miles away from the center, shooting him multiple times. Furrow confessed that he murdered Ileto because he was non-White and a federal employee (CNN). Won-Joon Yoon was among the many two-state shooting victims of White supremacist Benjamin Smith. During the Fourth of July weekend in 1999, Smith went on a hunt for ethnic and racial minorities and Jews to target. Yoon was killed as he attempted to enter his place of worship. Smith committed suicide before he could be taken into custody.

The LCCREF report goes on to describe wide ranging anti-Asian attacks (LCCREF, paragraph 8–10):

- In August 2006, four New Yorkers of Chinese descent were attacked in Douglaston, Queens, New York by two White men shouting racial epithets. The White men beat two of the Chinese Americans with a steering wheel locking bar. Kevin M. Brown, 19, of Auburndale, and Paul A. Heavey, 20, of Little Neck, were charged with assault and hate crimes. Douglaston and other nearby communities are now almost one-third Asian, and tensions have escalated (paragraph 8).

   "It definitely doesn't shock me," said one White resident of the area about the attack. "The entire strip of Northern Boulevard in the past four or five years went from German and Italian to Korean" (paragraph 9).
- In Chicago in September 2007, Du Doan, a 62 year-old Vietnamese man, was pushed off a fishing pier into the icy waters of Lake Michigan, where he drowned. John Haley, aged 31, a self-described "skinhead," was charged with first degree murder after he told police how he "pushed our victim in the water." Earlier, Haley reportedly pushed a second Asian man into Lake Michigan who was able to swim safely to shore and also tried to shove a third Asian man off the pier who fought him off (paragraph 10).

The examination of these and other incidents suggest several characteristics of anti-Asian acts: attacks vary in seriousness and include murder; Asians are viewed by some as an economic threat; Asian youth might be among the most victimized students due to their high visibility as a minority group and relative few numbers in most school districts and; the constancy of their perception as *permanent* immigrants. This single factor, that of the constant misperception of Asian-Americans as immigrants or foreigners, seems to be most critical for understanding anti-Asian hate crime. Terri Yuh-Lin Chen's (2004) article, *Hate Violence as Border Patrol,* is a critical analysis of anti-Asian hate crime and situates the problem as the ongoing perception of Asians as foreign and dangerous. Historically, immigrant groups were subject to a period of scrutiny and suspicion until there were eventually welcomed to assimilate. Yet there is an unwillingness by dominant cultural groups to relinquish this attitude of wariness, even after a substantial period of time, for immigrant groups of color. Legal scholar Angelo Ancheta argues that, "Asian Americans, Latinos, and Arab Americans are racially categorized as foreign-born outsiders, *regardless* of actual citizenship status" (Chen, 2004, 252). Chen adds that because Asian-Americans are continuously viewed as immigrants, they are frequently distrusted and closely watched. This social process of policing the Asian "immigrant" and keeping that group within certain social boundaries explains why hate-motivated violence is directed towards them. This function of policing or monitoring is what Robert S. Chang and Keith Aoki refer to as maintaining "figurative borders"):

Foreignness is inscribed upon our bodies in such a way that Asian Americans and Latinas/os carry a figurative border with us. This figurative border, in addition to confirming the belonging-ness of the 'real' Americans, marks Asian Americans and Latinas/os as targets of nativistic racism. It renders us suspect, subject to the violence of heightened scrutiny at the border, in the workplace, in hospitals, and elsewhere.

(Chen, 2004, 59)

The persistent view that Asian-Americans reflect the presence of a sinister alien or "foreign" presence may be the driving force behind why they have been targeted by hate crime perpetrators in the United States for decades.

Latinos (anti-Hispanic animus)

The term "beaner-hopping," became known during the investigation of the 2008 murder of Marcelo Lucero in Long Island, New York. Similar to the "Paki-bashing" attacks by London skinhead gangs in the 1980s, "beaner-hopping" refers to the brutal attack of Hispanics, usually by racist youths for the purposes of humiliation and intimidation. On November 8, 2008 Lucero was walking near the Patchogue train station in Long Island when he was confronted by a group of White teens who were intent on targeting him. Ethnic slurs were hurled at him followed by a physical attack. While Lucero was defending himself, he was fatally stabbed in the chest by one of the assailants.

According to FBI hate crime statistics, Latinos are the largest recipients of anti-ethnic motivated crimes. Anti-ethnic hate crime is reported in two categories: anti-Hispanic and anti-other ethnicity/national origin. The anti-Hispanic category is consistently the larger (see Table 6.3).

Marcelo Lucero was not the first person attacked by this particular group of thugs. According to investigators, this gang was involved in similar attacks viewing "beaner-hopping" as a type of "sport." This is similar to the *thrill* hate crimes category discussed by Levin and McDevitt (2002). Part of the reasoning for this type of boldness is awareness that due to fear of detention and possible deportation, some Latinos are reluctant to report any crime victimization to police. Thus,

Table 6.3 Anti-Hispanic incident rates

Year	No. of anti-ethnic hate incidents	No. of anti-Hispanic hate incidents	Percentage
2010	847	534	63
2009	777	483	62
2008	894	561	63
2007	1,007	595	59
2006	984	576	58
2005	944	522	55

Source: DOJ, FBI Hate Crime Statistics 2005–10

with little fear of discovery and legal repercussions, these offenders are unrestrained in their attacks.

However, one of the most important demographic changes occurring in the US is the growing presence of Hispanics. In fact, the most recent census reports indicate that Hispanics outnumber Whites today in two states: New Mexico and California (Pew Research Center, 2014a). The so-called demise of the White majority is how White nationalists interpret these changes. The question is whether this potential power shift will incite further violence against Hispanics particularly in light of the current crisis of illegal immigration. Stacey, Carbone-López, and Rosenfeld (2011) examine immigration patterns and use Blalock's (1967) group threat theory to hypothesize that an increase in Hispanic immigration is associated with *increases* in anti-Hispanic acts; the result of "new nativism" sentiments, as described by these researchers.

Results supported their hypothesis concluding that changes in immigration is a sound predictor of anti-Hispanic hate crime.

In 2010 there was a series of violent attacks on Latinos on Staten Island. Alejandro Galindo, a Mexican immigrant was attacked while coming home from work as a day laborer in the Port Richmond area of Staten Island. The assailants, who attacked without any provocation, caused a fractured eye socket and brain trauma to Galindo. New York police classified the assault as a hate crime. Earlier in the year, Rodolfo Olmedo, also a Mexican immigrant, was attacked in the same community. Ethnic slurs were shouted as a group comprised of several individuals beat and assaulted Olmedo with a baseball bat and a metal chain (DiBranco, 2010). This rash of hate crimes occurred during the recent debates regarding US immigration policy and Arizona's controversial immigration law. There is no definitive empirical evidence to link public discourse on these issues and the occurrence of these crimes, but the possibility of its influence can't be ruled out.

In April 2010, Arizona adopted a new law to address the problem of illegal immigration. Senate Bill 1070 is at the heart of the current immigration debate, which in its wake may have stimulated interest in extremist groups and membership growth in such groups according to the Southern Poverty Law Center (*Intelligence Report*, 2008). The law expands police powers and permits law enforcement officers to stop, question the immigration status and detain those who police have *reasonable suspicion* are "illegal" immigrants, until their legal status is determined. The law also makes it a state crime to be without immigration papers. Critics were concerned that this law legalizes racial profiling and the general harassment of Latinos. But on June 25, 2012 the US Supreme Court sustained that part of the Arizona law, affirming the provision permitting state law enforcement officials to determine the immigration status of individuals they stop or arrest if they also suspect they are in the US illegally. Still controversial, the ongoing debate opened the door to the expression of racist and xenophobic sentiments. In fact, the Office of Intelligence and Analysis at the US Department of Homeland Security (DHS) reported concern in 2009 that the effects of venomous public discourse could result in the targeting of Hispanics for violent crime (LCCREF, 2009).

High profile media personalities contributed to a negative atmosphere further fueling anti-immigrant fears and hostilities. Conservative talk show host, Rush Limbaugh reportedly offered the following comments:

> On April 1, 2005, Limbaugh described undocumented immigrants as an "invasive species," saying:
> So invasive species like mollusks and spermatozoa are not good, and we've Got a federal judge say, "You can't bring it in here," but invasive species in the form of illegal immigration is fine and dandy—bring 'em on, as many as possible, legalize them wherever we can, wherever they go, no matter what they clog up [paragraph 5].

> On January 31, 2011, Limbaugh asked:
> [H]as the CDC ever published a story about the dangers of catching diseases when you sleep with illegal aliens? [paragragh 6].
>
> (Media Matters for America, 2012)

Media Matters recently examined the content of cable news programs regarding immigration. An excerpt of their findings follows:

> Dobbs, O'Reilly, and Beck serve up a steady diet of fear, anger, and resentment on the topic of illegal immigration [paragraph 4].

> During 2007, the alleged connection between illegal immigration and crime was discussed on 94 episodes of *Lou Dobbs Tonight*, 66 episodes of *The O'Reilly Factor*, and 29 episodes of *Glenn Beck* [paragraph 6].

> *Lou Dobbs Tonight* has also been the show on which viewers are told about a mythical explosion of leprosy cases due to illegal immigration, and a mythical epidemic of voter fraud due to illegal immigration [paragraph 10].
>
> (Media Matters, n.d., Executive Summary)

With Arizona serving as ground zero for the confluence of a troubled public policy, mounting consequences albeit mixed for all affected parties, exploitation of public fears, local and national politicians with political agendas, well-intentioned law enforcement personnel being praised and vilified and White nationalists on the sidelines with their own agendas—did any of this impact the rate of anti-Latino hate crime? (see Table 6.4).

We see from these data that anti-Hispanic hate crimes were erratic until 2005. Since that year, the numbers have somewhat trended upward. Whether or not that trend is driven by the ugly climate in and around Arizona as well as group-threat dynamics can only be determined by a careful analysis of the triggers that motivated perpetrators who committed anti-Hispanic hate crimes in that area since 2005.

The 2005 NCVS provided data including per capita rates of hate crime victimization: 0.9 per 1,000 Whites, 0.7 per 1,000 blacks, and 0.9 per 1,000 Hispanics; suggesting little variation among racial and ethnic groups that would negate

Table 6.4 Anti-Hispanic incident rates in Arizona

Year	Total number of hate crimes	No. of anti-ethnic hate crimes	No. of racially motivated hate crimes
2010	236	37	98
2009	219	42	85
2008	185	46	80
2007	161	29	82
2006	149	38	52
2005	138	27	61
2004	224	45	101
2003	246	54	99
2002	238	47	106
2001	384	128	159
2000	240	36	129

Source: DOJ, FBI Hate Crime Statistics 2000–10

concern over the uptick of anti-Hispanic hate crime. But these data may be some-what misleading regarding victimization rates. The critical factor about hate crime is that it serves to reinforce marginalization; the marginalization of groups that have historically experienced oppression on a significant scale (meaning institutionalized and cultural racism) in the United States. This degree of subordination (social, political, and economical) is possible because racial minority groups—by definition—have always been fewer in numbers relative to European Americans and possess less political capital. Thus per capita representations fail to reflect the significance of proportionality between victim/perpetrator groups when reporting these crimes.

The prevalence of anti-Latino attacks must be viewed as a product of several things: multiple fears and prejudices, a less than stellar history of relations between Anglos and Hispanics, long-held unjust institutional practices, in addition to new tensions over economic uncertainty and the real issue of a failed immigration policy.

Sexual orientation

Gay men are often targeted for brutal attacks due to sexual orientation bias. Such was the case with Dwan Prince in Brooklyn, New York on June 8, 2005. Prince, who is Black and gay was viciously attacked in front of his own home following what his attacker, Steven Pomie, believed was a flirtatious remark made toward him by Prince. Prince sustained very serious brain trauma which required several surgeries yet resulted in partial paralysis. Pomie was eventually convicted of first degree assault as a hate crime and sentenced to 25 years (The LGBTQ Hate Crimes Project, 2007).

Similar to other victim groups discussed thus far in this chapter, sexual minorities also have a history of targeted victimization in the United States, including systematic discriminatory practices by social institutions. But unlike other groups, the LGBTQ community's response to these oppressive acts—which will be discussed later—should be considered unique in its focus, goals, political savvy, stratagem, and efficacy.

The Stonewall rebellion was a pivotal crisis that gave birth to the gay rights movement in the United States (LCCREF, 2009).

In response to a police raid at the Stonewall Inn, a gay bar in Greenwich, New York, June 27, 1969, many gay patrons resolved to no longer accept abusive treatment at the hands of police or others because of sexual orientation. They fought with police and ignited several days of riots, protests, demonstrations, and marches that would expand beyond the Stonewall Inn area into New York. Subsequently this incident inspired members of the LGBTQ community throughout the country to organize and advocate for social and legal equality. Perhaps the birth of this social movement would serve as the template for community activism that would be used to mount a campaign against sexual bias motivated hate crime.

This new assertive sociopolitical stance made the LGBTQ community more visible to the general public. It also encouraged gays and lesbians to not only privately express their sexuality, but to do so publicly as well. The cost of challenging cultural norms made the LGBTQ community a greater target for hate crime (Herek & Berrill, 1992). It would be more than 25 years after the Stonewall riots before sexual orientation hate crimes would be systematically reported and published by the DOJ. Current FBI crime data shows a steady pattern of these incidents (see Table 6.5).

Sexual orientation hate crimes are on average, 17 percent (or 1 out of 6) of all reported hate incidents. Anti-gay attacks are the largest category of sexual orientation-motivated hate crimes. The second largest category is anti-homosexual, which includes incidents reflecting hostility toward multiple sexual minority

Table 6.5 Sexual orientation hate crimes

Year	Total number of hate crime incidents	Total number of sexual orientation incidents	% of hate crimes incidents	Number of anti-male homosexual	% of sexual orientation incidents
2010	6,628	1,277	19	739	58
2009	6,604	1,223	18	682	56
2008	7,783	1,297	17	776	59
2007	7,624	1,265	17	772	61
2006	7,722	1,195	15	747	62
2005	7,163	1,017	14	621	61
2004	7,649	1,197	16	738	62
2003	7,489	1,239	16	783	63
2002	7,462	1,244	17	825	66
2001	9,730	1,393	14	980	70
2000	8,063	1,299	16	896	69

Source: DOJ, FBI Hate Crime Statistics 2000–10

groups. Frequency of occurrence is debatable despite official statistics. We know that reported crime does not capture all crime and that this reality is exacerbated with hate crimes (Levin & McDevitt, 1993, 2002). What may be more important is the nature of sexual orientation hate crime. What are the contours of these crimes? What are the various impacts of it on its victims?

Greg Herek (2002) and his colleagues have contributed much to the understanding of the victimization of sexual minorities in the United States. I will highlight some of his findings from his survey research of respondents from the Sacramento, California area, which compared their victimization experiences on hate and non-hate crimes. Study participants more often reported multiple perpetrators for hate-motivated crimes against persons, as well as property. Perpetrators were described primarily as young White males who carried out their crimes in a variety of settings, "in schools, in the workplace, and in and around their homes" (Herek, et al. 2002, 336). There is nothing unusual about the profile of offenders who attack sexual minorities. These individuals also participate in attacks against other targeted groups. What might be more unique is the relationship of some perpetrators to victims of these crimes. Herek, Cogan, and Gillis reported that perpetrators seem to have a variety of relationships to the victim—"neighbors, schoolmates, coworkers, *and relatives*" (2002, 336). It is disturbing to recognize that one's attacker is also a family member—but that was reported among Herek's study participants. Hate crime that is motivated by race, ethnicity, or even religion is more likely to impact a victim whose family also shares that status condition. But it is not likely that a minority sexual orientation characterizes an entire family. Thus, within the family itself, the victim is a minority. In addition, there are family members who are hostile toward the homosexual lifestyle. Therefore, it would not be out of the realm of possibility for a family member to also be an attacker. This could be particularly isolating and even more traumatic for some victims. It was also commonly reported among study participants that perpetrators uttered ugly comments and slurs during the attack that identified that their acts were hate-motivated.

Participants who experienced violent attacks described them as particularly brutal. For some of these victims, the psychological distress left in the wake of the crime was pronounced and distinct from the impact of non-hate violent crimes. Herek, Cogan, and Gillis contend that, as a result, recovery for these victims may be of longer duration.

Faulker (2009) provides additional information on the victimization experiences of sexual minorities. Highlights from the survey research are listed below:

• Gay men, from low socioeconomic backgrounds, and from 15–19 years of age experienced higher rates of victimization (122).
• Gay men experienced more verbal harassment by non-family members; and were more frequently exposed to intimidation and physical violence (e.g. weapon assaults, hit with objects, spat upon, followed or chased) (132).

- Lesbians more often reported fear of future victimization, which affected their day-to-day behavior (122). They were also more likely to know their attacker (144).
- Respondents were more likely to seek help from friends and partners than formal institutions, due to fear of secondary victimization (122).

Here we see different victimization patterns according to gender, but there is also evidence of race effects. The National Coalition of Anti-Violence Programs' 2011 report, *Hate Violence Against Lesbian, Gay, Transgender, Queer, and HIV affected Communities in the United States*, also reported on race effects:

- 87 percent of all anti-Lesbian, Gay, Bisexual, Transgender, Queer and HIV-affected Communities (LGBTQH) murder victims in 2011 were people of color.
- Transgendered women, people of color, non-transgendered men, and transgendered people of color experience a greater risk of serious hate violence than other LGBTQH people.

(NCAVP, 2011, 9, 20)

Dunbar and Molina (2004) examined a number of factors regarding the victims of hate crimes that occurred in Los Angeles County. The researchers posed a number of questions: (1) does the type of bias motive determined the severity of the crime committed?; (2) do race and gender affect reportage behavior?; and (3) do hate crime victims who hold multiple memberships in out-groups experience more severe attacks? Results indicated that compared to others, sexual orientation crimes were more severe than racial-motivated or religious-motivated crimes. For victims who hold multiple memberships in out-groups, lesbians of color experienced more violent crime than the other victim groups (gay White males, White lesbians or gay men of color). The study also indicated a high level of reportage across the board. Upwards of 72 percent of gay and lesbian victims reported to police. When race was factored in, gay White men reported more frequently (81 percent); followed by White lesbians (71 percent); then gay men of color (66 percent) ending with 52 percent of lesbians of color reporting the least often. Lesbians of color experienced the most violent sexual bias acts and they are less likely to report their victimization to police. Multiple memberships of out-groups may act as an additive effect and strongly suppresses victim reportage.

Overall, the victimization of sexual minorities is characterized as more violent and more virulent for gay men and LGBTQ members of color (NCAVP, 2000; Bell & Vila, 1996; Comstock, 1991). Poverty and the influence of a subculture of violence may also be contributing factors. As mentioned earlier, the LGBTQ community has developed an effective network of support groups and organizations to respond to multiple areas of need, including resources for victims of hate crime.

Religious bigotry: anti-Jewish and anti-Muslim acts

Anti-Jewish

In January 2008, more than 50 headstones were overturned and vandalized in a northwest Chicago Jewish cemetery. The headstones were sprayed with anti-Semitic images, such as swastikas and the Star of David hanging from a gallows. A 21 year-old self-professed neo-Nazi was arrested and charged with felony hate crime and felony criminal damage to property.

(LCCREF, 2009, 28)

On May 20, 2009, four New York residents were arrested for an alleged plot to attack two synagogues in the Bronx and to shoot down planes at a military base in Newburgh, New York. They were arrested after planting what they believed to be bombs in cars outside of the Riverdale Temple and the nearby Riverdale Jewish Center. Evidence indicates that the four perpetrators were Muslims who were motivated to act because of their hatred of America and Jews.

(LCCREF, 2009, 28)

Anti-Muslim

In Berkeley, California in September 2004, eight female Muslim students at the University of California were accosted by three White males who sprayed water on them, pelted them with water bottles, screamed derogatory statements, and mocked the traditional hijabs worn by some Muslim women. One woman was called an "East Oakland nigger." Two of the Muslim women reported that while this was the first time they have been physically confronted in Berkeley, verbal racial taunts are frequent.

(LCCREF, 2009, 30)

On a Lake Tahoe beach in July 2007, Vishal Wadhwa, 38, suffered fractures of several facial bones and an orbital fracture in one eye after being kicked and beaten by Joseph and Georgia Silva. Wadhwa approached the Silvas after they called him, his fiancée, and her cousin "terrorists," "relatives of Osama Bin Laden," and other slurs. The Silvas mistakenly believed the three victims "were Iraqi or Iranian or Middle Eastern"—in fact, they are all Indian American.

(LCCREF, 2009, 30)

On April 17, 2011 William Blackford was charged with simple criminal damage to property and committing a hate crime in Houma, Louisiana for allegedly kicking a glass door of a shop out because the owners are Muslim. Police said Blackford called them to say he did it because of the owners' heritage, saying, "I want to kill them all. We need to get them out of our country."

(Intelligence Report, 2011, 47–48)

Of these five descriptions of religious-motivated hate crimes, the first three involve incidents where highly recognizable symbols of the victim's community are present, (Jewish cemetery, Jewish Temple and Community Center, and a traditional hijab dress). The last two involved assumptions made by the perpetrator apparently based on skin color. This demonstrates that religion-bias hate crimes are not always clearly discerned. In fact, what is assumed to be anti-Jewish, or anti-Muslim crimes may actually involve a different motive altogether. I will return to this point later.

The Department of Justice reports religious bias data in seven categories: anti-Jewish, anti-Catholic, anti-Protestant, anti-Islamic, anti-other religions, anti-multiple religions, and anti-atheism/agnostic. Anti-Jewish and anti-Islamic incidents are the largest categories of specified religious faiths. The category, "anti-other religions" is often the third highest category (see Table 6.6). For the last decade, anti-Jewish acts make up at least 65 percent to as much as 75 percent of all religious motivated hate crimes (see Figure 6.2).

Jewish people have been the recipients of extraordinary hatred and persecution for centuries. The reality of this bleak fact is well document and need not be argued here (see such works as Wyman (1984), *The Abandonment of the Jews*; Prager and Telushkin (1983), *Why the Jews?* Fischer (2001), *The History of an Obsession*, for example). What is unique about anti-Semitism is its *multi-dimensional aspects*. The history of Jewish persecution includes the perpetual view of Jews as the foreigner to be suspicious of, the stranger, not truly belonging—even if native born. It also consists of old superstitions about Judaism, primarily that Jews were responsible for the crucifixion of Jesus Christ and were the enemies

Table 6.6 Anti-Jewish and anti-Islamic incidents

Year	Total number of anti-religion incidents	Anti-Jewish incidents	Anti-Islamic incidents
2010	1,322	887	160
2009	1,303	931	107
2008	1,519	1,013	105
2007	1,400	969	115
2006	1,462	967	156
2005	1,227	848	128
2004	1,374	954	156
2003	1,343	927	149
2002	1,426	931 (65%)	155
2001	1,828	1,043	481
2000	1,472	1,109 (75%)	28

Source: DOJ, FBI Hate Crime Statistics 2000–2010

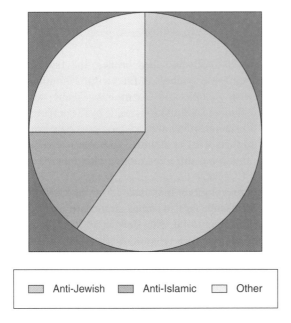

Figure 6.2 Religious bias hate crime 2011

Source: National Center for Victims of Crime. http://victimsofcrime.org/docs/default-source/
ncvrw2014/hate-crime-statistics-2014.pdf?sfvrsn=2

Note: Anti-Jewish 62.5 percent; Anti-Islamic 12.7 percent; Other 24.7 percent

of Christianity. Another longstanding myth is that Jews wielded much power and
influence in the political and financial worlds—and seek to manipulate these institutions to ensure Jewish wealth while undermining the interests of White Anglo-
Saxon heterosexual males. These prejudices and suspicions can still be found
among ordinary individuals. According to a recent national survey administered
by the Anti-Defamation League, anti-Semitism has increased in the United States
with "15 percent of the population holding deeply anti-Semitic views" (Benari,
2011, paragraph 2). Among White supremacists and adherents of Christian Identity, Jews are not viewed as real human beings but rather as the literal spawn of
Satan—the serpent. They view Jewish people as the arch enemy of the White
race; that they encourage homosexuality, inter-racial relationships (miscegena-
tion), feminism, abortion, and anti-Christian beliefs.

What seems to be very clear is that anti-Semitism represents classic stereotypes, beliefs, prejudices, and hatreds toward Jewish people that extend well
beyond Judaism. Anti-Black acts are motivated primarily by animus against Black
people; acts committed against sexual minorities are fueled by hostilities toward
same-sex sexual practices and values. But anti-Semitism is directed at Jews as a
people—which includes superstitions about Judaism, the religion—*but it clearly*

does not end there. It is larger than religion. As a result of this realization—that anti-Semitism is more than the condemnation of Judaism—this category of hate crime may be more accurately represented as an ethnic hate crime rather than one based on antipathy toward Judaism.

Anti-Islamic incidents, the second largest anti-religion category occurs far less often than anti-Semitic acts (in terms of reported incidents). The occurrence of the September 11th Al-Qaeda attacks likely explains the high number of anti-Islamic attacks that occurred in 2001. In those incidents where the offender expressed or revealed motive, the victim was held responsible for the 9/11 attacks and for possible future attacks on American soil. To those offenders, they were carrying out on-the-spot vigilante justice. The following is an excerpt from a hate crime reported by the Chicago Crime Examiner (www.examiner.com November 18, 2009, paragraph 2–3): "Valerie Kenney . . . of Tinley Park, was shopping at Jewel Foods . . . when she saw the Muslim woman in her aisle. . . . Kenney said something disparaging to the woman in regards to a Muslim being responsible for the massacre at Fort Hood two days earlier. Kenney then allegedly tried to pull off the woman's hijab (headscarf)." This act typifies the suspicion and anger that some feel towards those who are perceived to be of the Muslim faith.

The complicating factor in anti-Muslim acts is that hate crime perpetrators identify any Muslim as representative of radicalized Islamic terrorists. Muslim terrorists see their acts as part of a "jihad," a term with religious connotation (i.e. a holy and sacred act). Thus, the Muslim religion itself is viewed as a threat worthy of attack. The Council on American–Islamic Relations (CAIR) recent report, *Same Hate, New Target. Islamophobia and its Impact in the United States*, describes highlights from national polls on attitudes towards Muslims. The following is from a CBS News poll published September 2010, (CAIR, 2009/10, 23): " . . . a majority of Americans (fifty-five percent) know someone who has negative feelings toward Muslims as a result of the terrorist attacks of 9/11. Approximately one in five say they themselves have such feelings." In addition, "the Gallup Center for Muslim Studies reported, 43% of Americans admit to feeling some prejudice toward followers of Islam," (CAIR, 24). The report also describes a sample of anti-Muslim acts (CAIR, 30): "September 9, 2010—A vandal scrawled anti-Muslim hate graffiti across a retaining wall in Reno, Nev. The graffiti read, "Don't burn the Koran. Why? Just burn Muslims."

It appears that anti-Muslim hate crimes are more accurately categorized in the anti-religion category than anti-Semitism. The bigot equates Islam with radical fundamentalism, which seems to help fuel the jihadists and terrorism. Nevertheless, we have yet to read that a hate crime was actually carried out against a terrorist. Victims of anti-Muslim-motivated hate crimes are innocent victims, undeserving of this infliction.

Current research tells us that the victims of hate crime are uniquely impacted by these crimes. In addition to the trauma of being a crime victim, they realize that they were chosen for victimization because of who they are and not from something they did or some goods that they possess. They cannot change this vulnerability but must find the determination to recover. Individuals are attacked in hate crimes and sometimes cultural institutions, but there is a larger community that often responds to these acts. How do communities respond to hate incidents?

When we speak of community response, we are referring to two aspects of it. The victim represents a targeted community—the Hispanic community, the LGBTQ community, and so on. Then there is the greater community—the vicinity where the hate crime occurred. Both should be concerned with the crime, but this discussion focuses on the greater community.

The general consensus among academics, advocacy groups, and local officials is that the community has a moral and pragmatic responsibility following the occurrence of a hate crime. After dealing with the shock and possible embarrassment that a hate crime occurred in their town, local officials and community leaders should publically assemble for the purpose of sending a strong and unified message condemning the act and then to follow up with an educational campaign describing the importance of standing up to hate. This is a very powerful and symbolic action that diminishes the perpetrator (and potential perpetrators) and encourages the victim and members of the targeted community—a perspective supported by the National Institute Against Prejudice and Violence as well as the Anti-Defamation League. The intent of the perpetrator is to demean, isolate, and objectify the victim but a strong community response negates this attempt. Examples of educational initiatives in which communities can participate include "Mix it Up at Lunch Day." This program originated with the Teaching Tolerance arm of the Southern Poverty Law Center. The program challenges students to sit with someone new during lunch periods. The objective is for students to broaden their social networks as a way of breaking down boundaries (SPLC, 2003). "No Place for Hate" programs are supported by the Anti-Defamation League. These programs focus on creating community coalitions which then work to create various anti-hate activities that enhance multiculturalism and the value of inclusion.

Communities that fail to follow this model and ignore these acts embolden the perpetrator, diminish the quality of life of the targeted community and facilitate the continuation of hate crime activity. Instead, establishing a coalition of community-based groups and governing officials to promote the celebration of diversity and taking a strong stand against hate crimes and acts of bigotry is the more constructive path for communities.

Hate crimes against the homeless and those with disabilities

The nature of hate crime against disabled persons

The Matthew Shepard and James Byrd, Jr. Hate Crimes Prevention Act of 2009, 18 U.S.C. paragraph 249, the most recent federal hate crime law, contains a larger class of protected statuses, including the actual or perceived race, color, religion, national origin, gender, sexual orientation, gender identity, or *disability* of the targeted victim.

In some ways, this category of hate crime may be considered to be even more despicable since these victims have less capacity to defend themselves. The DOJ

Hate Crime Statistics 2012 report anti-disability-motivated crimes in two catego-ries: anti-physical disability and anti-mental disability. Types of disabilities may include limitations in areas of hearing, vision, cognitive, ambulatory, and self-care. It is interesting to note that the number of crimes reported as anti-mental dis-ability is four times that of anti-physical disability. In fact, anti-mental disability hate crimes have been the consistently larger category for at least the last nine years. The following describes a particularly heinous anti-mental disability hate crime reported originally in the online British daily newspaper, the *Daily Mail.*

> Steven Simpson died from severe burns that he suffered at the hands of some of the supposed guests at his own 18th birthday party. These individuals peri-odically harassed Simpson, who had been diagnosed with Asperger's and other related mental impairments. Simpson had been the frequent victim of bullying.
>
> (*Daily Mail*, 2012)

Other news reports state that on the night of the crime, the victim who suffered from Asperger's syndrome, a speech impairment and epilepsy, was dared to strip down to his underpants before being doused in tanning oil and set on fire at his own party. Prosecutors reported that this was considered a case of bullying (not hate crime) but that the sentence received by the offender was within the sentencing range for a similar hate crime conviction.

Another crime illustrating the vulnerability of the disabled and the cruelty at times exacted upon them was reported in the *New York Times* in February, 1999. The following summarizes the incident:

> A group of men and women premeditated and carried out the torture of a men-tally disabled man. The crime, which was motivated by disdain for the disa-bled, occurred in Monmouth County New Jersey. The victim was stripped of his clothing and beaten by the group. He was eventually tied to a chair where the abuse continued for hours, causing numerous wounds across his body. Eventually the victim was driven to another area where he was permitted to leave. Police investigators noted that due to the victim's mental limitations, he failed to even understand the reason behind his brutalization.
>
> (*New York Times*, 1999)

According to the National Center for Victims of Crime, individuals with disabilities are often targeted *because of* their disabilities. Too often, the perpetrators of these crimes are known to the victims because they are third party (paid) care givers or perhaps are family members. Due to these circumstances, these victims report to police less often, as they are unfortunately more dependent upon abusers and may be fearful of retaliation. In addition, due to the nature of the disability, particularly mental and/or cognitive disabilities, victims may be less able to fully appreciate their ill-treatment, and to follow up by reporting it. Likewise, anti-disability hate crimes may be more often recognized as instances of abuse, mishandling or ill-treatment, rather than hate-motivated crimes; furthering the problem of under-reporting.

Statistics show a consistently higher crime victimization rate of disabled persons in comparison to non-disabled crime victims (see Figure 6.3).

But how often are these victimizations due to perpetrator bias or hatred against disabled persons?

The Center reports disability bias crimes utilizing a compilation of Uniform Crime Reports (UCR) and the National Crime Victimization (NCVS) data. The following are a few highlights from the Center's report:

- In 2011, a total of 53 anti-disability hate crimes were reported. 19 were motivated by bias against persons with physical disabilities and 34 by bias against those with mental disabilities.
- What is particularly disturbing is that of all disabled crime victimizations, those with cognitive disabilities had the highest rate of violent victimization (23.7 per 1,000) as shown in Figure 6.4.

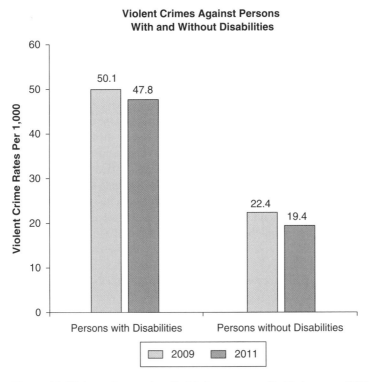

Figure 6.3 Violent crime against disabled versus non-disabled persons 2011

Source: National Center for Victims of Crime

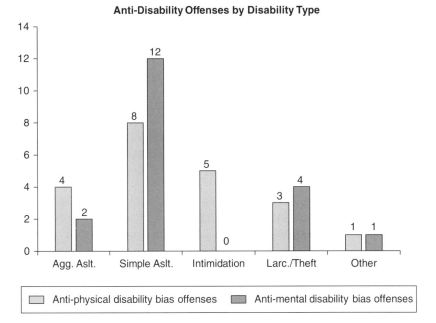

Figure 6.4 Anti-disability hate crimes by disability type 2010
Source: National Center for Victims of Crime

This category of hate crime needs a good deal more of systematic research. A basic question which needs further clarification is what distinguishes the victimization of the disabled when they are viewed as easier targets by perpetrators from victimization primarily due to the perpetrators animus towards this community? Another question involves that of ideology. Where in the ideology found in the hate movement is there the perspective of the disabled as a threat of enemy of White civilization? Whereas the historic view of Nazism emphasized racial and genetic purity, today's neo-Nazi seems less inclined to focus on those with physical and mental disabilities as a rationale for attack or separation. Pursuing these and other relevant lines of inquiry would permit more understanding of anti-disability hate crime.

The nature of hate crime against the homeless

According to the National Coalition for the Homeless:

- 633,782 people were homeless on a single night in January 2012. Most homeless persons (62 percent) are individuals.
- 62,619 veterans were homeless on a single night in January 2012.
- Street homelessness (the unsheltered population) was unchanged since January 2011.

- Five states accounted for nearly half of the nation's homeless population in 2012: California (20.7 percent), New York (11.0 percent), Florida (8.7 percent), Texas (5.4 percent), and Georgia (3.2 percent).

There are many factors that contribute to the problem of homelessness in the United States. Two of the most significant include poverty caused by the lack of opportunity for gainful employment and deficiency of affordable housing. None of these factors seem to represent a well-crafted Jewish conspiracy to undo White Christian civilization. Still, the homeless have become victims of hate crime. Currently the federal government does not include "homelessness" as a protected status so the ability to assess the prevalence of this type of hate crime is challenging. So we turn to other sources to obtain some insight into this category:

> Hours after they murdered a homeless man because of the color of his skin . . . white supremacists celebrated by planning to get lightning bolts tattooed on their arms, prosecutors said . . . the bolts represent the slaying of a minority. . . . Walker's death was part of a "campaign . . . " designed to create an all-white state . . . nation.
>
> (LATimes.com, 1998)

While the victim was homeless at the time that he was attacked, it appears that homelessness was merely incidental to the fact that his race was the primary reason he was targeted. Eight years later, a similar crime occurred in Tacoma, Washington. In March 2003, racist skinheads attacked and killed a homeless man. According to news reports, Randall Mark Townsend was not the first choice of the murderous group. They were seeking African-American drug addicts when they encountered Townsend, a homeless White male who suffered from schizophrenia:

> four assailants, all members of a white supremacist gang, attacked Townsend with baseball bats, a boulder, their fists and boots . . . Pillatos . . . hit the victim in the face with a bat and a [40-lb.] . . . rock, while Butters, Monschke and Frye . . . punched, stomped and kicked him repeatedly. Townsend died on April 12.
>
> (ADL, 2003)

During the trial, Monschke testified that this attack was carried out to establish a presence in the Tacoma area and a new chapter of the neo-Nazi skinhead group Volksfront. Again, we see where the preferred target was a *Black* drug addict— someone who is a member of one of the more commonly targeted groups. Instead, a White homeless man, with mental illness, became the more convenient target. So the intentional targeting of a homeless person is not reflected in the Tacoma case.

Criminologist Sandra Wachholz (2005) conducted a very informative study on the victimization of the homeless due to bias. She interviewed 30 individuals regarding the treatment they encountered during homelessness. Wachholz argues that the individual instances of discriminatory treatment, from the verbal harassment to the outright assaults, collectively send the message "you are not welcome or wanted in this public space, vacate it now." This is tantamount to the historical act of "warning-out" (Wachholz, 2005). Warning-out and other similar social practices ensured that the poor, the unemployed, the unestablished immigrant— were required to pass through a community; being prohibited from settling. Such individuals were deemed undesirables who represented a potential threat to the *established* community.

Similarly, Barbara Perry (2001) argues that modern hate crimes are about maintaining the hegemonic bloc enjoyed by White, Protestant, heterosexual males. Thus the hostile treatment acted upon the homeless is about contesting and controlling access to desirable public spaces in a given community. But because the homeless population is truly diverse in all respects (gender, sexual orientation, ethnicity, race, religion, disability, etc.), bigots cannot rely on the familiar derogatory tags to easily castigate this group (e.g. "spics, niggers, fags, dirty Jews"). The obvious attribute that most homeless share is indigence.

Wachholz's study participants primarily described ordinary citizens, business owners, and some law enforcement officers as the assailants who treated them in an abusive manner. Not racist skinheads or those spewing ugly epithets as they harangued or attacked the homeless. It is interesting that just as in the more typical hate crimes, it is the ordinary citizen who commits these crimes far more often than members of hate groups. We see the same pattern in hate crimes committed against the disabled as well as the homeless. Nevertheless, we also see the same grey areas in attacks against the homeless. Are they truly hated for their state of homelessness? Or are other dynamics at play? What is again absent is a clear rationale that views the homeless as the type of threat imagined about racial minorities, illegal "brown" immigrants, sexual minorities and Jews. Further study is needed to discern how the targeting of the homeless fits into the context of "legitimate" targets for hate crime perpetrators.

Conclusion

Hate crime victims are of every gender, race, ethnicity, religion, physical, and mental ability imaginable. Just as offenders come from various walks of life—so do victims. Appreciating this variation reiterates the complexity of bias motivations and the astounding ignorance of hate crime perpetrators about people, social problems and themselves. It is quite ironic but an unrecognized reality is that the perpetrator likely has more in common with the individual targeted than he realizes. But viewing the history and constancy of hate crime also reaffirms the resilience of those who are victimized. The more that victims are aware of the large field of persons victimized by these acts, the less they will feel isolated, stigmatized, and helpless. The response of communities-as-victims with a resounding "no" and condemnation of these crimes, sets an example to individual victims to feel empowered and strengthened as members of such communities.

Chapter summary

- The impact of hate crime victimization exceeds that of ordinary crime victimization. The realization that one was targeted for harm because of immutable or prominent *personal* characteristics diminishes feelings of safety and security.
- These crimes distinguish themselves in two critical areas: (1) there is a *historical* continuity of hate-motivated victimization of racial minorities, Jews, and homosexuals; and (2) a continuing complicity of social institutions and mainstream culture in the targeting of victim groups.
- Racial bias is the most frequently occurring hate-motivation category. Within this category of hate crime anti-Black incidents are usually several times that of the other racial categories combined.
- Anti-Black hate crime occurs across the country, even in states where few Black Americans live. The animus involved in these crimes at times causes a complete disregard for both Black women and children who are viewed as valid targets.
- Asian-Americans and Asian immigrants are subject to racially motivated attack for a variety of reasons. They are sometimes viewed by bigots as an economic threat and unfair competition in a troubled jobs market.
- Regardless of their status as American citizens, Asians are often viewed as *permanent* immigrants, foreigners who are viewed with suspicion. They are subjected to treatment identified by scholars as *figurative boarders.*
- Often anti-immigrant sentiments are compounded by racist attitudes. Asians, Latinos, and Arab-Americans are frequently viewed with the double status of a racial minority and a foreigner.
- Hispanics are the largest recipients of anti-ethnic motivated crimes. Ethnicity is reported in two categories: anti-Hispanic and anti-other ethnicity/national origin. The anti-Hispanic category is consistently the larger.
- Some social scientists are concerned that the ongoing debate and hyperbole at times interjected regarding immigration policy has opened the door to the expression of racist and xenophobic sentiments, which may impact the occurrence of anti-Hispanic hate crime.
- Sexual minorities have a history of targeted victimization in the United States. But this community has waged effective campaigns for social and legal equality. Ironically, the movement for equality has also increased the likelihood of more victimization by hate crime perpetrators.
- Anti-gay attacks are the largest category of sexual orientation-motivated hate crimes. There are also race effects in this category with 87 percent of all LGBTQH murder victims in 2011 were people of color.
- Gay White males continue to be the group most often victimized in violent sexual orientation hate crime.
- Anti-Semitism represents classic stereotypes, beliefs, prejudices, and hatreds toward Jewish people that extend beyond Judaism. Therefore, this category of hate crime may be more accurately represented as ethnic rather than religion bias.

- Those who target people of Middle-Eastern descent assume that they practice Islam and are followers of radical Islam. Thus, some of these perpetrators see their acts as carrying out on-the-spot vigilante justice because of terrorist attacks on the US.
- Attacks against persons with disabilities and the homeless are at times identified as hate-motivated. While there are clear examples of such acts, there needs to be much more research on the theoretical links between these attacks and more conventional hate crimes.

Case study 6.1 Woman charged with hate crime in Queen Anne attack

Many would argue that all hate crimes are bizarre acts in and of themselves. But this act which occurred in Seattle's Queen Ann neighborhood is untypical even for a hate crime. An African-American man was engaged in a pleasant conversation with two friends on First Avenue North and Mercer Street.

When a female resident of the neighborhood, who was inebriated, and her male companion walked past the group of friends, the Black male addressed them in a friendly way saying, 'How are you doing?' With that, the female screamed racist epithets at the Black male and then proceeded to kick at his groin area, grabbing at his clothing, while spitting in his face.

The entire incident was witnessed by police officers who were patrolling in the area at the time. The officers intervened in order to restrain the female attacker. The victim was visibly shaken and distraught following the attack; even crying from shock and stress as he recounted what happened to police.

The attacker was charged with malicious harassment as a hate crime, in addition to misdemeanor assault.

(Source: http://blog.seattlepi.com/seattle911/2013/05/20/woman-charged-
with-hate-crime-in-queen-anne-attack/)

Discussion questions

1   In what way, if any, did the victim in this incident provoke his own attack by the perpetrator?
2   From the account, the victim was distraught as a result. In what way did this attack distress him and how does it compare with a similar non-hate-motivated attack?

Bibliography

Anti-Defamation League (ADL). (2003). White Supremacists Charged in Brutal Tacoma Murder. Available from http://archive.adl.org/learn/news/tacoma_murder.html [Accessed June 12, 2014].

Babineck, M. (2004). Byrd Killing Still Touchy Subject. Chron.com. Available from www. chron.com/disp/story.mpl/special/jasper/latestnews/1931474.html [Accessed September 13, 2007].

Barnes, S. (May 12, 2004). Teenagers Charged in Grave Desecration. *New York Times.* Available from http://query.nytimes.com/gst/fullpage.html ?res=9F0DE6D8103CF931 A25756C0A9629C8B63 [Accessed September 13, 2007].

Bell, J. (2002). *Policing Hatred: Law Enforcement, Civil Rights, and Hate Crime.* New York: New York University Press.

Bell, M.D. & Vila, R.I. (1996). Homicide in Homosexual Victims: A Study of 67 Cases from the Broward County, Florida, Medical Examiner's Office (1982–1992), with Special Emphasis on "Overkill". *American Journal of Forensic Medicine and Pathology,* 17(1), 65–69.

Benari, E. (2011). ADL Survey: 15% of Americans Are Anti-Semitic. Survey Conducted by the Anti-Defamation League Finds That Nearly 35 Million Americans Harbor Deeply Anti-Semitic Views. Available from www.israelnationalnews.com [Accessed July 12, 2012].

Blalock, H. M. (1973). *Toward a Theory of Minority Group Relations.* Gilbert, AZ: Perigee Publishing.

Bobo, L., Schuman, H., & Steeh, C. (1986). Changing Racial Attitudes Toward Residential Integration. In J.M. Goering (ed.) *Housing Desegregation and Federal Policy* (pp. 152–69). Chapel Hill, NC: University of North Carolina Press.

Bowling, B. (1999). *Violent Racism: Victimisation, Policing and Social Context.* (Revised Edition). Oxford: Oxford University Press.

Bureau of Justice Services. (2003). Hate Crime Victimization, 2003–11. Special Report. March. N. Sandholtz, L. Langton, and M. Planty. US Department of Justice. NCJ 241291.

Bureau of Justice Services. (2005). Hate Crime Reported by Victims and Police. National Criminal Victimization Survey and Uniform Crime Reporting. November. NCJ 209911.

Chen, T. Y. (2004). Hate Violence as Border Patrol. In P. B. Gerstenfeld & D. R. Grant (eds.) *Crimes of Hate: Selected Readings* (pp. 250–69). Thousand Oaks, CA: Sage Publications.

Chicago Crime Examiner. (2009). Woman Charged with Hate Crime Muslim Headscarf Incident. Available from www.examiner.com/article/woman-charged-with-hate-crime-muslim-headscarf-incident [Accessed June 9, 2014].

CNN. (n.d.). Postal Worker Joseph Ileto Mourned as President Clinton Sends Condolences. Available from www.cnn.com/US/9908/15/california.shooting.01/ [Accessed June 12, 2014].

Comstock, G. D. (1991). *Violence Against Lesbians and Gay Men.* New York: Columbia University Press.

Council on American–Islamic Relations (2009/10) (CAIR). *Same Hate, New Target: Islamophobia and Its Impact in the United States.* Available from www.cair.com/islam-ophobia/legislating-fear-2013-reort.html [Accessed June 13, 2014].

Crump, J. R. (2004). Producing and Enforcing the Geography of Hate: Race, Housing Segregation and Housing-Related Hate Crimes. In C. Flint (ed.) *Spaces of Hate* (pp. 227–44). New York: Routledge.

Daily Mail. (2012). Autistic Teenager "Was Murdered by Thugs who Set Him on Fire With Self-tanning Spray at his Own 18th Birthday Party." June 29. Available from www.dailymail.co.uk/news/article-2166327/Autistic-teenager-Steven-Simpson-dies-burn-injuries-tanning-oil-prank-went-wrong.html#ixzz34BpfCfuj [Accessed June 9, 2014].

Department of Justice. (DOJ). (n.d.). Hate Crime Statistics 2000. Available from www.fbi.gov/about-us/cjis/ucr/hate-crime/2000/hatecrime00.pdf [Accessed February 7, 2015].

Department of Justice. (DOJ). (n.d.). Hate Crime Statistics 2001. Available from www.fbi.gov/about-us/cjis/ucr/hate-crime/2001/hatecrime01.pdf [Accessed February 7, 2015].

Department of Justice. (DOJ). (n.d.). Hate Crime Statistics 2002. Available from www.fbi.gov/about-us/cjis/ucr/hate-crime/2002/ [Accessed February 7, 2015].

Department of Justice. (DOJ). (n.d.). Hate Crime Statistics 2003. Available from www.fbi.gov/about-us/cjis/ucr/hate-crime/2003/hatecrime03.pdf [Accessed February 7, 2015].

Department of Justice. (DOJ). (n.d.). Hate Crime Statistics 2004. Available from www.2.fbi.gov/ucr/hc2004 [Accessed February 7, 2015].

Department of Justice. (DOJ). (October 2006). Hate Crime Statistics 2005. Available from www.2.fbi.gov/ucr/hc2005 [Accessed February 7, 2015].

Department of Justice. (DOJ). (November 2007). Hate Crime Statistics 2006. Available from www.2.fbi.gov/ucr/hc2006 [Accessed February 7, 2015].

Department of Justice. (DOJ). (October 2008). Hate Crime Statistics 2007. Available from www.fbi.gov/about-us/cjis/ucr/hate-crime/2007 [Accessed February 7, 2015].

Department of Justice. (DOJ). (November 2009). Hate Crime Statistics 2008. Available from www.2.fbi.gov/ucr/hc2008 [Accessed February 7, 2015].

Department of Justice. (DOJ). (November 2010). Hate Crime Statistics 2009. Available from www.2.fbi.gov/ucr/hc2009 [Accessed February 7, 2015].

Department of Justice. (DOJ). (n.d.). Hate Crime Statistics 2010. Available from www.2.fbi.gov/about-us/cjis/ucr/hate-crime/2010 [Accessed February 7, 2015].

DiBranco, A. (2010). From Long Island to Staten Island: Another Hate Crime in NY. Change.org. Available from http://news.change.org/stories/from-long-island-to-staten-island-another-hate-crime-in-ny [Accessed June 21, 2012].

Dunbar, E. & Nikolova, N. L. (2004). *Community Factors in Hate Crime Victimization*. Presented at the 112th Annual Convention of the American Psychological Association in Honolulu.

Dunbar, E. & Molina, A. (2004). Opposition to the Legitimacy of Hate Crime Laws: The Role of Argument Acceptance, Knowledge, Individual Differences, and Peer Influence. *Analyses of Social Issues and Public Policy*, 4(1), 91–113.

Eitle, D., D'Alessio, S. J., & Stolzenberg, L. (2002). Racial Threat and Social Control: A Test of The Political, Economic, and Threat of Black Crime Hypotheses. *Social Forces*, 81(2), 557–76.

Feagin, J. R. (2001). *Racist America: Roots, Current Realities and Reparations*. New York: Routledge.

Fischer, K. P. (2001). *History of an Obsession: German Judeophobia and the Holocaust*. New York: Bloomsbury Academic.

Garcia, L. & McDevitt, J. (1999). *The Psychological and Behavioral Effects of Bias and Nonbias Motivated Assault*. Washington, DC: US Department of Justice, National Institute of Justice.

Green, D. P., Strolovitch, D. Z., & Wong, J. S. (1998). Defended Neighborhoods, Integration, and Racially Motivated Crime. *American Journal of Sociology*, 104(2), 372–403.

Hall, N. (2005). *Hate Crime*. Portland, OR: Willan Publishing.

Herek, G. M. & Berrill, K. T. (eds.) (1992). *Hate Crimes. Confronting Violence Against Lesbians and Gay Men*. Newbury Park, CA: Sage.

Herek, G. M., Cogan, J. C., & Gillis, J. R. (2002). Victim Experiences in Hate Crimes Based on Sexual Orientation. *Journal of Social Issues*, 58(2), 319–39.

Ho, C. (n.d.). The Model Minority Awakened (Murder of Vincent Chin) Pt. 1. Available from http://us_asians.tripod.com/articles-vincentchin.html [Accessed June 14, 2012].

Horowitz, D. (1985). *Ethnic Groups in Conflict*. Berkeley, CA: University of California Press.

Intelligence Report. (2008). Hate Crimes—Anti-Latino Hate Crime Up for Fourth Year. *Intelligence Report*. Winter, Issue 132.

Intelligence Report. (2011). For the Record. Fall, Issue 143.

LATimes.com (1998). Teen to be Tried as Adult in Hate Crime. March 28. Available from www.articles.latimes.com/1998/mar/28/local/me-33531 [Accessed June 9, 2014].

Leadership Conference on Civil Rights Education Fund (LCCREF). (2009). *Confronting the New Faces of Hate: Hate Crimes in America*. Authored by Jonathan Rintels, President, Heathcote Strategies, and Peter Loge, Principal, Milo Public Affairs LLC.

Levin, J. & McDevitt, J. (1993). *Hate Crimes: The Rising Tide of Bigotry and Bloodshed*. New York: Plenum Press.

Levin, J. & McDevitt, J. (2002). *Hate Crimes Revisited: America's War against Those Who Are Different*. Boulder, CO: Westview Press.

LGBT Hate Crimes Project. (2007). Dwan Prince. Available from www.lgbthate crimes.org/doku.php/dwan_prince [Accessed June 28, 2012].

Media Matters. (n.d.). Fear and Loathing in Prime Time. Immigration Myths and Cable News. Executive Summary. Available at http://mediamattersaction.org/reports/fear-andloathing/online_version [Accessed March 6, 2015].

Media Matters for America. (2012). 15 of Limbaugh's Most Offensive and Controversial Comments Targets Immigrants. Available from http://mediamatters.org/blog/2012/03/10/15-of-limbaughs-most-offensive-and-controversia/186214 [Accessed March 6, 2015].

National Center for Victims of Crime. (n.d.). Hate Crimes Motivated by Religious Bias. March 10. Available from www.victimsofcrime.org/library/crime-information-and-statistics/hate-and-bias-crime [Accessed June 13, 2014].

National Center for Victims of Crime. (n.d.) Crime and Victimization in the United States. Statistical Overviews. Available from http://victimsofcrime.org/docs/defaultsource/ncvrw 2015/2015ncvrw_6_statisticaloverviews.pdf?sfvrsn=2 [Accessed on March 6, 2015].

National Coalition of Anti-Violence Programs (NCAVP). (2000). Anti-lesbian, gay, transgender and bisexual violence in 2000. Available from http://www.avp.org/storage/documents/Reports/2000_NCAVP_Bias_Report.pdf [Accessed on March 6, 2015].

National Coalition of Anti-Violence Programs (NCAVP). (2011). Hate Violence Against Lesbian, Gay, Bisexual, Transgender, Queer and HIV-Infected Communities in the United States in 2011. Available from http://www.cuav.org/wp-content/uploads/2012/08/4379_NCAVPHVReport2011Final_Updated.pdf [Accessed March 6, 2015].

New York Times (1997). Ex-G.I. at Fort Bragg Is Convicted in Killing of 2 Blacks. February 28. *New York Times*. Available from http://query.nytimes.com/gst/fullpage.html?res=9A02E3DB1331F93BA15751C0A961958260&n=Top/Reference/Times%20Topics/Subjects/H/Hate%20Crimes [Accessed September 16, 2007].

New York Times. (1999). 8 Are Charged in Tormenting of Learning-Disabled Man. February 17. Available from www.nytimes.com/1999/02/17/nyregion/8-are-charged-in-tormenting-of-learning-disabled-man [Accessed June 12, 2014].

Perry, B. (2001). *In the Name of Hate: Understanding Hate Crimes*. New York: Routledge.

Petrosino, C. (1999). Connecting the Past to the Future. *Journal of Contemporary Criminal Justice*, 15, 271–92.

Pew Research Center. (2014a). In 2014, Latinos Will Surpass Whites as Largest Racial/Ethnic Group in California. Available from www.pewresearch.org/fact-tank/2014/01/24 [Accessed June 13, 2014].

Pew Research Center. (2014b). The Rise of Asian Americans. Available from www.pew
socialtrends.org/asianamericans-graphics [Accessed June 13, 2014].

Prager, D. and Telushkin, J. (1983). *Why the Jews? The Reason for Antisemitism*. New
York: Touchstone.

Race Relations Reporter, The. (1994). Residential Terrorism. Vol. 2, No. 3.

Race Relations Reporter, The. (1995). Residential Terrorism. Vol. 3, No. 7.

RW ONLINE. (1997). Chicago: The Streets Where Black Kids Ain't Allowed. The Racist
Beating of Lenard Clark. Available from http://rwor.org/a/firstvol/900-905/901/lenard.
htm [Accessed June 26, 2009].

San Francisco Chronicle in Education. (2007). A Murder in Jasper, Texas, Brings Back Haunt-
ing Memories. Available from www.kqed.org/programs/tv/niot/KQEDCIC-NIOT4.pdf
[Accessed September 7, 2007].

Southern Poverty Law Center (SPLC). (2003). Mix It Up Day Hit from Coast to Coast.
Available from http://www.splcenter.org/get-informed/news/mix-it-up-day-hit-from-
coast-to-coast [Accessed March 6, 2015].

Southern Poverty Law Center (SPLC). (2013). Hate Watch Headlines for May 23, 2013.

Stacey, M., Carbone-López, K., & Rosenfeld, R. (2011). Demographic Change and
Ethnically Motivated Crime: The Impact of Immigration on Anti-Hispanic Hate
Crime in the United States. *Journal of Contemporary Criminal Justice*, 27(3), 278–98.
Doi: 10.1177/1043986211412560.

Tolnay, S. E., Beck, E. M., & Massey, J. L. (1989). The Power Threat Hypothesis and
Black Lynchings: Wither the Evidence? *Social Forces*, 67(3), 634–40.

Turpin-Petrosino, C. (2009). Black Victimization: Perceptions and Realities. In B. Perry's
(Ed.) *Hate Crimes: The Victims of Hate Crimes*. Vol. 3 (pp. 19–44). Westport, CT:
Praeger Publications.

United States Census Bureau. (2010). The Black Population 2010. Available from www.
census.gov/prod/cen2010/briefs/c2010br-06.pdf [Accessed June 5, 2014].

US Census 2000 Bureau. (n.d.). The Black Population: 2000. Available from http://www.
census.gov/prod/2001pubs/c2kbr01-5.pdf [Accessed March 6, 2015].

Wachholz, S. (2005). Hate Crimes Against the Homeless: Warning-Out New England
Style. *Journal of Sociology and Social Welfare*, 32(4), 141–63.

Wyman, D. S. (2007). *The Abandonment of the Jews: America and the Holocaust
1941–1945*. New York: The New Press.

7 Criminal justice system responses

Introduction

Modern hate crime laws have been in existence for the last thirty years. With that, we are able to make some observations on how the criminal justice system formally responds to hate crimes from the initial police investigation to the determination of guilt and the requisite punishment and or treatment of the offender. Due to the nature of hate crime and the unique harms it causes, the justice system's response to it is particularly crucial. Considering that hate crimes are often committed to diminish the social place of those victimized, contesting their very liberty—it is vitally important that the justice system "get it right" not only for the victim and the victim's community but also for a society that values equality. In fact, the stakes are even higher because historically the US justice system has devalued the very groups usually victimized in hate crime and at times participated in their victimization (Higginbotham, 1978; Takaki, 1989; Jaimes, 1999). This chapter reviews the responses of the justice system according to its principal organizational components: police, courts, and corrections.

Law enforcement prevention and control initiatives

Police are the first officials to arrive at scenes where crime victims, witnesses and sometimes attackers are present. Whether the incident under investigation is designated as a hate-motivated act is determined by law enforcement personnel. What complicates this task are a number of vagaries. First, hate crime statutes and local ordinances vary across jurisdictions; therefore what constitutes a hate crime in Illinois is not the same in Alabama. Second, there are over 12,500 local police departments in the United States. The degree of training required of police for the investigation of alleged hate crimes will differ enormously among departments. Third, even if police are effective in investigating hate crime in the community, local prosecutors may be reluctant to follow through with these charges.

   Police are critical in this initial investigative determination. It is important for them to get it right if a hate crime has occurred and it is equally important for them to resist the hate crime label if the evidence fails to substantiate the charge. In April 2009, two men were attacked on the same evening and in the same vicinity in Broward County, Florida. They were both beaten, one fatally, and robbed.

Both victims were gay. At first glance, one might suspect that these attacks probably occurred due to the perpetrator's bias toward gays. The Broward Sheriff's office came to a different conclusion and did not treat either crime as hate-motivated because of insufficient evidence. The police saw the sexual orientation of the victims as *coincidental* and maintained this position despite pressure by LGBTQ advocacy organizations (Marino, 2009).

The International Association of Chiefs of Police (IACP), a professional organization for sworn law enforcement officers in supervisory positions, provides protocols for the investigation of alleged hate crimes. Their website offers a rationale for why police must respond to these acts and respond to them effectively. They contend that hate crimes have the potential to not only make the victim feel devalued but also to some extent destabilize the communities most impacted. There are at least two communities potentially affected: the victim's social community of which he or she holds membership and the community where the crime took place. In light of this possibility, the IACP emphasizes the need for a "swift and strong response by law enforcement . . . to stabilize and calm the community" (International Association of Chiefs of Police, 1999, paragraphs 8–11). Investigation of these acts must be approached in an aggressive manner to accomplish two objectives; first, to send a message that law enforcement takes these acts seriously and, second, to uncover all available evidence so that a successful prosecution can be achieved. With this perspective guiding investigating officers, the IACP further acknowledge the importance of preserving evidence, including "hate literature, threatening letters, and symbolic objects (e.g. swastikas, crosses)" (International Association of Chiefs of Police, 1999, paragraphs 14–15). The professional standards of procedure offered on the website are sufficiently detailed and comprehensive. It provides specific approaches to securing and preserving evidence, responding to the victim in a reassuring and constructive manner, interviewing witnesses/canvassing the community, corresponding with other police departments to determine any patterns of hate activity in the area including the presence of hate groups, and interacting with the community and the victim in the wake of incident.

Particularly conspicuous on the website is a statement addressing the likely emotional state of the victim. It is a much more nuanced description of how the victim may be processing the attack. This is invaluable as a heuristic tool for police to better understand hate crime victims. It has been observed that a significant obstacle to more reporting of hate crimes is the perception by victims that police are unsympathetic, uncaring, and possibly hostile to the victim due to police bias. The website describes how the manner of investigation should be mindful of the emotional vulnerabilities operating in all those affected. Some of these tips include:

- request the assistance of translators when needed;
- reassure victim that they are not to blame for what happened;
- voice your support of the actions the victim took to protect themselves and defuse the situation;

- allow them to vent feelings about the incident or crime;
- provide information about community and department resources available to protect and support victim, their families and members of the community;
- avoid being abrupt or rushed;
- avoid belittling the seriousness of the incident, especially if the perpetrator was a juvenile;
- support or coordinate community clean-up efforts;
- participate in meetings or other forums designed to address the community-wide impact of hate incidents or crimes;
- share information, as appropriate, with schools about cases where students or staff were victims or perpetrators of hate crimes; and
- collaborate with community leaders to mobilize resources that can be used to assist victims and prevent future hate incidents and crimes.

(International Association of Chiefs of Police, 1999, paragraphs 12–13)

Professional guidelines like the ones described above are only one aspect of a set of factors that underscore the importance of policing hate crime (Haider-Markel, 2002). Adequate police training and awareness that an effective response may prevent retaliatory or subsequent hate crimes is also needed (Phillips, 2009). Still, police investigations must be approached in a careful and balanced manner; the welfare of the crime victim and the public's confidence in police depend upon it.

Law enforcement in Phoenix, Arizona appeared to be reluctant to investigate a 2009 homicide as a possible hate crime. The *Phoenix New Times* reported a killing that seemed to meet many of the indicators outlined by the IACP, but the police downplayed them early in their investigation. On October 3, 2009 an inter-racial couple walking in a park was confronted and harassed by a tattooed White male who questioned why they were walking together—according to victim statements. The couple saw the individual again drive past them, but this time a shot-gun was fired, which injured the Black male and killed the White female, Kelley Ann Jaeger. Despite each of these telling indicators (who the victims were, who confronted them, and why) the police at that time stated that the crime was not being investigated as a hate crime "because it could skew the focus of the investigation. We just don't have enough information to call it a hate crime and isolate a single group" (King, 2009; paragraphs 7–8). Eleven months later, the Phoenix police announced the indictment on first-degree murder charges of two members of a violent racist skinhead group, the Vinlanders Social Club, now identifying the attack as a hate crime (Lemons, 2010).

Provincetown is a summer resort town on Cape Cod in Massachusetts; it also has a significant LGBTQ community, some quotes are as high as 50 percent of the residents. It is a socially progressive community that is supportive of the LGBTQ community. Nevertheless, there are hate crimes that occur in Provincetown; some of which are motivated by sexual orientation bias. A recent attack on two lesbians in Provincetown, MA reveals additional insight into how the system may respond (Sowers, 2009). The Provincetown community responded with well-organized activities. The police department participated in the anti-bias program, "No Place for Hate." According to news reports, the police department scheduled a public forum on hate crimes prior to the next court appearance of the suspect. Activities like this reassure the victim and the community that this type of crime is taken seriously be police and that they are willing participants in coalitions that fight against hate. In addition, Provincetown police sent the case files to the state Attorney General's office and advocated for a civil injunction to be brought against the suspect who was released on bail. The purpose of the injunction is to encourage the suspect to avoid contact with the victims and also "limit his access to any homosexuals in Provincetown . . . and perhaps ban him from Provincetown" itself (Sowers, 2009, 6–7).

Some police departments have created specialized units to respond to hate crimes. They may be referred to as community disorder units, hate crimes task force units or bias crime units. The Metropolitan Police Department in Washington, DC formed a Gay and Lesbian Liaison Unit, which was solely staffed with LGBTQ officers, to respond to alleged hate crime incidents (Labbe-DeBose, 2009). The unit was well received by the public but budgetary restraints forced significant changes. Specialized units were determined to be too costly to maintain for the DC police department and have been replaced by patrol officer volunteers who are trained to respond to sexual orientation hate crimes.

Courts and legal advocates

The work of prosecutors reflect the extent and manner of the public's denouncement of a hate crime. If prosecutors respond to an aggressive investigation by police of an alleged hate crime by either failing to charge appropriately by entering a lesser offense absent the bias motive when evidence supports otherwise, they may lose public confidence. Conversely, when prosecutors pursue charges on a hate crime with as much determination as they do with non-hate serious offenses, it sends a strong message to potential violators and potential targets. Federal prosecutors were persistent in their efforts to charge and convict Bill White, a former National Socialist Movement leader and neo-Nazi. Bill White used the Internet as a means to threaten and intimidate others. Some of the more offensive comments that he published on his website, *Overthrow.com*, used as evidence in this case, includes the following, found in a SPLC's Intelligence Project's article:

> Lynch the Jena 6. If these niggers are released or acquitted, we will find out where they live and make sure that . . . white citizens . . . know it, we'll mail directions to their homes to every white man in Louisiana if we have to in order to find someone willing to deliver justice.
>
> (SPLC, Intelligence files, paragraph 2)

> Sometimes you just have to murder blacks—and, frankly, the killing needs to start with the black leaders and NAACP activists . . . I know where my local NAACP 'leaders' live—do you?
>
> (SPLC, Intelligence files, paragraph 3)

Federal prosecutors brought the case against White with "Threat by Instrument of Interstate Commerce" which involved violation of Federal law 18 U.S.C. paragraph 875(c) "Whoever transmits in interstate or foreign commerce any communication containing any threat to kidnap any person or any threat to injure the person of another, shall be fined under this title or imprisoned not more than five years, or both" (Findlaw.com). A jury convicted White and he was sentenced to 30 months in prison, followed by 3 years of community supervision and restricted use of the Internet. White was also charged and convicted of threatening the jury foreman in the trial of fellow White supremacist Matt Hale, who was subsequently convicted and sentenced to 40 years. White blamed the foreman for the Hale verdict and posted personal information about him on his website, including his address, phone number, and photograph. The foreman reported that he received disturbing phone calls as a result of White's efforts. However, this conviction was subsequently thrown out by a US District judge who determined that prosecutors failed to provide sufficient evidence to support solicitation to harm the foreman and that White's postings were protected by the First Amendment. Despite this outcome, federal prosecutors showed by their actions that they fully appreciated the dangerous nature of White's hate-motivated actions; and they responded accordingly.

But not all prosecutors fully understand hate crime laws. There can be confusion and misinterpretations which would hinder the prosecution of these crimes. The federal government did not include gender as a protected status until the enactment of the Local Law Enforcement Hate Crimes Prevention Act of 2009. Even today, the Justice Department's annual hate crimes report does not reflect gender-motivated incidents. Spousal battery, domestic violence causing severe bodily injury or resulting in death, sexual assault, and rape offenses are commonly recognized as crimes that are primarily carried out against females. Disturbing crimes all, but which are motivated by bias or hatred against women? One could make the argument that a hate motive is at work more often than we think. But that would be speculative. Until there is a consensus of clear indicators of misogyny as the cause of a crime, there will be uneven responses by the criminal justice system toward these crimes. To illustrate this uncertainty, the Massachusetts Attorney General's office administers a policy that requires at least two restraining orders from two different victims against a gender-bias suspect before an alleged incident is identified as motivated by gender bias (Jenness, 2003; Levin & McDevitt, 2002). This policy seems to act as an administrative screening device to differentiate gender hate crimes from the more common crimes that primarily victimize women.

This cautious approach and uncertainty regarding gender hate crime is evident among some prosecutors. McPhail and DiNitto's 2005 study investigated the familiarity of Texas prosecutors with gender hate crime laws. Using a convenience sample (N = 16), a diverse group of prosecutors participated in semi-structured interviews. The objective of the interviews was two-fold: to understand what prompts the decision to charge an offense as hate-motivated and to obtain their professional opinions on gender as a protected status in hate crime law.

Study findings revealed three themes: (1) interviewees see hate crime prosecutions as generally problematic and that the inclusion of gender as a protected status was essentially unnecessary; (2) they also tended to view crimes against women as not motivated by prejudice but by issues of power and control and; (3) these prosecutors were not well informed about gender-bias laws which were enacted in Texas law within the last several years. Gender or ethnicity of the prosecutor did not make any difference. Female prosecutors and prosecutors of color were just as uncertain about the legitimacy of gender-motivated hate crime as their male and White counterparts. This study reflects what appears to be uncertainty among prosecutors regarding gender-motivated hate crimes. Moreover, although about 24 states now include gender as a protected status in hate crime laws, there have been few cases prosecuted on charges of gender hate crime.

There are guidelines and other decision aides written for prosecutors that could be useful. The American Prosecutor's Research Institute (APRI) published *A Local Prosecutor's Guide for Responding to Hate Crimes* (2000). The document provides to prosecutors the fundamentals of establishing and effectively prosecuting hate-motivated crimes. In it, evidentiary issues are reviewed including the appropriateness of mixed motives. A mixed-motive hate crime includes both the animus plus an additional motive such as economic gain. This could be helpful to prosecutors who are shaky on pursuing gender hate crimes; (APRI, 2000, 40) "a hate crime can be charged even if the underlying offense resulted from a mixture of discriminatory and non-discriminatory motives." It also underscores the fact that in each and every instance, prosecutors must establish the bias motive and have the ability to evaluate the "totality of the circumstances" (offender's acts before, during, and after the crime; offense history, beliefs, social activities, social network, music and literature tastes and relevant habits, etc.). Evidence to support gender hate against a female victim would include verbal slurs like "slut," "bitch," "whore" or any other relevant evidence of hatred towards women.

Another guideline of sorts for prosecutors and police was published in a 2002 article by McDevitt, Levin, and Bennett. It is an expanded typology or categorization of hate crimes, first described in 1993 (see *Hate Crimes: The Rising Tide of Bigotry and Bloodshed*, Levin & McDevitt). The purpose of the typology is to aid the investigation and prosecution of hate crimes by suggesting motive through specifying aspects of the crime. McDevitt and his colleagues identify an additional fourth category of hate crimes (i.e. thrill, defensive, reactive, and mission). Thrill hate crimes are committed for excitement—experience a rush from frightening or hurting others and for peer approval. Acts committed to "defend" one's neighborhood, school, recreational area, or even workplace that is perceived as being "encroached" upon by "outsiders" represents defensive hate crimes. While defensive hate crime occurs when change is viewed as threatening to the offender, reactive (or retaliatory) hate crime occurs when the perpetrator believes that a member of his or her group has been assaulted or humiliated by a specific action committed by the "other." Finally, mission hate crime occurs when the perpetrator takes on the responsibility of ridding the world of evil (i.e. gays, Muslims, Jews, etc.) and sets out to murder and destroy the targets.

Although this typology is widely recognized by prosecutors and it is referenced in law enforcement training manuals, it may have limited application. Phillips (2009) conducted a study to measure the effectiveness of the typology when applied to a set of hate crime cases referred for prosecution between 2001 and 2004 in one New Jersey County. The primary question posed by Phillips is how well does the typology classify or identify the criminal cases included in the study. Additional questions posed were whether such classification assists prosecutors in the charging decision and what types of hate crime cases tend to be prosecuted. Phillips' sample of thirty cases not only met the statutory criteria for hate crimes but also achieved consensus from both investigators and prosecutors from the hate crime unit. These were unambiguous cases and therefore should be classifiable by the typology. However, the typology had utility for only 19 of the 30 cases and could not be applied to the remaining 11 cases. Some of the dynamics in the unclassifiable cases did not neatly fit the McDevitt, Levin, and Bennett typology. It appears that the chronology of events presented some murkiness. Phillips reports that what might have been reactive/retaliatory was illusive because the bias component presented after the actions began. Likewise, Phillips found that the classified cases more likely ended in conviction whereas the unclassified cases did not have that outcome. For hate crimes where the bias motive competes with other non-biased motives that are also present, the typology itself loses effectiveness.

Still, the determination of whether the offender's bias is central, subordinate or peripheral is a matter of evidence and perhaps a matter for the jury. The circumstances of competing motives are probably more typical than not. If a criminal robs a woman before he rapes her—who would argue that the rape held less importance? Likewise, an offender that robs an Asian before he proceeds to kick and bludgeon him while shouting anti-Asian sentiments would likely be perceived as committing a hate crime regardless of the robbery occurring first. What might be more central to the explanation of the unclassifiable cases is that there is disagreement among lawmakers and prosecutors on the extent to which bias is needed as an element of the crime before it can be viewed as a bona fide hate crime in this jurisdiction. But this is a separate issue from the typology itself. The typology does not argue for evidentiary standards or makes arguments of evidentiary sufficiency—it merely offers qualities of offender motives and the types of hate crime acts that tend to be forthcoming from these types of motives. That is not to say that there are no problems with the typology. It is probably at best a relatively crude measure of broad categories and the categories themselves are not mutually exclusive. Therein lies the limitations of its usefulness. Nevertheless, the culture of the courtroom working group in a jurisdiction may be more determinative of hate crime charging and conviction rates than anything else—including the utility of a typology.

The Phillips (2009) study shows that the lack of clear policy may create a type of chilling effect on a vigorous prosecution of hate crime. But it is also apparent that even in extremely serious hate crime acts such as murder, some prosecutors will not neglect charging the bias element that triggers the enhancement of an already severe sentence. For example, on November 14, 2008 transsexual Moses Cannon was shot and killed while sitting in a car in Syracuse, New York (O'Hara, 2009). The defendant, Dwight DeLee was convicted of first degree manslaughter as a hate crime and sentenced nine months later to the maximum sentence of 25 years. In New York State, a first degree manslaughter conviction carries a 25 year maximum sentence but the enhancement for a hate crime conviction for a serious violent felony is 20 years. Although the enhancement is less than the maximum for the underlying offense, the District Attorney's office sent a clear message about the seriousness of violent hate crimes in Onondaga County, New York by attaching the hate crimes element to the case.

In the DeLee case, the hate crime enhancement was symbolic only. But in other jurisdictions, the enhancement could have very real effects on the length of a sentence. Angie Zapata, a transgendered woman, was brutally murdered on July 17, 2008 in Greeley, Colorado by Allen Andrade after he discovered she had been born male. Andrade, a habitual offender, was convicted of first degree murder, which brought a life sentence. In addition, Andrade was convicted of other charges from the crime, including a hate crime. He received an additional sixty years to run consecutive to the life sentence; this included a 12 year sentence for the hate crime conviction (Sandeen, 2009). In this case, we see that the sentencing enhancement feature from the hate crime conviction added actual time to the defendant's life sentence.

Among the many options available to prosecutors in Massachusetts is the civil rights injunction that requires an individual to immediately refrain from a specified act. Injunctive actions in hate crime cases act no differently than in any other civil or criminal case. In Boston, a superior court judge issued a five-year civil rights injunction against a defendant charged with a hate crime. The defendant was accused of assaulting and beating a gay man, of which he pleaded guilty. The injunction prohibits the defendant from committing acts of intimidation motivated by sexual orientation bias against anyone, not just the victim who he assaulted (*The Patriot Ledger*, 2009). If he breaches the injunction, the penalties include a $5,000 fine and a two-and-a-half year term of incarceration for each violation.

The Local Law Enforcement Enhancement Act of 2005 permits the US Attorney's office to support state or local law enforcement authorities when they request federal assistance in the investigation and or prosecution of hate crime cases. There are a variety of reasons for which local authorities do not have the resources to investigate effectively or the particular hate crime statute does not fully recognize this category of crime. For example, the FBI's Indiana office is very actively involved in hate crimes that occur in that state (as well as Arkansas, Georgia, South Carolina, and Wyoming) as Indiana currently lacks state hate crime laws. This office prosecuted three defendants in 2008 for a cross-burning committed on the property of an African-American family who recently moved into a predominately white neighborhood (Murray, 2009). With the FBI's involvement, the defendants were charged and convicted on federal crimes, the conspiracy to violate the civil rights of the victims and interfering with housing rights.

The job of the defense attorney is to challenge the state's case against the defendant. This is no less true for those accused of a hate crime. There are defense attorneys that advertise their services for hate crime defendants especially on the Internet. For example, one website provides the following practical advice: hate crimes occur because bigotry and prejudice still exist in our society. While some may hold prejudiced attitudes, others go further and act on them. Hate crimes are despicable acts that should be punished, sometimes these acts can be inappropriately charged.

The website for attorney Jeremy Goldman describes himself as having experience in "handling hate crime cases" and offers this advice:

> If you have been arrested for a hate crime in California, the aggressive Irvine violent crime defense attorney Jeremy N. Goldman can build a strong defense on your behalf. To learn more about getting the charges against you reduced or dropped entirely, contact Mr. Goldman today.
>
> (jeremygoldmanlaw.com)

Attorney Goldman's ad suggests a number of defense strategies including misleading evidence and lack of bias among others. More specific defense arguments emphasize the psychological state of the defendant and, if successfully argued, this could mitigate criminal liability or even win acquittals. Two broad categories include diminished competency and stress-induced arguments (Dunbar, 1999). Diminished competency states that due to reasons of mental impairment, the defendant lacks the capacity to form the *mens rea* or mental state required to commit a specific crime. These arguments may result in a conviction on lesser charges. One of the arguments used in diminished competency is based upon the "racial paranoia-induced delusional disorder" (RPIDD). Here, the defense argues that the defendant's thought process and criminal behavior is a product of racial paranoia which produces the delusion that he or she is being persecuted by a member of the race at issue. For example in *State v. Simon* (1982), the defendant is described as an elderly racist man who shot his Asian neighbor believing he was a threat due to the neighbor's *expertise in martial arts*. This belief was a product of stereotypical and racist thinking. He was charged with aggravated assault. But due to his mental state, which caused him to "reasonably" believe he was in danger—a self-defense claim based on a subjective standard was entered and based on that, he was acquitted by a jury (Tesner, 1991). The mental competency argument succeeded in, not only minimizing exposure to a more severe punishment, but in achieving an acquittal.

Homosexual panic has been utilized also as a diminished capacity defense in anti-gay hate crime cases. It suggests that when the victim makes unwanted sexual advances to the heterosexual defendant, a severe adverse reaction interferes with rational judgment and facilitates violent defensive actions. Historically, it was believed that a heterosexual with an ongoing internal struggle with latent homosexuality, could react with violence toward a gay person, to defend against these complex psychological emotions and conflicts (Lee, 2008).

An example of a successful use of homosexual panic or threat as a defense strategy is illustrated in the trial of Jonathan Schmitz for the killing of Scott Amedure, also known as the Jenny Jones murder case. Lee (2008) provides a succinct discussion of the event and trial.

Jonathan Schmitz killed his gay friend Scott Amedure after an appearance on the Jenny Jones Show in 1995. Schmitz had been invited to appear on the show and knew the show's theme that day was *Secret Admirers*. Schmitz thought an ex-girlfriend was going to be revealed as his secret admirer. In fact, Schmitz's male friend Scott Amedure appeared on the show as his secret admirer.

Even though he was surprised and apparently embarrassed to find that his secret admirer was a man, Schmitz hugged Amedure on the air. Before they left the Detroit Metropolitan Airport, Amedure snatched a flashing construction light and stashed it in Schmitz's car. On March 9, 1995, three days after appearing on the show, Schmitz came home from work and found the flashing construction light and an unsigned note in front of his apartment that read, "John. If you want it 'off' you'll have to ask me. P.S. It takes a special tool. Guess Who." Believing the note to be a crude sexual come-on from Amedure, Schmitz drove to his bank, withdrew money from his savings account, purchased a twelve-gauge shotgun and some ammunition. He drove to Amedure's house, and after Amedure admitted to writing the note, Schmitz shot Amedure twice in the chest, killing him.

Schmitz was charged with first degree murder. At trial, Schmitz's attorney argued that Schmitz was suffering from diminished capacity when he shot and killed Scott Amedure, stemming from his embarrassment on the Jenny Jones Show when Amedure appeared as his secret admirer. At that time, diminished capacity was allowed in Michigan as a partial defense to first degree murder. Despite the overwhelming evidence of premeditation and deliberation, the jury found Schmitz's claim of diminished capacity stemming from homosexual panic credible and found him guilty of second degree murder rather than first degree murder (Lee, 2008, 495–96).

The use of diminished competency (or insanity) in general has decreased significantly for a variety of reasons for criminal defendants and concomitantly the argument of homosexual panic or threat as well. More evident today is the legal use of provocation and self-defense as a justification of violent crime committed by a heterosexual man upon a gay one. Self-defense requires that the defendant shows that there was little opportunity to thwart an imminent threat of death or serious bodily injury at the hands of the aggressor other than the use of deadly force. In September 1997, Stephen Bright killed Kenneth Brewer, a gay man, when he believed Brewer was about to sexually assault him. The two men met in a gay bar and, when invited, Bright voluntarily went with Brewer back to his residence and even to his bedroom. However, the convivial nature of the evening came to an abrupt end when Brewer re-entered the bedroom "naked, erect and stating that he wanted to f_____ Bright" (Lee, 2008; 518). Bright's defense was that he panicked and sought to defend himself in order to avoid being raped. He was charged with second degree murder but he was acquitted of murder and found guilty of third degree sexual assault punishable by one year in jail.

The tasks of policing, prosecuting, or defending hate crime defendants range across and within state jurisdictions. This variability is reflective of a range of factors including the robustness of state statutes, cultural factors within the justice system and attitudes of public officials regarding hate crimes and hate crime laws, the existence of countervailing political costs and the vigilance of civil rights advocacy groups. We end this discussion on defense strategies by highlighting the first anti-gay case prosecuted under the Local Law Enforcement Enhancement Act (LLEEA). We will see that because the bias motive itself is the linchpin of these crimes, defense attorneys will challenge the existence of the defendant's bias and/or its connection to the act when possible.

Kevin Pennington was kidnapped and beaten last year in Kentucky by two men as they shouted anti-gay epithets. As the assault was taking place, two relatives of the perpetrators witnessed the attack and corroborated that the beating and slurs occurred. A federal prosecutor tried the case under the LLEEA. The two male perpetrators were found guilty of kidnapping, but not of the bias element of the charges. The defense was successful in attacking the hate motive by interjecting that the defendants themselves were bisexual and that the incident was actually about a drug deal (Shapiro, 2012).

Corrections

Sentences handed down for hate crime convictions range greatly and reflect the differences found in statutes governing hate crime offenses, crime seriousness, aggravating or mitigating offense features, and offender culpability. Sentencing options include probation, fines, restitution, community service, diversion, and terms of incarceration that include a sentence enhancement. Penalty enhancement statutes allow a sentence to be increased by modifying the degree of criminal liability (e.g. from third degree to second degree) for the underlying offense when the hate motive has been established. Some state statutes also provide that the offender may be subject to civil action brought by the victim who is seeking some form of relief for damages sustained (Franklin, 2002). Prosecutors can and do make specific sentencing recommendations and judges may intend specific sentencing objectives that include aspects of retribution, deterrence, incapacitation, or rehabilitation.

However, even when the prosecutor pursues hate crime charges, there is no guarantee that a conviction will be forthcoming. Triers of fact may not see evidence of a hate motive as particularly compelling, and there may be a reluctance on their part for convicting on these charges if the offense circumstances lack undeniable clarity.

In this section, we briefly review a sample of sentences handed down following hate crime convictions.

On August 24, 2008, Boston, Massachusetts, four persons (three men and one woman) were attacked by several men after leaving a local nightclub. Anti-gay slurs were repeatedly yelled during the assault. The victims were left with cuts, bruises, and concussions from kicks to the head. Fabio Brandao pleaded guilty to nine charges including four civil rights violations and hate crime (Jacobs, 2009). Despite a recommendation by the District Attorney for a term of incarceration, the judge "imposed a two-year suspended sentence and the mandatory completion of an anger management program" (Jacobs, 2009, paragraph 2). The judge also ordered Brandao to pay $4,250 in medical costs to the victims. It was reported that Brandao lacked a prior criminal record.

Lenard Clark, a 13-year-old African-American boy, was attacked on March 21, 1997 in a predominately White suburb in Chicago while riding his bike back home. He was brutally torn from his bike and beaten by three White teenagers. The perpetrators motivation was to "keep their neighborhood white." The victim's head was slammed into a building and he was kicked repeatedly before being left unconscious in an alley (Slater, 1999). As a result of the racially motivated attack, the 13 year-old became comatose. Following hospitalization for brain injury, he spent six weeks in the Rehabilitation Institute of Chicago and required outpatient treatment to recover physical and speech functions. The perpetrators, Frank Caruso, 18, Michael Kwidzinski, 19, and Victor Jasas, 17, were charged with attempted murder, aggravated battery, and committing a hate crime. These charges could have brought a 30 year sentence. Jasas and Kwidzinski pled guilty to reduced charges of aggravated battery and each received a 30-month probation term and 300 hours of community service. Caruso was convicted of aggravated battery and hate crime and was sentenced to eight years in prison.

Levin, Rabrenovic, Ferraro, Doran, and Methe (2007) searched major US newspapers to record reported hate crime charges and their dispositions in court. They were interested in whether teenage hate crime offenders were treated less severely than their adult counterparts (Levin & McDevitt, 2002). More specifically, they investigated whether prosecutors and judges view teenage offenders' hate-motivated acts as less serious and therefore hand down sanctions that are equivalent to the proverbial "slap on the wrist." However, their findings show that:

- 66 percent of teens and 59 percent of adult cases were resolved by plea bargaining.
- Hate crime convictions were achieved in 72 percent of the teen cases and 63 percent of adult cases.
- Teen offenders received longer sentences than their adult counterparts for crimes of vandalism or destruction of property: 3.83 years compared to 1.89 years, respectively; for intimidation, 1.88 years compared to 1.53 years.
- Even for the more serious offenses of murder and manslaughter, the researchers report that teen offenders received longer sentences than adult offenders.
- Fines were rarely assigned in any of the sentences (adult or teen) and few were required to enter anger management or similar programs (only 7 percent of adults and 11 percent of teens).
- Sentences: 56 percent of teens received probation and community service including restitution; whereas 36 percent of adults received probation but few received community service and restitution.

- Although some teens received a prison sentence, they mostly received a community-based corrections sentence; still the researchers noted that few teens received inappropriately minor sentences.

This study revealed that young hate crime offenders were punished as rigorously as their adult counterparts and that possibly high media coverage of crimes committed by youthful perpetrators influenced a more severe outcome.

Managing hate gangs behind prison walls

It has been proposed that some judges are very careful about sending youthful hate crime offenders to prison. The concern is that prison gangs are persistent problems for correctional management and that such gangs have the capacity to recruit new inmates into their ranks (Levin & McDevitt, 1993; Hamm, 2007). Moreover, prison gangs tend to coalesce around race, ethnicity, and to some extent political ideology. White racist gangs, which is estimated to be 10 percent of the total prison population, such as the Nazi Low-Riders, Public Enemy Number 1, European Kindred, and the Aryan Brotherhood (AB) are real concerns and cannot be overlooked as potential magnets for incoming unseasoned offenders. The Southern Poverty Law Center reported on a large scale 2005 federal indictment levied against multiple members of the AB. The following is a quote from a member of the AB which suggests why judges may prefer not to send younger hate crime offenders to prison (Holthouse, 2005, paragraph 14): "My brothers and I have went to war, (make no mistake it is war) with all of the mongoloid races at one time or another, using knives, pipes, locks/rocks in socks," a member of the Aryan Brotherhood in Oklahoma who identified himself as "tree 1488" posted to a forum on prison gangs on the White supremacist Stormfront website in June.

Currently the AB and other such groups are established in the federal prison system and have affiliated groups both inside and outside of state correctional systems across the country. Although the majority of those convicted of hate crimes are not affiliated with hate groups, once these offenders are incarcerated, they may very well become members. Thus the management of White supremacist gangs (often referred to as "security threat groups") as well as other non-racist gangs should be a significant concern to most judges and correctional officials.

There are few studies concerning the recruitment dynamics of White supremacist prison gangs; however, Randy Blazak (2009) provides a well-reasoned argument that this area should receive more attention from correctional administrators. As we consider appropriate correctional responses for hate crime offenders— Blazak's argument should be heeded. He makes several important points. First, the existence of these groups in the correctional system can facilitate the radicalization of some into the violent hate movement. Second, for some White inmates, prison conditions and the failure of officials to manage potential conflicts and tensions among and between prisoners could actually expedite affiliation or membership in a White racist prison gang. Finally, these newly acquired members into hate groups may remain active and now ideologically rooted following release from prison.

The enforcement of drug laws has created a disproportionately Black prison population. Some of these individuals have ties to street gangs. Just like White supremacist prison gangs there are likewise Black, Hispanic, Asian, and Mexican prison gangs. These patterns set the stage for incoming White inmates to choose to either remain unaffiliated and therefore without protection in a violent environment, or to associate with White racist prison gangs in order to gain security. These groups are involved in criminal enterprises—both inside and outside of prisons—and they advocate the ideological beliefs found in the hate movement. Once a White inmate joins with these groups, they are expected to carry out the group's agenda while in prison and afterwards. These groups pride themselves with a "blood in, blood out" oath of allegiance (Leyden, 2008). Inmates who are incarcerated for committing a hate crime would be well received and even celebrated inside for the acts that brought them there. This new found acceptance and approval could encourage future exploits. Today, White racist prison gangs are found not only in federal and state prison systems, but also in county jails (Blazak, 2009).

Considering the potential dangers of these groups, do prison administrators monitor and effectively control their activities? Recent research indicates that some prison superintendents isolate problematic or "extremist prisoners" rather than increase surveillance of them (Merola & Vovak, 2012). Merola and Vovak report that nearly one in five superintendents state that their facilities separate "extremist prisoners" from the general population. But the overwhelming majority (at least 77 percent) reports that their primary strategy is to keep a closer watch on members of these groups and perhaps pair monitoring with other tactics.

Other management practices of security threat groups—which include members of hate gangs/groups—involve segregating individuals *only if they are actively recruiting others* or conducting other questionable behaviors; maintaining them in the general population but ensuring that their housing assignments are scattered throughout the facility and lastly treating them no differently than any other inmate. Whether or not these policies merely cause a temporary halt to the activities of White racist gangs or effectively contain and diminish their ability to add to their ranks can only be determined by careful monitoring by correctional administrators.

Rehabilitation: restorative justice models

Restorative Justice may be described as a forward-looking approach to dealing with all affected parties touched by crime: forward-looking because the objective is one of healing, restoration and prevention. The victim has the opportunity to express the extent of the crime's impact and to inquire more specifically of the offender as to why the victimization occurred. The offender has the opportunity to become more aware of the harm he or she caused, to express remorse, ask forgiveness and to make efforts to compensate the victim. Community members participate by affirming community standards and values and extending support to both the victim as well as the offender. The techniques found in restorative justice approaches include: victim-offender mediation; conferencing; peacemaking circles; reparative boards; victim services, community services, restitution and reintegration services. Is this a viable alternative for hate crime offenders? The literature suggests that there is more use of restorative justice programs and activities for hate crime offenders in the United Kingdom (UK) and Australia than in the United States. This likely reflects the establishment of restorative justice as an alternative to conventional criminal processes in the UK than in the states. Gavrielides (2012) conducted a three-year study which explored the effectiveness of restorative justice as a means to mediate, repair or restore social and other damages caused by hate crime. At first glance, one may not see much potential in using this approach for hate crimes. The very definition of hate crime suggests that the perpetrator does not see the victim as an equal. Restorative justice approaches require that all parties acknowledge some degree of egalitarianism among those involved in order to engage in this process. Therefore one might conclude that hate crime perpetrators who are entrenched in White supremacy, anti-Semitism, homophobia and other *isms* would be less likely to volunteer for a restorative justice implementation.

Drawing from a variety of participants, Gavrielides obtained feedback from victims and perpetrators of hate crime through focus groups, and with policy makers and practitioners through semi-structured interviews. In addition, direct observations were made of two UK restorative justice programs. Of the twenty-one participants in the focus group, only two reported exposure to restorative justice with face-to-face mediation. Study findings indicated:

- Focus group participants and other interviewees were familiar with restorative justice aims in general and most believed it could shed light on why a hate crime occurred.
- It was expressed that perhaps both the offender and victim are "victims," that perpetrators are often individuals who've felt wronged by society and reciprocate by committing bias acts.
- interviewees recognized the importance of the community being part of the restorative justice process, referencing the emotional impact of the crime on the community.

However, what might be the most profound finding from the Gavrielides study is the consensus among study participants that restorative justice has the capacity to be effective for hate *incidents* as well as criminal offenses motivated by bigotry. Incidents that have not reached the threshold of a crime and have not come to the attention of law enforcement are just as injurious to the victim and the community as criminal acts and could well profit from restorative justice interventions. Participants noted that these very same incidents, if left unattended, could escalate into fully-fledged serious criminal acts. Participants who were victims of hate crime emphasized the importance of restorative justice involvement for those offensive acts that are not crimes.

Conclusion

After several decades of hate crime laws in the United States, we see patterns of actions that are similar to the processing of non-hate crimes and some that may be out of the norm. Even with clear statutory language, there are instances where prosecutors and/or law enforcement will only identify and prosecute a hate crime in the most blatant cases. Perhaps due to the local political climate or uncertainty of public support of hate crime laws, prosecutors may be inclined to only charge and prosecute hate crimes when there is little doubt that such charges are well substantiated. A similar cautious approach is taken by some police departments who prefer *stark* evidence surrounding an alleged crime before they identify it as a hate crime investigation. This reluctance may occur with other criminal offenses but it appears to be heightened with hate crimes. Federal prosecutors are the most aggressive when it comes to this crime category. With the enactment of the 2009 federal law, the Matthew Shepard and James Byrd, Jr., Hate Crimes Prevention Act, federal prosecutors have wider access to involvement in more criminal prosecutions of hate crimes. In addition, federal prosecutors are less affected by local sentiments (by public officials or the public) which negatively impact local prosecutors.

Once a hate crime conviction is obtained, judges make full use of an array of sentences—as they do in any other criminal case. However, there are some concerns over sending younger White hate crime offenders to a term of incarceration. Prison populations have become increasingly impacted by prison gangs. Therefore, the bigoted tendencies of these offenders may be hardened with exposure to racist prison groups like the Aryan Brotherhood. Interestingly, there does not seem to be a parallel concern for minority hate crime offenders.

Finally, restorative justice may be a viable alternative for some hate crime offenders in receptive jurisdictions. This is an area yet to be fully explored for these offenders in the United States, as it has been in the UK. Overall, there is a lack of research on the effectiveness of either incarceration or community-based sentences on the hate crime offender. This gap in the literature must be addressed because the possibility of radicalization during incarceration is a real possibility.

Chapter summary

- Police are critical in the initial investigative determination of an alleged hate crime incident. It is important for them to get it right if a hate crime has occurred and it is equally important for them to resist the hate crime label if the evidence fails to substantiate the charge.
- Professional guidelines like the one provided by the International Association of Chiefs of Police describe only one aspect of many that heighten the importance of hate crime to police. Additional factors include hate crime statutes and local ordinances in a jurisdiction; training for police officers and police supervisors and line officers that understand that the enforcement of hate crime laws prevents or diminishes subsequent hate crimes.

- Some police departments have created specialized units to respond to reported hate crimes. They may be referred to as community disorder units, hate crimes task force units or hate crime units.
- The work of prosecutors reflects the public's denouncement of a hate crime act. If prosecutors respond to an aggressive investigation by police of an alleged hate crime by failing to charge appropriately, they may undermine public confidence. Conversely, when prosecutors pursue charges on a hate crime case, it sends a strong message to potential violators and potential targets.
- The question of when violence against a woman is a hate crime has been long debated. There is the perspective that crimes against women are mostly due to issues of power and control, which are the most common explanations for acts of sexual assault and domestic violence. These crimes that disproportionately impact women are not perceived as hate-motivated.
- The Local Law Enforcement Enhancement Act of 2005 permits the US Attorney's office to support state or local law enforcement authorities when they request federal assistance in the investigation and or prosecution of hate crime cases.
- The use of diminished competency for hate crime defendants has decreased significantly for a variety of reasons. More evident today is the legal use of provocation and self-defense as a justification or defense strategy. Self-defense requires that the defendant shows that there was little opportunity to thwart an imminent threat of death or serious bodily injury at the hands of the aggressor other than the use of deadly force.
- Sentences handed down for hate crime convictions range greatly and reflect the variation found in statutes governing hate crime offenses, crime seriousness, aggravating or mitigating offense features, and offender culpability. Sentencing options include probation, fines, restitution, community service, diversion and terms of incarceration that could include a sentence enhancement. Penalty enhancement statutes allow a sentence to be increased by modifying the degree of criminal liability (e.g. from third degree to second degree) for the underlying offense when the hate motive has been established.
- Some judges are careful about sending youthful hate crime offenders to a prison. The concern is that prison gangs are problems and tend to coalesce around race, ethnicity, and political ideology. White racist prison gangs, such as the Nazi Low-Riders, Public Enemy Number 1, European Kindred and the Aryan Brotherhood (AB) cannot be overlooked as potential magnets for incoming unseasoned offenders.
- Randy Blazak warns about the potential harm of racist prison gangs and recruitment inside prison walls. First, the existence of these groups can facilitate the radicalization of some into the violent hate movement. Second, prison conditions and the failure of officials to manage potential conflicts and tensions among prisoners could expedite affiliation with a White racist prison gang. Finally, these new members may remain active and now ideologically rooted following release from prison.
- Restorative justice may be a viable alternative for some hate crime offenders in receptive jurisdictions.

Case study 7.1 White supremacist pleads innocent to burning Black family's home

Committed white supremacists often leave little to the imagination of where their loyalties lie. Brian Moudry of Joliet, Illinois, made clear his self-acclaim as a white supremacist by the tattoo in his scalp, "Blue-eyed Devil," in addition to the countless other tattoos which cover his face, neck, and arms.

Moudry is in federal court to answer charges that in 2007 he set the home of his Black neighbors on fire in the middle of the night. Included in the house were eight children. The alleged motive—to rid his neighborhood of African-Americans.

This is not his first involvement with hate crime but has a history of racially motivated acts. Moudry was incarcerated for a prior hate crime that targeted Blacks. In addition to the current federal charges, he also has a pending weapons charges in Will County, Illinois Circuit Court.

Known in the white power rock and white nationalist netherworld, Moudry has edited and self-published Hatemonger Warzine, subscribing to the name, Rev. Brian 'Warhead von Jewgrinder' Moudry. He acknowledged involvement in the white power movement since age 18 eventually earning the position of reverend in the Creativity Movement. Another indicator of his mindset is the sign hung on his own house which reads, "English spoken here."

Ironically, his federal public defender is a female African-American attorney. Defense attorney MiAngel Cody entered the federal courtroom, met with Moudry—who qualified for a public defender—and then accepted the appointment to defend him as issued by Magistrate Judge J. Gilbert.

Moudry faces three federal charges which upon conviction brings a mandatory 10-year sentence. He was ordered held without bail as he is viewed as a threat to the community and a flight risk.

(Source: Fitzpatrick, L. and Seidel, J. Sun-Times Media,
May 31, 2012. www.suntimes.com/news/12886580-418/white-
supremacist-pleads-innocent-to-burning-black-familys-home.html)

Discussion questions

1 In what ways would the background of defendant Moudry assist police and prosecutors in the investigation and prosecution of this crime?
2 What should police and prosecutors be wary of in identifying Moudry as the suspect?
3 Would restorative justice be a possible option in this case? Why or why not?
4 If defendant Moudry is convicted and sentenced to federal prison, what could correctional officials do to minimize his ability to recruit others into the hate movement?

Bibliography

American Prosecutor's Research Institute (APRI). (2000). A Local Prosecutor's Guide for Responding to Hate Crimes. Available from www.ndaa.org/pdf/hate_crimes.pdf [Accessed June 14, 2014].

Blazak, R. (2009). The Prison Hate Machine. *Criminology and Public Policy*, 8(3), 633–40.

Dunbar, E. (1999). Defending the Indefensible: A Critique and Analysis of Psycholegal Defense Arguments of Hate Crime Perpetrators. *Journal of Contemporary Criminal Justice*, 15(1), 64–77.

Findlaw.com. (n.d.). 18 U.S.C. paragraph 875: US Code—Section 875: Interstate Communications. Available from http://codes.lp.findlaw.com/uscode/18/I/41/875 [Accessed November 2, 2012].

Franklin, K. (2002). Good Intentions: The Enforcement of Hate Crime Penalty-Enhancement Statutes. In P. Gerstenfeld & D. Grant (eds.) *Crimes of Hate: Selected Readings* (pp. 79–92). Thousand Oaks, CA: Sage Publications.

Gavrielides, T. (2012). Contextualizing Restorative Justice for Hate Crime. *Journal of Interpersonal Violence*, 20(10), 1–20.

Goldman, J. N. (n.d.). Law Offices of Jeremy N. Goldman. Hate Crime Defense Lawyer in Irvine. Available from www.jeremygoldmanlaw.com/hate-crimes.shtml [Accessed February 22, 2011].

Haider-Markel, D. P. (2002). Regulating Hate: State and Local Influences on Law Enforcement Actions Related to Hate Crime. *State Politics and Policy Quarterly*, 2(2), 126–60.

Hamm, M. S. (2007). Terrorist Recruitment in American Correctional Institutions: An Exploratory Study of Non-Traditional Faith Groups. Final report. Sponsored by the National Institute of Justice, Washington, DC.

Higginbotham, A. L. (1978). *In the Matter of Color: Race and the American Legal Process: The Colonial Period.* New York: Oxford University Press.

Holthouse, D. (2005). Leaders of Racist Prison Gang Aryan Brotherhood Face Federal Indictment. *Intelligence Report*, Issue 119. Southern Poverty Law Center. Available from www.splcenter.org/get-informed/intelligence-report/browse-all-issues/2005/fall/smashing-the-shamrock [Accessed February 8, 2015].

International Association of Chiefs of Police. (1999). Responding to Hate Crimes: A Police Officer's Guide to Investigation and Prevention. Available from www.theiacp.org/PublicationsGuides/LawEnforcementIssues/Hatecrimes/tabid/191/Default.aspx#respond [Accessed November 1, 2012].

Jacobs, E. (2009). Backlash to Lenient Sentence in Gay Bashing Case. June 4. Available from http://baywindows.com/backlash-to-lenient-sentence-in-gay-bashing-case-92092 [Accessed January 20, 2013].

Jaimes, M. A. (1999). *The State of Native America: Genocide, Colonization and Resistance.* Brooklyn, NY: South End Press.

Jenness, V. (2003). Engendering Hate Crime Policy: Gender, the "Dilemma of Difference," and the Creation of Legal Subjects. *Journal of Hate Studies*, 2(73), 73–97.

Jeremygoldmanlaw.com. (n.d.). Available from www.jeremygoldmanlaw.com/hate-crimes.shtml [Accessed February 22, 2011].

King, J. (2009). Death Valley: Phoenix Police Won't Label Murder a Hate Crime but Suggest There Were Racial Overtones. *Phoenix New Times*. Available from http://blogs.phoenixnewtimes.com/valleyfever/2009/10/death_valley_phoenix_police_in.php [Accessed November 1, 2012].

Labbe-DeBose, T. (October 13, 2009). No New Hires in Gay Police Unit: Residents Point to Rise in Hate Crimes As D.C. Initiative Is Diluted to Cut Costs. *The Washington*

Post. Available from www.washingtonpost.com/wpdyn/content/article/2009/10/12/ AR2009101201450.html [Accessed February 8, 2015].

Lee, C. (2008). The Gay Panic Defense. *The UC Davis Law Review*, 42(2), 471–566.

Lemons, S. (2010). Kelly Jaeger's Alleged Killers: Phoenix PD Issues Circumspect Press Release. *Phoenix New Times*. Available from http://blogs.phoenixnewtimes.com/bastard/2010/09/kelly_jaegers_alleged_killers.php [Accessed November 1, 2012].

Levin, J. & McDevitt, J. (1993). *Hate Crimes: The Rising Tide of Bigotry and Bloodshed*. New York: Plenum Press.

Levin, J. & McDevitt, J. (2002). *Hate Crimes Revisited: America's War on Those Who Are Different*. Boulder, CO: Westview Press.

Levin, J., Rabrenovic, G., Ferraro, V., Doran, T., & Methe, D. (2007). When a Crime Committed by a Teenager Becomes a Hate Crime Results from Two Studies. *American Behavioral Scientist*, 51, 246. Doi: 10.1177/0002764207306057.

Leyden, T. J. (2008). *Skinhead Confessions: From Hate to Hope*. Springfield, UT: Sweetwater Books.

McDevitt, J., Levin, J., & Bennett, S. (2002). Hate Crimes Offenders: An Expanded Typology. *Journal of Social Issues*, 58(2), 303–17.

McPhail, B. A. and DiNitto, D. M. (2005). Prosecutorial Perspectives on Gender-Bias Hate Crimes. *Violence Against Women*, 11, 1162–85. Doi: 10.1177/1077801205277086.

Marino, J. (2009). Death Won't be Investigated as Hate Crime. South Florida Sun-Sentinel. com. Available from www.topix.com/news/gay/2009/10/death-wont-be-investigated-as-hate-crime [Accessed December 12, 2009].

Merola, L. M. and Vovak, H. (2012). The Challenges of Terrorist and Extremist Prisoners: A Survey of U.S. Prisons. *Criminal Justice Policy Review*, November 28, 1–24. DOI: 10.1177/0887403412463048.

Murray, J. (2009). Feds in Indianapolis Says Hate Crimes are Top Priority. Available from www.indy.com/posts/feds-in-indianapolis-say-hate-crimes-are-top-priority [Accessed December 28, 2009].

O'Hara, J. (2009). Onondaga County's First Hate Crime Murder Trial Starts Monday. *The Post-Standard*. Published July 12, 2009. Available from www.syracuse.com/news/index. ssf/2009/07/onondaga_countys_first_hate_cr.html [Accessed December 28, 2009].

Patriot Ledger, The. (2009). Injunction Issued Against Quincy Man under Hate-Crime Law. Available from www.wickedlocal.com/quincy/news/x1795889451/Injunction-issued-against-Quincy-man-under-hate-crime-law [Accessed December 28, 2009].

Phillips, N. D. (2009). The Prosecution of Hate Crimes: The Limitations of the Hate Crime Typology. *Interpersonal Violence*, 24(5), 883–905.

Sandeen, A. (2009). Breaking: Angie Zapata's Killer Sentenced to 60 Additional Years. Available from http://pamshouseblend.firedoglake.com/2009/05/08/breaking-angie-zapatas-killer-sentenced-to-60-additional-years/ [Accessed January 10, 2013].

Shapiro, L. (2012). Gay Hate Crime Acquittal in Kentucky Throws Fuel on Hate Crime Debate. *Huffingtonpost.com*. Available from www.huffingtonpost.com/2012/10/26/ gay-hate-crime-acquittal-kentucky_n_2024569.html [Accessed January 14, 2013].

Slater, E. (1999). Beating Case Is a Bizarre Tale of Mafiosi and a Racial Divide. *Los Angeles Times*. Available from http://articles.latimes.com/1999/jul/01/news/mn-51916 [Accessed January 20, 2013].

Southern Poverty Law Center (SPLC). (n.d.). Bill White. Intelligence Files. Available from www.splcenter.org/get-informed/intelligence-files/profiles/bill-white [Accessed November 1, 2012].

Sowers, P. (2009). Lopes Leads Way on Provincetown No Place for Hate Forum. Wicked Local.com. Available from www.wickedlocal.com/capecod/news/x986608239/

Lopes-leads-way-on-Provincetown-No-Place-for-Hate-forum#axzz2AzuRiII9   [Accessed November 1, 2012].

Takaki, R. (1989). *Strangers from a Different Shore: A History of Asian Americans*. New York: Little, Brown.

Tesner, M. (1991). Racial Paranoia as a Defense to Racial Violence. *Boston College Third World Law Journal*, 11, 307–33.

8   International perspectives

Introduction

Hate crime occurs globally and although perpetrators and targeted groups may vary to some degree, the general dynamics underlying this crime remain unchanged. This chapter describes the nature of hate crimes abroad, the principal parties involved in these crimes, the types of laws enacted to address them, and the policies and programs offered to combat them. In some instances, we see laws similar to those found in the United States particularly around the need to document hate crime prevalence and to establish national statistics. However, in some nations hate crime laws are far more stringent than those of the US. For example, the possession and dissemination of hate literature in Germany is outlawed, which is not the case in the United States. Or in several nations, the very denial of the Holocaust could be prosecuted as a criminal offense. But what may be more interesting is the variety of ways in which different nations, peoples, and cultures conceptualize and respond to this social problem. Following a brief overview of hate crimes that occur by selected countries, we examine crime policies that are in place to suppress these activities. As mentioned earlier, hate crimes are universal, with countless examples across the world. The countries included in this chapter were selected in part to show that whether we focus on modern industrialized nations or developing ones—there is evidence of hate crime. Finally, we discuss the larger picture of these problems from a global perspective.

Humankind's capacity to develop prejudiced attitudes and to act on them dates back to the time of ancient civilizations. With the evolution of tribalism and the subsequent development of organized and competitive societies, some argue that the practice of devaluing others due to group differences is biological (Flohr, 1987; Mills & Polanowski, 1997).

Unfortunately history provides many clear examples of one group's persecution of another due to religious, ethnic, racial, socioeconomic class, ideology, or other status differences. Genocide is the most extreme case of intergroup hatred and these acts have occurred throughout human history and are no respecter of geography or social progress. These cases often include the systematic and increasing dehumanization of a minority group that ends in mass murder. Besides the Holocaust, there have been many genocides including the Lakota Sioux,

Yuki, Arapaho, and Cheyenne, tribes that were decimated by military and other authorities throughout early (North) American history; through the execution of periodic pogroms during the nineteenth and twentieth centuries, the Ottoman Turks murdered thousands of Armenians (Europe); Stalin killed millions of Ukrainians during the 1930s (Asia); millions of ethnic minorities and other "undesirables" were eradicated by the Khmer Rouge in the infamous "killing fields" of Cambodia from 1975–79 (Asia) and; the Rwandan genocide saw nearly a million Tutsi killed in about 100 days (Africa). These examples and others teach us that suspicion of the *other* and bigotry are universal experiences. Left unimpeded, their culmination—genocide—occurs globally; thus it should not be surprising that hate crimes also occur in many nations and among many people.

A report published by the Leadership Conference on Civil and Human Rights—The Leadership Conference on Civil Rights Education Fund (LCCREF), *Hate Knows No Borders—The International Perspective* (2009), indicates that hate crimes increased in several European countries as well as the Russian Federation since the start of the twenty-first century. These findings are based on official governmental statistics, media reports and hate crime accounts reported by NGO organizations. There is a range of hate-motivated crimes described in the report including anti-Semitic, anti-immigrant (xenophobia), racism, homophobia and anti-Roma. An increase in racially motivated hate crime was reported for years 2006 and 2007 in the United Kingdom, Ireland, Slovakia, Sweden, and Finland, (LCCREF, 2009, 22). But there are problems in some instances with official data not reflecting incidents or crimes that occurred but remain unreported to local authorities. Just as in the United States, there is a gap between official reports and victimization surveys conducted by non-governmental monitors. Such surveys showed larger numbers of anti-immigrant hate crime in countries such as Italy, Spain, Portugal, and Greece than what is represented in official data.

Who are the reported victims? There are hosts of groups targeted for abuse due to their actual or perceived status. Asylum seekers and immigrants are mentioned in the LCCREF report as are Muslims, Jews, and Christians, homosexuals, Africans, and Roma. There is also the reality that hate motives for some attacks could fit more than one category. For example, asylum seekers may also be attacked for racial reasons or even for xenophobic reasons. Similarly, persons of Middle-Eastern descent may be targeted for their perceived religion or due to their ethnicity. Until data collection becomes more refined, standardized, and consistently applied, all of these data sources can only be viewed, at best, as estimates. Anti-Muslim-motivated hate crime is at high levels in Germany, the UK as well as France and "anti-Semitic violence has increased in Canada, Germany, the Russian Federation, Ukraine and the UK" (LCCREF, 2009, 22). What might be surprising to some is the targeting of Christians for their religious beliefs. Turkey, Sudan and the Central Asian republics, as well as the Russian Federation are areas were Christians are relegated to a subordinate social status due to their "non-traditional" faith.

Who commits these crimes? While the perpetrators of these crimes were not discussed in this report, it did describe how public officials at times fueled racist violence. If government officials or other political or popular leaders used anti-Roma or anti-immigrant rhetoric during public statements or campaign stops that were inflammatory or proposed legislation that scapegoated vulnerable groups; violent and at times deadly attacks on members of these groups occurred. Pogroms targeting Roma in multiple metropolitan areas in Italy are examples.

Another non-governmental international organization which monitors hate crime and other abuses around the world is *Human Rights First.* Through its work and advocacy of human equality and human dignity, Human Rights First engages governments and governmental institutions to aspire to these values and address systemic problems of abuse and discrimination. Several noteworthy publications are produced by this organization and are referenced throughout this chapter. According to Human Rights First and other watch groups, far too few nations are monitoring hate crime activity, and even fewer are taking serious action to combat it. The stance of benign neglect by governments is a dangerous one as inaction is clearly an action and may signal to perpetrators that no one cares what they do and that the state will not intervene. In the twenty-first century, is this an effective strategy to manage hate crimes?

The nature of hate crime in other nations

China

There are some who argue that the cultural practice of devaluing female but not male infants even to the point of literally throwing them away soon after birth— fits the theoretical definition of hate crime. Female infanticide or abandonment has occurred in China and India.

S. K. Horn (2001) presents this argument in *Femicide in Global Perspective.* These babies are discarded by their families because they are *female.* While the current government has criminalized this act since 1949, it was an institutionalized social practice especially among the poor. Furthermore, China's more recent One-Child policy, established in 1979, might be interpreted by some as a rationale for female infanticide or abandonment. As this policy came into effect, the development of hundreds of "missing women" has been documented (Gendercide Watch). According to Gendercide, millions of women are unaccounted for because of the "institutionalized killing and neglect of girls" due to the One-Child policy (paragraph 16). Families failing to observe the policy are penalized by wage-cuts and are less eligible for social services. But other researchers indicate that the "missing women" number can be explained by reasons other than female infanticide and include "underreporting of female births, prenatal sex determination testing and subsequent aborting of females" which account for most of this missing population (Gendercide Watch, paragraph 18). A much smaller percentage therefore would be attributable to female infanticide.

The dynamics of this practice has some similarities with hate crime, but it also has some clear differences. Similarities include: first, the attitude and belief that females are inferior to males and therefore are inherently less valuable; second, it is implicit in female infanticide that the very existence of female persons somehow takes away from superior males; third, that female infants are interchangeable; meaning their individuality is not recognized nor does individuality make any difference. Females, as a group are neglected, abandoned, or killed by virtue of an immutable characteristic.

While these factors echo those of victimized groups, there are important differences. The motive behind these acts are complex. Are female babies actually hated or despised or is this an economically driven act? Are there extremist (or traditional) views and ideologies in Chinese culture that situates females as a threat to Chinese civilization? Another important difference is that the perpetrator(s) is/are likely to be the parents of the child, which situates these acts in a very different social context from traditional hate crimes. It is an act that in a very broad sense, however, might be construed as a type of hate crime—but upon closer examination, it does diverge from the traditional characteristics, despite the same result. It is important to stress that at this point in time female infanticide has been drastically reduced in China.

India

Northeast Indians are the most frequent targets of institutionalized cultural, economic and political discrimination in India. This pervasive mistreatment is a result of India's caste system, which for generations determined the occupations and limited the social interactions for those negatively impacted by this social system. India has moved away from the caste system but there are remnants of it that continue to thrive in Indian society. The caste system has been officially dismantled, but equal opportunity for all citizens has not been prioritized by India's government. After legal barriers which prevented Northeast Indians and other ethnic groups' access to education and job opportunities were removed, these groups migrated to metropolitan areas where opportunities became more available. But with this move came a backlash against the newcomers. Hate-motivated victimizations became regular occurrences. These attacks included aggravated assaults, sexual assaults, rape, murder, and human trafficking in addition to conventional discriminatory practices (Chandra, 2012). Groups identified previously as the "untouchables" are today the victims of social isolation, marginalization, considerable discrimination, and hate crimes. The perpetrators of these crimes and other forms of harassment are largely carried out by those from the more dominant and upper classes (Sharma, 2012).

The Scheduled Castes and Scheduled Tribes Prevention of Atrocities Act of 1989 was enacted to combat these hate crimes. This law, which is similar in spirit to the US Civil Rights Act of 1964, criminalizes an array of crimes perpetrated against this population based on discrimination. It also criminalizes the practice of untouchability that include treating this population in ways similar to indentured servitude. A prior study on hate crimes against the SC and ST populations reported that there are higher incidence rates in those regions where the upper classes must now share water sources with the SC and ST population. Under the caste system, this sharing was forbidden as it was considered "ritualistic pollution" for the upper castes according to Bros and Coutennier, 2010 (as cited in Sharma, 2012).

Sharma (2012) investigated the effect of economic disparity between upper classes (castes) and the lowest classes (castes)—the SC and ST populations. Findings indicate a positive relationship between the narrowing of the economic gap between the upper and lower castes and hate crime incidence. This result suggests that as the upper castes perceive an economic threat from subaltern groups, hate crimes are committed to reinforce boundaries (social and economic). The hate crimes committed are primarily violent in nature but property crimes also occur as the acquisition of property by SC and ST members is highly resented by the upper castes. At times, whole communities are targeted for harassment and victimization when one of its residents has progressed economically.

Class discrimination is still a potent legacy from the caste system, which leaves the SC and ST populations very much vulnerable to disparaging treatment, subordination and hate crimes. This ongoing problem is compounded by the apparent lack of commitment by governmental and criminal justice authorities in India to respond to systematic discrimination and vigorously prosecute hate crimes.

Russia

International students from the developing world are not entirely welcomed by everyone in Russia. Watch groups report that in 2008 alone nearly 100 murders that were racial- or other hate-motivated incidents occurred in Russia (LCCREF, 2009). The victims were not just international students but included citizens of the Russian Federation. Even more disturbing are reports that hate-motivated murders are at times videotaped by perpetrators and placed on the Internet and on social media to chronicle their crimes and to inspire others. A *New York Times* article reported a videotaped beheading placed on the Internet in August 2007 that showed a masked person decapitating a bound, dark-skinned man. The video, entitled "Execution of Tajik and Dagestani," also shows another individual shot in the head and ends with two masked people giving Nazi salutes in front of a red banner with a swastika (Schwirtz, 2008). This horrific video was supposedly authenticated by the Russian Investigative Committee. The perpetrators are alleged to be Russian neo-Nazis, the victims are ethnic minorities from the Caucasus region. The use of social media as a tool used in hate crimes was also noted in the recent criminal trial of nine racist skinheads, the "White Wolves," who planned, coordinated, and subsequently videotaped their attacks by using the Internet and smartphones (RT News, 2009). Skinheads are among the growing number of extremist groups found in Russian cities. The Ministry of Internal Affairs report that there are over 400 extremist groups in Russia, including 147 skinhead groups—numbering 20,000 to 50,000 members (McClintock, 2005, 34). The group referenced earlier, the White Wolves, a violent neo-Nazi group, were found responsible for approximately 11 murders and multiple brutal attacks; members received sentences of nine years and the leader, a 23-year term (Liss, 2010).

African and Asian international students are frequently targeted by violent skinhead groups. Victimization of these students occurs with such regularity that they travel to off-campus classes in groups to fend off attacks (McClintock, 2005). In response to this problem, ambassadors from several African nations sent a petition to Russian President Putin in 2002, demanding protection for the students. Americans are not omitted as possible targets. African-American exchange student Stanley Robinson was stabbed several times in Volgograd in southern Russia on December 5, 2008 while attempting to return to the residence of his host family. Two neo-Nazi skinheads were subsequently arrested and charged with the attack.

Perpetrators are becoming bolder as they appear to systematically target human rights activists including anti-fascists for contract-style executions. These killings are carried out openly for maximum effect of intimidation and to terrorize those who would speak out against their nationalist agenda. The recent murder of Ivan Khutorskoi, a critic of neo-Nazis and other nationalist groups and an active anti-racist is being investigated as a possible hate-motivated crime according to the Prosecutor General's investigative unit (WSVN.com, 2009). Nationalist groups who advocate xenophobic agendas are targeting those who are not Slavic in appearance, which includes international students, migrant workers, ethnic minorities, Russians who have darker complexions as well as those who challenge their ideology (Schwirtz, 2009). Media reports describe several recent murders involving human rights activists as the victims and members of ultra-nationalist groups as the perpetrators. SOVA the Center for Information and Analysis states that the primary objectives of these groups are to provoke a "nationalist revolution" and to establish a neo-Nazi regime in Russia (SOVA, 2010, paragraph 4). More recent reports indicate that Russian officials have begun to be more responsive to the crimes and other activities of extremist groups.

South Africa

A discussion about hate crime in South Africa must be placed in proper context by acknowledging two historical policies of this country: the enactment of apartheid and its dismantlement. Apartheid was the institutionalization of legalized racial segregation, racial oppression, civil rights suppression, and discrimination against all groups in the Republic of South Africa who were categorized as non-White. Many (this author included) would consider apartheid itself as systematic hate crime perpetrated by the South African government. This official policy was the law of the land from 1948 until 1994; ending with the prison release and eventual election of Nelson Mandela, the first Black South African President of the country. Despite this seismic shift in formal public policy and all of its social ramifications, crimes motivated by bias and hatred occur in South Africa today and this country has not enacted legislation that identifies these behaviors as "hate crime." A report published by South Africa's Center for the Study of Violence and Reconciliation states that "acts of prejudice are not framed as hate crime" in South Africa (Harris, 2004, 24). Several explanations are offered for this: violent crime occurs frequently in South Africa and hate-motivated violence is just one aspect of it; there is a general presumption that prejudice is at the root of most violence in South Africa and; there is a reluctance to grapple with the consequences of apartheid on contemporary South African society and on racially motivated acts and; finally, prejudice is perceived as both multifaceted and ubiquitous and thus difficult to conceptualize as an aspect of criminal behavior.

Nevertheless, there are hate groups in South Africa. Perhaps among the most organized is the Afrikaner Resistance Movement or AWB (Afrikaner Weerstandsbeweging). Included in its ideological platform are neo-Nazism and White supremacy. The founder of the group, Eugene Terre Blanche, advocated a White-led South African government (apartheid) and the group worked to thwart government efforts to transition to a democratic process that permitted the participation of all citizens, White, Black, and "Coloured." The group used terrorism to influence government leaders by planting bombs and explosive devices over a two-year period, killing at least twenty people. The emblem of the AWB bears a strong resemblance to the Nazi swastika. It is comprised of three Black-colored 7s arranged in a clockwise fashion on a white circle that's placed on a red field. Since the murder of Blanche in 2010, the AWB continues to strive for a White homeland in South Africa. But racial hate is not the only form of hate-motivated acts in South Africa.

Corrective rape is the term used to describe vicious sexual assaults committed against women in general and lesbians in particular. Perpetrators explain their victimization of lesbians by stating that it is their attempt to "cure" lesbians of their homosexuality. These acts of violence have also included murder. It's reported that since 1998 at least 31 lesbians have been killed in acts that began as rape (Hunter-Gault, 2012, paragraph 2). Despite South Africa's history of entrenched discrimination, bigotry aimed at the gay and lesbian community continues to be prevalent. But it is also important to note that the rate of violent crime in South Africa in general is among the highest in the world. Murder and rape are significant problems in this country where the legacy of apartheid has created overwhelming poverty, substandard housing, and inadequate education and health systems. So, hate-motivated sexual violence against lesbians is a fraction of all rapes and sexual assaults that occur routinely. Nevertheless, sexual minority groups do not have many strongholds of support in this culture where masculinity and aggressive expressions of it dominates. South Africa's GLBTI (gays, lesbians, bisexuals, transgendered, and intersexed) community is among those targeted for hate-motivated crime; not unlike patterns of victimization that is seen elsewhere in the world. However, there is also anti-HIV bias in South Africa that motivates attacks on this community. Just as the 1998 killing of Matthew Shepard brought national attention to the abusive treatment of LGBTQ youth in the United States, the murder of AIDS activist Gugu Dlamini, also in 1998, focused attention on this community. Ms. Dlamini was beaten and stoned to death by a crowd of individuals because of her HIV status (Harris, 2004). Despite efforts to educate the public about AIDs, there continues to be the occasional expression of hostility towards HIV-infected persons in this region.

With increased pressure from internal advocacy groups and international organizations, the government of South Africa has begun to focus on these crimes, including corrective rape. Cape Town is the site of several recent meetings attended by government officials and community group representatives to develop effective interventions and prevention initiatives. Results from these meetings includes the establishment of the National Task Team, which is charged with the responsibility of proposing policies to meet both short- and long-term solutions (Department of Justice and Constitutional Development, 2011). Working with the National Task Team are the South African Law Reform Commission and the Human Rights Commission.

A recent review of this collaboration by the Human Rights First organization produced several recommendations for the South African government: the government should initiate changes in a more expedient manner; hate crime legislation should be drafted and enacted to more effectively deal with these crimes; government officials should speak out against hate crimes more often; hate crime statistics should be uniformly collected and monitored on a consistent basis and law enforcement should strengthen ties to community groups in an effort to build trust and encourage the reporting of hate crimes to authorities (LeGendre, 2012).

Australia

Similar to the occurrences in Russia, international students are also frequent targets in Australia. There are approximately 600,000 international students in Australia from over 200 countries according to government authorities. The largest proportions of these students are from China and India. However, within the last several years, Indian students, as well as Indian Australians, have experienced racially motivated attacks particularly in Melbourne and Sydney. The response by government officials to this trend has been lackluster. In fact, Dunn, Pelleri, and Maeder-Han (2011) put forth a credible argument that states government actions by Australian officials were prompted by economic rather than public safety concerns.

International Indian students as well as Indian-Australians have been the victims of violent and other hate-motivated crimes including stabbings, beatings and robberies. Dunn and colleagues report that Indian-born and Sri Lankan-born Indians were targeted more often than all other foreign-born residents and that Indian Australians reported higher victimization rates than other Australian ethnic groups in recent surveys. Moreover, Indian-Australians describe racist incivilities as "common" to their daily experiences. These victimizations triggered persistent media coverage in India. Indian government officials voiced much concern over the safety of their students studying in Australia, causing a corresponding dip in the number of Indian students applying to Australian universities. Decreased enrollments in Australia's international education export market resulted in economic losses which impacted the country's economy. According to Dunn and colleagues, a 5–10 percent drop in enrollments from Indian students translated to a loss of $600 million in tuition and related costs and a loss of 6,300 jobs neither of which would be well tolerated by the Australian economy.

At the time of these developments, Australia had not enacted hate crime laws. In fact, there appeared to be a general reluctance among legislators to formally recognize such crimes. Some of the sentiments expressed were that such laws provided preferential legal treatment to the victimization of some and not others; or even that hate crime laws would somehow disadvantage White male heterosexuals. Initial reactions by police to these crimes included the perspective that Indian students were "soft" or "weak" targets; a blaming-the-victim social construction of these crimes. These terms used to describe the victims hearken to stereotypical pejorative notions of Asian-Indians as weak, impotent, and passive individuals with quiet natures—who also possess and carry expensive electronics or other gadgetry. Other depictions were that these crimes naturally occur in urban settings and are not reflective of prejudiced or racist attitudes.

Both Victoria and New South Wales saw the highest numbers of Indian student victimization, but it was Victoria that subsequently enacted comprehensive policies to respond to these acts as hate crimes. For example, the Victorian Sentencing Act was amended to recognize hate-motivated acts as an aggravating feature which would trigger sentencing enhancements. Police surveillance was stepped up through the Operation Safe Stations program, which significantly increased the use of cameras at train stations. Other initiatives included the establishment of police-community groups to improve working relationships and the installment of a call line to support the public (and victims) reporting these crimes.

The Australian federal government responded by holding several high-profile meetings to determine a response of sufficient scope. One result included the establishment of the Australian Indian Institute (AII) located in the University of Melbourne in 2008. Its primary purpose is to further collaboration and partnership endeavors between India and Australia on a whole host of issues. It also serves to increase deeper understanding and appreciation of Indian history, culture and public policy. Another result included the AII hosting roundtable events to encourage Indian students to voice their concerns and to discuss their experiences of harassment and victimization. Still, despite these actions undertaken by the Victorian and federal governments, there remains concern by some of the apparent lack of consistent and strong leadership among government officials to denounce racial violence and advocate for multicultural understanding. This reaction towards Indian student victimization is somewhat surprising considering that victimization studies in Australia dating back to the 1990s indicate that Jews, Asians, Aboriginal persons, the disabled, Muslims, and members of the LGBTQ community are targeted groups for hate crime.

Modern hate crime laws have been enacted only recently in Australia. In 2003, New South Wales passed revisions to its Crimes Act of 1999 to incorporate hate crime provisions. It utilizes a sentence aggravation model that provides judges the option of taking hate motivation into account when determining the proper sentence. A penalty enhancement model was adopted in Western Australia in 2004. Still, despite the availability of these new statutory provisions, prosecutions using these laws appear to be infrequent in Australia at best (Mason, 2010).

France

The following account was published in a *New York Times* article in 2006:

> Ianis Roder . . . history teacher in a middle school (in) Paris . . . was stunned
> by what he witnessed after Sept. 11, 2001. . . . someone spray-painted in a
> stairwell of the school the image of an airplane crashing into the World Trade
> Center beside the words "Death to the U.S., Death to Jews."
>
> (Smith, 2006)

This incident illustrates a resurgence of anti-Semitism among the children
of immigrants in France and unfortunately such sentiments are described as
"ubiquitous" among students by an inspector general of education. Attitudes like
the one represented in the *New York Times* article provides some social context
to the problem of hate crimes in France. The number of Muslim immigrants from
Northern Africa has increased dramatically in France, as has the number of Jews
from the same region. The Israeli–Palestinian conflict also plays a role in this
backdrop that is resulting in offenses resembling hate crime.

It appears that anti-Semitic, anti-immigrant, or xenophobic and racially motivated hate crimes are most typical in France. The Commission Nationale Consultative des Droits de L'Homme or National Consultative Commission on Human
Rights (CNCDH) is the French Human Rights organization and its role is to advise
the government on matters impacting human rights and international humanitar-
ian law. As a result, it addresses the problem of hate crimes and related matters.
The organization publishes annual reports on hate crimes, bigotry and discrimination that occur in France and comments on proposed policies that address human
rights concerns. In a recent report published by the CNCDH the prevalence and
nature of hate crimes in France is briefly described (see Table 8.1).

These data indicate that anti-Semitic hate crime is the only category that saw
some reduction over the last four years. This trend may be the result of effective
targeted campaigns against anti-Semitism. For example, reports indicate that both
Jewish and Muslim communities were engaged by officials to help focus on these
crimes. Jewish institutions received more attention by police through increased
surveillance and a more visible police presence. France has also appointed special
prosecutors tasked with the aim to respond persistently and robustly to anti-Semitic

Table 8.1 Trends in racial violence and anti-Semitism in France since 2008

	2008	2009	2010	2011	*Trend over 4 years*
Anti-Semitism	459	815	466	389	−15.25%
Racism and xenophobia	467	1026	770	710	+52.68%
Anti-Muslim racism*			116	155	+33.6% (over two years)
TOTAL	926	1,841	1,352	1,254	+35.42 %

Source: CNCDH (2013). Commission Nationale Consultative Des Droits de L'Homme
Note: *Before 2010 anti-Muslim acts were included in the category racism and xenophobia.

and racially motivated hate crimes. Jewish communities are encouraged to work with these prosecutors in moving anti-Semitic cases forward in the criminal justice system. For example the Representative Council of French Jewish Institutions (CRIF) works collaboratively with the Interministerial Committee to fight racism and Anti-Semitism to further diminish anti-Semitism and anti-Jewish hate crime. The French government has also required schools to observe a teaching tolerance day that focuses on the harms of anti-Semitism as well as the Holocaust.

In addition to engaging communities and schools, the law itself has been revamped to address hate crimes. The enactment of Loi Lellouche amended French law in 2003 allowing for harsher punishment for racially motivated violent hate crime. Soon after, sexual orientation was added for increased punishment as well. A particularly horrendous incident helped to justify changes in French law. A young homosexual, Sebastian Nouchet, was nearly burned to death when a juvenile gang doused him with gasoline and set him ablaze due to his sexual orientation. Moreover, anti-homosexual crimes had increased substantially in France. Legislative efforts to stem these and other hate crimes also led to the criminalization of hate speech in 2004. According to France's penal code, defaming, insulting, or inciting discrimination or worse against another due to their perceived group membership is a crime. The laws referenced follow:

Criminal Code
Article R. 624-3 Discriminatory Defamation

- Defamation committed in private against a person or a group of people on account of their origin or their actual or supposed membership or nonmembership of a particular ethnic group, nation, race or religion shall carry the fine for fourth-class summary offenses.

Article R. 624-4 Discriminatory Insults

- Insults committed in private against a person or a group of people on account of their origin or their actual or supposed membership or nonmembership of a particular ethnic group, nation, race or religion shall carry the fine for fourth-class summary offenses.

Article R. 625-7

- Incitement committed in private to discrimination against or hatred or violence towards a person or a group of people on account of their origin or their actual or supposed membership or nonmembership of a particular ethnic group, nation, race or religion shall carry the fine for fifth-class summary offenses.

While the United States has not criminalized repugnant or offensive speech per se, constitutional protections stop short with the "fighting words" doctrine. In accordance with *Chaplinsky v. New Hampshire,* 315 U.S. 568 (1942), words that inflict injury upon hearing or could incite retaliatory actions are not protected speech. In France, prosecutors make that determination and have the Discriminatory Insult laws as tools to punish this category of speech.

The precedent for these laws may be traced to the 1990 Gayssot Act (Act 90-615) which prohibits the public expression of Holocaust denial.

France also has developed measures to minimize the impact of right-wing extremist groups. Recent estimates indicate that there are from 2,500 to 3,500 individuals who are members or are actively involved in these groups. But local government officials now have the legal power to ban their public meetings and to take down neo-Nazi internet websites (McClintock, 2005, 73). It is clear that France has made considerable policy changes to reflect a commitment to combat hate crime; however, for some critics, the extent in which officials make use of these tools and prosecute these crimes remains to be seen (Bleich, 2007).

Germany

The world will likely always see Germany as the ultimate lesson in unaddressed hate gone amuck. As a result of its unique history, Germany has developed public policies aimed at stifling anti-Semitism. Nevertheless, since reunification, there has been an escalation in xenophobic and racist hate crime (Bleich, 2007). Human Rights First reported the following observations (see McClintock, 2005; 83–84):

- Crime attributed to right-wing extremists has increased since 2002. Of the 10,902 crimes in this category, 772 were described as violent. These crimes are identified as politically motivated and is defined in Germany as any offense "directed against a person on account of their political opinion, nationality, ethnic origin, race, color, religion, ideology, sexual orientation, disability, appearance or social status."
- Crimes against foreign nationals and minorities have sharply escalated. Anti-Semitic violence against individuals and property has also increased in Germany.
- The European Union Monitoring Centre on Racism (EUMC) reported a decade ago that two-thirds of the victims of hate offenses were foreign nationals, half of which were asylum seekers. Currently these are individuals mostly from Serbia, Macedonia, Bosnia-Herzegovina, Afghanistan, Syria and Iraq.
- The EUMC further stressed that persons whom are easily identifiable due to physical characteristics as nonGermans (e.g. Turks, Africans, Sinti and Roma or Vietnamese nationals) were more likely to be victimized by extremists.

Black minority groups are also vulnerable for racially motivated violence. Human Rights First adds that poor treatment received by these groups at the hands of ordinary citizens is attributed in part by discriminatory treatment by authorities. Members of these groups are disproportionately stopped by police for questioning in public venues such as train stations and airports. This public treatment is akin to racial profiling behaviors, which is negatively viewed by most in the United States. Roma and Sinti are also subject to discriminatory and shabby treatment by both authorities and ordinary citizens and experience racially motivated violence as well. Finally, anti-Semitic hate crime still occurs in Germany. The following account describes an ugly incident that is particularly repugnant because it occurred in the country where the near genocide of European Jewry took place:

> Marinus Schöberl, age 16, was murdered in Germany in July 2002. Schöberl, who was learning-disabled, was killed because his assailants thought he was a Jew (although he was not). His three young assailants shouted antisemitic epithets and then repeatedly kicked and beat him. They then dragged him to an abandoned farm where they beat his head repeatedly against a stone pig trough. Schöberl's murderers, members of a right-wing organization, later confessed to the crime.
>
> (McClintock, 2005, 10)

Germany has also taken measures to respond to hate crime in all of its manifestations. Instead of putting substantial effort into creating a special category of criminal offenses, the federal government chooses to focus upon impacting cultural beliefs and practices. The government funded four programs to provide a variety of initiatives that were designed to support victims of political violence (hate crime), advocate diversity and multiculturalism and democratic ideals while educating the public on the threat posed by intolerance and bigotry. However, while these programs are apparently constructive, the funding to support them is not permanent. If state and local jurisdictions are unable to pick up and sustain the costs of these programs, the programs will be short-lived.

Hate crime laws are not provided in Germany's criminal code but statutes criminalizing hate speech have been incorporated. Incitement of 'popular' hatred against a segment of the population (Volksverhetzung) is a punishable offense under section 130 of Germany's criminal code. The specifics of this law include the following: a person is guilty of this offense if he or she in a manner qualified for disturbing public peace:

1   incites hatred against segments of the population or calls for violent or arbitrary measures against them; or
2   assaults the human dignity of others by insulting, maliciously maligning, or defaming segments of the population.

An individual may be guilty of this crime even if the act was not committed by a German citizen.

Holocaust denial is also included in this offense. Other than the specifics provided in Volksverhetzung, the German Criminal Code does provide judges the ability to consider the perpetrator's hate and bias toward the victim when determining the appropriate sentence.

United Kingdom

The United Kingdom's population is increasingly diverse. The Office of National Statistics reports that the nation's White population has fallen below 90 percent for the first time; with Asians making up 7.5 percent and Blacks 3.4 percent of the population. Immigrants have made their way into Great Britain since the 1960s and this remains unchanged in the twenty-first century. Currently, London has the largest amount of immigrants with 37 percent of its residents identified as foreign born. White British are now in the minority in London: white British 44.9 percent, Asian 18.4 percent, other White 14.9 percent, Black 13.3 percent, mixed race 5 percent, and Arab 1.3 percent (Gye, 2012). But along with the fact that the presence of immigrants and ethnic minorities are not a recent development in the UK, neither is their victimization. Discriminatory and racist treatment of these groups has occurred with some regularity and so has racially motivated and anti-immigrant violence. But with the 1981 Home Office Report, *Racist Attacks*, the criminal victimization of ethnic minorities due to racial bigotry became officially recognized. The 2011 Home Office Crime in England and Wales reports data on various racially or religiously aggravated offenses and shows decreased trends in most categories from 2009 to 2010. Other hate motives appear to be absent from this report. Also not reported is the racial or ethnic identities of the victims of these crimes, and neither are the type of religious communities that were victimized identified. However, a recent report submitted by *UK NGOs Against Racism* as well as the *European Council Against Racism Intolerance* provide an overview of hate crime in England that describes the targeting of the above mentioned groups and others. Media sources and other published accounts of 600 events of racially motivated hate crime yields the following description of targeted groups in 2009 (in descending order): (racially motivated) 45 percent were Asian, 18 percent Black, 10 percent White British, 7 percent Polish, 1.25 percent Chinese, and 1.25 percent from Traveller communities; (religious motivated): 7 percent of the cases the victims were Muslim and 1.8 percent anti-Semitic. Ninety-three percent of the perpetrators were White, 3.8 percent were Asian, and 2.8 percent were Black. Up to half of all members of minority groups who reside in England's rural areas report to have experienced racial harassment or attacks. NGOs estimate that Blacks are 4.5 times and Asians are 1.7 times more likely to be victims of racially motivated manslaughter and murder than are Whites.

The UK's Public Order Act 1986 and the Racial and Religious Hatred Act 2006 proscribe acts that stir up or incite hatred against persons on racial or religious grounds. This includes using words or behaviors or displaying or distributing written material which is threatening and intended to stir up racial or religious hatred against persons defined by reference to color, race, nationality (including citizenship), or ethnic or national origins or religious beliefs (or lack of beliefs). In the 1990s, the definition of a racial "incident" for investigatory and documenting purposes is defined as any incident which is perceived to be racist by the victim or any other person in accordance with the 1999 Macpherson report. With the advent of these laws and policy changes the prosecution and criminal punishment of racial- and religious-motivated hate crimes progressed.

The number of these cases that are prosecuted increased accordingly. In 2006–07 60 percent of racially and religious motivated crimes were criminally charged. The following year saw 73 percent charged (UK NGOs Against Racism, 2011, 23). But despite this development, these reports also note that part of the difficulty in mounting an effective response to hate crime in the United Kingdom is the existence of institutional and cultural bigotry. Examples of this include anti-immigration and ethnically coded public policies that fan both xenophobic and anti-Muslim attitudes. Hate groups use such official positions to further legitimize their ideologies of intolerance. In fact, UK NGOs observe that because of such official rhetoric, the British National Party (BNP) has made political gains in local and national elections. This group has its roots in Nazi ideology and all that it embraces. Even though the BNP has determined to take on a more moderate position, it continues to advocate White nationalism and anti-Semitism. This change has made them more attractive to ordinary citizens. It's reported that 48 percent of over 5,000 respondents to a 2011 survey acknowledged that they would support BNP candidates if they "cracked down on immigration and on Islamic extremists, but gave up violence" (UK NGOs Against Racism, 2011, 19). An ominous observation made in this report is that since the government does not react to domestic terrorism with the same vigilance as it does Islamic terrorist groups, the UK is more vulnerable to home-grown dangers. NGOs recommendations to improve government response to hate crime include: collect and report hate crime victimization by ethnicity and immigration status; increase partnerships between government agencies and civic groups on hate-motivated crimes; victims should be more involved with the criminal prosecution of their attackers and government should work to develop the trust and confidence in police response to these crimes. The need to build confidence in police is critically important due to the checkered past of the Metropolitan Police. The Policy Studies Institute published a commissioned report in 1983 on London's Metropolitan Police describing "many in the force as bigoted, racist, sexist, bored, dishonest, and often drunk" (Bleich, 2007, 151). While this finding did prompt changes within the law enforcement community, improving relationships with minority communities is still of paramount importance overall and uniquely critical for confronting the problem of hate crimes.

Canada

Sections 318 and 319 of the Criminal Code of Canada places hate crime laws in two categories: crimes that fall under the Hate Propaganda category and then all other offenses motivated by bias make up the second category. Hate Propaganda crimes include Advocating Genocide, Public Incitement of Hatred, and Willful Promotion of Hatred against persons from an identifiable group. Identifiable groups are defined as persons *distinguished* by color, race, religion, ethnicity, or sexual orientation. The second category of hate crime laws is defined as offenses that were motivated solely or in part by hatred, bias or prejudice regarding a person's race, ethnicity/nationality, language, color, religion, sex, age, mental or physical disability, age, or sexual orientation. Canada's hate crime laws also allows for sentencing enhancement when the hate element is proven.

There are over 50 police departments just within the Ontario province of Canada. Many of these departments publish annual reports on hate crime in their respective areas. One of the deficiencies in Canadian hate crime is from police departments using different definitions of hate crimes or hate incidents. This inhibits the ability to fully integrate these data and analyze the state of hate crime in Canada. Hamilton Police Service publishes statistics in a manner similar to that of the US Uniform Crime Reports but a distinction lies in the source of the reported data. UCR data is generated by police reports, but the Hamilton Police Service includes incidents generated by persons involved. According to 2008 data, most hate crimes were due to racial bias (Blacks with the highest victimization rate) with religion (mostly comprised of the targeting of Jews) as the next largest category followed by sexual orientation (Hamilton Police Service, 2010). This is similar to the pattern reported by the Toronto Police force in their 1993 hate crime victimization survey. At that time racial bias comprised 50 percent (Blacks 48 percent, East Indians 22 percent, Asians 8 percent, and Whites 8 percent) of reported incidents, religious bias was 35 percent (anti-Semitism 89 percent) and sexual orientation bias was reported by 10 percent (gay men 94 percent) of survey respondents (Canadian Department of Justice). The typical offenders in Toronto are young males, first offenders, under the age of 20. The Montreal Police department also reported the association between the nature of the hate crime and the targeted group. For example, hate crimes committed against gay men were more inclined to be violent; 69 percent of anti-Black hate crimes were against persons and not property, and finally, anti-Semitic acts were carried out more likely by members of hate groups (Canadian Department of Justice).

A series of attacks on Asian-Canadian fishermen in Ontario resulted in a large-scale collaborative effort that reflects the important role of community in combating hate crime. From 2007 through 2008, a number of attacks occurred on this group while fishing and included brutal assaults followed by victims being thrown into the waters. Following an inquiry by the Ontario Human Rights Commission, a comprehensive initiative, titled, *Fishing Without Fear*, was embarked upon. These efforts produced an investigative report FISHING WITHOUT FEAR: Report on the Inquiry into Assaults on Asian Canadian Anglers. Ontario Human Rights Commission. The following are some of the study's findings:

- The confirmation that Asian fisherman were viewed stereotypically and negatively. Because they were Asian it was assumed that their fishing habits were self-serving, criminal and thus harmful to the industry.
- These stereotypes were used to justify the attacks but were reflective of a broader problem of racist attitudes and bigotry in Ontario.

- The Commission determined that to combat racism and discrimination, institutions in Ontario had to play key roles and show leadership in denouncing these attitudes and behaviors.
- The Commission worked with over 20 organizations including police departments, local government officials and community groups to determine solutions and to lead in educating the public on racial intolerance, racial profiling, and bigotry.
- Efforts were made to support victims by identifying resources to assist and restore them and to emphasize the importance of the inclusion of these and other racial minority groups in the region.
- The Commission did not merely ask for these organizations to contribute ideas but to also make commitments of action to engage in active anti-racism work within their respective organizations.

These efforts were successful in that the Ontario Human Rights Commission was able to frame the problem of hate crime as not just a crime issue but a social one in need of solutions from the community and not merely the criminal justice system. It also effectively engaged multiple stakeholders to form real partnerships and become significantly involved in public educational campaigns to impact bigoted ideas, attitudes and practices.

Conclusion: the global picture

While the media, advocacy groups, and political figures most often respond to the more sensationalized hate crimes, the most prevalent and common form of these crimes are no less repugnant and harmful. As described by McClintock (2005, 5), "low-level violence (includes) the broken window, the excrement through the letter box, late night banging on doors, and the pushes, kicks, and blows delivered to the passerby on the sidewalk. The accompanying epithets and threats, the frequent repetition, the threats that are both random and constant, and the likelihood of a blow becoming a beating, a beating becoming a stabbing or a shooting, adds to a pervasive *terror*" (emphasis added). Hate crime is clearly a global phenomenon but today there are efforts to establish criteria for governments to more effectively recognize, document, and address these problems. The Office for Democratic Institutions and Human Rights (ODIHR) publishes reports on the progress made by member states of the Organization for Security and Cooperation in Europe (OSCE), an office of the ODIHR on human rights and hate crime issues. Some of the major commitments made by the member states include: (1) establish and sustain data collection procedures; (2) maintain reliable hate crime data and make it available to the public; enact hate crime legislation; (3) encourage targeted groups to report hate crimes; (4) provide comprehensive training for law enforcement, prosecutors and other judicial officers and; (5) develop educational and awareness campaigns as recommended by the ODIHR.

The 2011 ODIHR progress report on countries implementing these standards discusses mixed findings. While some states have initiated or improved data collection, there are still significant gaps in data overall, which hinders a coherent picture of hate crimes in the OSCE region. For example, some states still do not collect hate crime data while others collect but do not make their reports available to the public. Another observation is that states will sometimes identify and code a hate motive differently. For instance in some countries, Islamaphobic-motivated crimes may be recorded as either a religious hate, racial hate, or a xenophobic hate.

The work of the ODIHR, NGOs and cooperative governments has produced much more transparency in hate crime policies and practices across multiple nations than had ever existed previously. Information provided in Table 8.2 shows information on cases reported, prosecuted and sentenced, is only possible because of these efforts.

Considerable progress has been made in several nations on their commitments to improving efforts to respond to hate crime, yet further improvements can be made. Fifty states reported to the ODIHR that they collect hate crime data, but only 33 of them has actually provided statistics for the year 2011. Also there are still many governments that have not enacted hate crime laws (McClintock, 2005). Due to these and other shortcomings, the following recommendations *continue* to be suggested to governments by the ODIHR (ODIHR, 2011, 94–96):

Data collection

- Collect, maintain and make public reliable data and statistics in sufficient detail on hate crimes and violent manifestations of intolerance. Such data and statistics should include the number of cases reported to law-enforcement authorities, the number of cases prosecuted and the sentences imposed.
- Consider creating systems for data collection that separate hate crimes from other crimes and that disaggregate hate motivations.

Legislation

- Enact legislation to combat hate crime, providing for effective penalties that take into account the gravity of such crimes.

Criminal Justice Agencies

- Promptly investigate hate crimes and ensure that the motives of those convicted of hate crimes are acknowledged and publicly condemned by the relevant authorities and by the political leadership.
- Provide adequate security to vulnerable communities and invest in necessary resources to protect vulnerable community institutions and places of worship, cemeteries, faith-based schools and religious heritage sites.

Table 8.2 Hate crimes in the OSCE region: police reports, prosecutions, and convictions in 2009, 2010, and 2011

Participating state	Type of data	Cases recorded by police 2011	Cases recorded by police 2010	Cases recorded by police 2009	Cases prosecuted 2011	Cases prosecuted 2010	Cases prosecuted 2009	Cases sentenced 2011	Cases sentenced 2010	Cases sentenced 2009
Albania										
Andorra										
Armenia										
Austria	Data includes crimes of incitement to hatred	57	99	61	38					
Azerbaijan										
Belarus	Police data include crimes of incitement to hatred and those of damaging historical/cultural values	1	1	72			3	1		
Belgium	Data refer to crimes with a racist/xenophobic motive and include crimes of incitement to hatred and crimes of discrimination	1152	815	1198	865	860	974	75		
Bosnia and Herzegovina	Data include crimes of incitement to hatred		15	15						

(continued)

Table 8.2 (continued)

Participating state	Type of data	Cases recorded by police 2011	Cases recorded by police 2010	Cases recorded by police 2009	Cases prosecuted 2011	Cases prosecuted 2010	Cases prosecuted 2009	Cases sentenced 2011	Cases sentenced 2010	Cases sentenced 2009
Bulgaria	Data include crimes of incitement to hatred and crimes of discrimination	29	20	20	41	34	22	10	4	9
Canada		not yet available	1401	1482						
Croatia	Data include crimes of incitement to hatred and discrimination	57	34	32	20	34		10	3	3
Cyprus	Data include crimes involving hate speech		32	8	not yet available	27	16		16	3
Czech Republic	Data represent total number of criminal offences with an extremist context	238 (including 31 crimes involving violence against people or property)	252 (including 55 crimes involving violence against people or property)	265 (including 34 crimes involving violence against people or property)	246 (including 31 crimes involving violence against people or property)	231 (including 48 crimes involving violence against people or property)	188 (including 66 crimes involving violence against people or property)	106 people	52 people	103 people
Denmark	Police data include discrimination and propaganda crimes. Prosecution and sentencing data refer only to cases of incitement to hatred	not yet available	334	306	not yet available	9	5	not yet available	4	1
Estonia	Data include crimes of incitement to hatred			2						

Table 8.2 (continued)

Participating state	Type of data	Cases recorded by police 2011	Cases recorded by police 2010	Cases recorded by police 2009	Cases prosecuted 2011	Cases prosecuted 2010	Cases prosecuted 2009	Cases sentenced 2011	Cases sentenced 2010	Cases sentenced 2009
Finland	Police data include crimes of incitement to hatred and crimes of discrimination. Prosecution and sentencing data only includes crimes of incitement to hatred and crimes of discrimination	not yet available	860 reports 1407 offences	1007 reports 1580 offences	29	38	41			
France	Data include discrimination and defamation crimes									
Georgia			19	41		1	11			
Germany	Police data include hate crimes, as well as those of incitement to hatred and of propaganda; Prosecution data only include crimes of incitement to hatred and those of propaganda	4040 (including 528 violent crimes)	3770 (including 467 violent crimes)	4583 (including 590 violent crimes)			3079			2221
Greece				2			2			

(continued)

Table 8.2 (continued)

Participating state	Type of data	Cases recorded by police 2011	Cases recorded by police 2010	Cases recorded by police 2009	Cases prosecuted 2011	Cases prosecuted 2010	Cases prosecuted 2009	Cases sentenced 2011	Cases sentenced 2010	Cases sentenced 2009
Hungary	Data include crimes of incitement to hatred and of discrimination			12			7			
Holy See	Data include crimes of incitement to hatred and of discrimination									
Iceland	Data include crimes of incitement to hatred and of discrimination						0			0
Ireland		162	141	164						
Italy	Data include crimes of incitement to hatred and those involving insults	68	63		31					
Kazakhstan	Data include crimes of incitement to hatred	10	5	5	10	4	4	4	1	3
Kyrgyzstan	Data include extremist crimes			79			58			41
Latvia	Data include crimes of incitement to hatred			6	4	6	5	4	3	6
Liechtenstein			6	6		3	3		3	1
Lithuania		5		3	2					
Luxembourg										
The Former Yugoslavia Republic of Macedonia										
Malta										
Moldava				2			0			
Monaco										0

Table 8.2 (continued)

Participating state	Type of data	Cases recorded by police 2011	Cases recorded by police 2010	Cases recorded by police 2009	Cases prosecuted 2011	Cases prosecuted 2010	Cases prosecuted 2009	Cases sentenced 2011	Cases sentenced 2010	Cases sentenced 2009
Montenegro										
Netherlands	Total data refer to all registered discrimination cases at the Prosecution Service					170	160 (including 15 cases involving violence or the threat of violence)		90	135
Norway	Data include crimes of incitement to hatred	128	236	213						
Poland	Data include crimes of incitement to hatred	222	251	194	43	30	28	24	30	28
Portugal										
Romania	Data refer to crimes of incitement to hatred and of discrimination						28			
Russian Federation	Data include crimes of incitement to hatred									

(continued)

Table 8.2 (continued)

Participating state	Type of data	Cases recorded by police 2011	Cases recorded by police 2010	Cases recorded by police 2009	Cases prosecuted 2011	Cases prosecuted 2010	Cases prosecuted 2009	Cases sentenced 2011	Cases sentenced 2010	Cases sentenced 2009
San Marino										
Serbia	Data include crimes of incitement to hatred			82	36	35	16	26	15	44
Slovakia	Data include crimes of incitement to hatred			132						18
Slovenia	Data include crimes of incitement to hatred	45	34	9						
Spain		115	98	121			246			
Sweden	Data include crimes of incitement to hatred crimes and of discrimination	5493	5139	5797	347	440	450			
Switzerland	Data include crimes involving discrimination	182	204	230	36	32			25	30
Tajikistan										

(continued)

Table 8.2 (continued)

Participating state	Type of data	Cases recorded by police 2011	Cases recorded by police 2010	Cases recorded by police 2009	Cases prosecuted 2011	Cases prosecuted 2010	Cases prosecuted 2009	Cases sentenced 2011	Cases sentenced 2010	Cases sentenced 2009
Turkey	Data only include crimes of incitement to hatred crimes and of discrimination				628	330	250	17	297	242
Turkmenistan										
Ukraine	Data include both hate crimes and of incitement to hatred crimes and of discrimination	5	5	2						
United Kingdom		44519 (in England, Wales and Nothern Ireland) 6169 (in Scotland)	48127 (in England, Wales and Nothern Ireland) 5819 (in Scotland)	52102 (in England and Wales) 6,590 (in Scotland)	15284 (in England, Wales and Nothern Ireland) 4518 (in Scotland)	15020 (in England, Wales and Nothern Ireland) 4322 (in Scotland)	13030 (in England and Wales)	12651 (in England and Wales)	11405 (in England, Wales and Northern Ireland)	10690 (in England and Wales)
United States		not yet available	7699	7789						
Uzbekistan		4								0

Source: Office for Democratic Institutions and Human Rights. Hate Crimes in the OSCE Region: Incidents and Responses. Annual Report for 2011, 23–25

- Conducting awareness-raising and education efforts, particularly with law enforcement authorities, directed towards communities and civil society groups that assist victims of hate crimes.

The problem of intolerance, bigotry, and thus hate-motivated crimes are entrenched social problems that will continue in many nations for some time to come. Nevertheless, inroads can be made with concerted and intelligent efforts to suppress and ultimately diminish the conditions that fuel these destructive motivations. Just as McDevitt, Levin and Bennett (2002) theorized that hate crimes have the capacity to create retaliatory responses; this dangerous cycle can take place within communities, across communities, and also within nations. The work of the ODHIR is important and necessary to prevent these dangerous crimes from erupting into something larger and even more lethal.

Chapter summary

- Suspicion of the *other* and bigotry are universal experiences. Left unimpeded, their culmination—genocide—occurs globally; thus it should not be surprising that hate crimes also occur in many nations and among many people.
- The Leadership Conference Education Fund (LCCREF) report, *Hate Knows No Borders—The International Perspective*, indicates that hate crimes increased in several European countries as well as the Russian Federation since the start of the twenty-first century.
- Who are the reported victims? There are hosts of groups targeted for abuse due to their actual or perceived status. Asylum seekers and immigrants are mentioned in the LCCREF report, as are Muslims, Jews, and Christians, homosexuals, Africans, and Roma.
- Hate motives for some attacks could fit more than one category. For example, asylum seekers may also be attacked for racial reasons or even for xenophobic reasons. Similarly, persons of Middle-Eastern descent may be targeted for their perceived religion or due to their ethnicity.
- The 2011 Office for Democratic Institutions and Human Rights progress report on countries implementing these standards discusses mixed findings. Some states have improved data collection, but there are still some states that do not collect hate crime data while others collect but do not make their reports available to the public.
- Considerable progress has been made in several nations on their commitments to improving efforts to respond to hate crime yet further improvements can be made.

Case study 8.1 Ukrainian Jews look to Israel as anti-Semitism escalates

There are reports which indicate an increase in anti-Semitism and anti-Jewish acts in Ukraine.

In the midst of the struggle between Ukrainian authorities and pro-Russian factions since the Russian takeover of Crimea, there have been some disturbing anti-Jewish incidents: a synagogue was fire-bombed in Nikolayev; the Holocaust memorial in Sevastopol was vandalized and; the desecration of the burial site of historic religious leader and teacher Dov Ber Schneerson.

What preceded these events was the distribution of leaflets to Jews residing in the eastern Ukrainian city of Donetsk that came under the control of pro-Russian authorities. The leaflets called for Jews to register with local authorities and provide a list of properties they owned since they would now be required to pay a "registration fee." The leaflet reportedly went on to state that should they refuse to comply, their property and other assets would be confiscated and they'd be subject to deportation. These developments have put the Jewish community in eastern Ukraine on edge. The increased possibility of Russian encroachment in the eastern areas of Ukraine is unsettling due to the history of Jewish oppression in the former Soviet Union. Subsequently their fears have generated increased interest in emigration to Israel. Sohnut, a Jewish agency that assists with repatriation reports more inquiries into the process by Ukrainian Jews. In fact the number of Jews emigrating from Ukraine to Israel has nearly doubled. From the leaflet distribution and the blatant anti-Jewish sentiment displayed by the hate crimes recently committed—people have become fearful and unsettled.

(Source: www.haaretz.com/jewish-world/jewish-world-news/1.587115)

Discussion questions

1   The anti-Semitic hate crimes occurring in Ukraine are designed to send a strong message to the Jewish residents. One of the more disturbing reports is an apparent request for Jews to "register" with pro-Russian authorities. How would you interpret the nature of this hate crime? Is it driven by extremist groups or is it government sanctioned?
2   Are there any recommendations made by the Organization for Security and Cooperation in Europe, (OSCE), that could help stem anti-Semitic hate crime in Ukraine? What are they?

Bibliography

Bleich, E. (2007). Hate Crime Policy in Western Europe. *American Behavioral Scientist*, 51(2), 149–65.

Canadian Department of Justice. (n.d.). Disproportionate Harm: Hate Crime in Canada. Available from www.justice.gc.ca/eng/rp-pr/csj-sjc/crime/wd95_11-dt95_11/p3.html#section3_2 [Accessed February 8, 2015].

Chandra, M. (2012). Social Profiling: The Root Causes of Racial Discrimination Against North East Indians. North East Support Centre and Helpline. Available from http://

nehelpline.net/?p=702 [Accessed March 20, 2013]. UGC Sponsored National Seminar on Gender and Racial Discrimination: The Paradigm of Women's Vulnerability, held on 7th and 8th September, 2012, *Organised by:* Human Rights Studies Centre, S. Kula Women's College in collaboration with Human Rights Alert, Imphal, and Manipur.

Commission Nationale Consultative Des Droits de L'Homme (CNCDH). (2013). National Consultative Commission on Human Rights. Contribution of the CNCDH to the 2nd cycle of the UPR of France, 4 January, p.12. Available from http://nhri.ohchr.org/EN/IHRS/UPR/Documents/CNCDH%20contribution%20for%20UPR%20Dec%202012.pdf [Accessed February 8, 2015].

Department of Justice and Constitutional Development. (2011). Task Team Is Set Up to Attend to Lesbians, Gays, Bisexuals, Transgendered and Intersexed (LGBTI) Issues and Corrective Rape. Available from www.info.gov.za/speech/DynamicAction?pageid=461&sid=18294&tid=33187 [Accessed April 12, 2013].

Dunn, K., Pelleri, D., & Maeder-Han, K. (2011). Attacks on Indian Students: The Commerce of Denial in Australia. *Race & Class*, 52, 71.

European Commission Against Racism and Intolerance. (2010). ECRI Report on the United Kingdom (Fourth Monitoring Cycle). Council of Europe. Available from www.coe.int/t/dghl/monitoring/ecri/default_en.asp [Accessed May 24, 2013].

Flohr, H. (1987). Biological Bases of Prejudice. *International Political Science Review*, 8 (2), 183–92.

Gendercide Watch. (n.d.). Case Study: Female Infanticide. Available from www.gendercide.org/case_infanticide.html [Accessed March 20, 2013].

Gye, H. (2012). British Whites' Are the Minority in London for the First Time as Census Shows Number of UK Immigrants Has Jumped by 3 Million in 10 Years. Available from www.dailymail.co.uk/news/article-2246288/Census-2011-UK-immigrant-population-jumps-THREE-MILLION-10-years.html#ixzz2U7B5PFHo [Accessed May 23, 2012].

Hamilton Police Service. (2010). Hate/Bias Statistical Report. Hamilton, Ontario, Canada. Available from www.hamiltonpolice.on.ca/NR/rdonlyres/7987F700-C4C4-4E84-935D-A7A097012D16/0/2010HateCrimeUnitAnnualReport.pdf [Accessed February 8, 2015].

Harris, B. (2004). *Arranging Prejudice: Exploring Hate Crime in Post-Apartheid South Africa*. Race and Citizenship in Transition Series. Johannesburg, South Africa: The Center for the Study of Violence and Reconciliation.

Horn, S. K. (2001). Female Infanticide in China: The Human Rights Specter and Thoughts Towards (An) Other Vision. In D. E. H. Russell & R. A. Harmes (eds.) *Femicide in Global Perspective* (pp. 138–46). New York: Teachers College Press.

Hunter-Gault, C. (2012). Violated Hopes: A Nation Confronts a Tide of Sexual Violence. Newyorker.com. Available from www.newyorker.com/reporting/2012/05/28/120528fa_fact_huntergault#ixzz2Mxfhdh8W [Accessed March 11, 2013].

Leadership Conference on Civil Rights Education Fund (LCCREF). (2009). Confronting the New Faces of Hate. Hate Knows No Borders: The International Component. Available from www.civilrights.org/publications/hatecrimes/borders.html [Accessed March 11, 2013].

LeGendre, P. (2012). Hate Crime in South Africa Gets International Scrutiny. Available from www.humanrightsfirst.org/2012/06/08/hate-crime-in-south-africa-gets-international-scrutiny/ [Accessed March 8, 2013].

Liss, A. (2010). Neo-Nazi Skinheads Jailed in Russia for Racist Killings. BBC News, Moscow. Available from http://news.bbc.co.uk/2/hi/europe/8537861.stm [Accessed April 10, 2013].

McClintock, M. (2005). Everyday Fears: A Survey of Violent Hate Crimes in Europe and North America. Available from www.humanrightsfirst.org/wp-content/uploads/pdf/everyday-fears-080805.pdf [Accessed March 12, 2013].

McDevitt, J., Levin, J., & Bennett, S. (2002). Hate Crime Offenders: An Expanded Typology. *Journal of Social Issues*, 58(2), 303–17.

Mason, G. (2010). Hate Crime Laws in Australia: Are They Achieving Their Goals? Sentencing Conference 2010. Canberra 6th and 7th February. National Judicial College of Australia. Available from http://papers.ssrn.com/sol3/papers.cfm?abstract_id=1601624 [Accessed May 20, 2013].

Mills, J. & Polanowski, J. A. (1997). *The Ontology of Prejudice*. Atlanta, GA: Rodopi Bv Eds.

Office for Democratic Institutions and Human Rights (ODIHR). (2011). Hate Crimes in the OSCE Region: Incidents and Responses. Annual Report for 2011. Available from http://tandis.odihr.pl/hcr2011/ [Accessed May 28, 2013].

RT News. (2009). Skinhead Gang of Ten Put on Trial. Published August 4, 2009. Available from http://rt.com/Top_News/2009-08-04/skinhead-gang-trial-attacks.html. RT News (Russia Today) [Accessed December 29, 2009].

Schwirtz, M. (2008). Police in Moscow Investigate Killing of a Migrant Worker. NYTimes.com. Available from www.nytimes.com/2008/12/14/world/europe/14russia.html [Accessed April 9, 2013].

Schwirtz, M. (2009). Nationalists Suspected in Russian Activist's Death. NYTimes.com. Available from www.nytimes.com/2009/11/18/world/europe/18moscow.html?_r=0 [Accessed April 9, 2013].

Sharma, S. (2012). Hate Crimes in India: An Economic Analysis of Violence and Atrocities Against Scheduled Castes and Scheduled Tribes. Centre for Development Economics, Department of Economics, Delhi School of Economics. Working Paper No. 213. Available from www.cdedse.org/pdf/work213.pdf [Accessed March 15, 2013].

Smith, C. S. (2006). Jews in France Feel Sting as Anti-Semitism Surges Among Children of Immigrants. Published March 26, 2006. *New York Times*. Available from www.nytimes.com/2006/03/26/international/26antisemitism.html [Accessed December 29, 2009].

SOVA. (The Center for Information and Analysis.) (2010). Galina Kozhevnikova: Under the Sign of Political Terror. Radical Nationalism and Efforts to Counteract It in 2009. Summary. Available from www.sova-center.ru/en/xenophobia/reports-analyses/2010/03/d18151/ [Accessed April 9, 2013].

UK NGOs Against Racism. (2011). Joint Submission by UK NGOs Against Racism to the UN Committee on the Elimination of Racial Discrimination (CERD) with Regard to the UK Government's 18th and 19th Periodic Reports. July. Available from www2.ohchr.org/english/bodies/cerd/docs/ngos/NGOsAgainstRacism_UK79.pdf [Accessed May 24, 2013].

WSVN.com. (2009). Campaigner Against Hate Crimes Killed in Moscow. November 20. LongIslandPress.com. Available from www.wsvn.com/news/articles/world/MI136664/ [Accessed December 31, 2009].

9 The future of hate crimes

Introduction

Hate crimes are contemptible acts. Their toll only begins with the victim. These crimes ultimately impact society itself by contesting the liberties and quality of life of some of its members. There are countless examples of perpetrator–victim combinations where the perpetrator is a member of a dominant social group and the victim a member of a minority one; there are also occurrences of the opposite. *Wisconsin v. Mitchell* 508 U.S. 476 (1993), the case that affirmed the constitutionality of hate crime statutes, involved an African-American perpetrator and a white victim. There are also examples of minority-on-minority hate crime as discussed earlier. In the last several years, there have been a number of hate crime convictions of Latinos who have targeted Blacks or Black families in various communities in Los Angeles and Compton, California. Undoubtedly, the opposite has occurred as well. Frank Collin (real name Cohen) a Jewish man, was a member of the American Nazi Party and later founded the National Socialist Party of America. Both organizations were strongly anti-Semitic and sought to agitate the Jewish community. There are even reports of neo-Nazis (some of them of Jewish ancestry) attacking Jews in the state of Israel. Although it can be argued that the impact of hate crime is far worse when the power differential between the perpetrator and the victim is perceived as large, the victimization experience is still harmful regardless of which social group the victim or perpetrator belongs.

Groups still erect social boundaries for one another when the distinctions between them are less evident and the two are from very similar backgrounds. The Rwandan genocide took place near the close of the twentieth century and its death toll was approximately 800,000. The principals involved were fellow Rwandans—Hutus and the Tutsi. Besides the enormity of the event itself, the realization that this ultimate hate crime occurred between fellow countrymen is very unsettling. The Rwandans were virtually the same people until colonial powers designated one of the two "more European-like" (Tutsi), than the other (Hutus); creating a socially constructed hierarchy within Rwandan society. This fueled social inequality and injustice and rationalized ugly tribalism, stereotyping, classism, profiling, resentment, and political exploitation. The eventual product of this was the total dehumanization and systematic murder of fellow countrymen.

As the history of humankind suggests that hate crimes will be with us for some time to come, future research should delve more into this natural proclivity. Why do social groups inherently construct binary relationships of *us versus them*? Does this process have a biological basis? What more can be learned about the triggers of these dynamics? It is easier to understand why group differences may generate fear and hostility. But when there are more similarities than differences between groups, why are these boundaries still created? Does tribalism underlie even the most advanced societies where resources are plentiful but self-seeking survivalist instincts (or greed) still produces the us (deserving) versus them (not deserving) dynamic? Because perceived differences, prejudices, and hostilities can ultimately lead to the loss of life, the systematic research of hate crime, its preconditions, effects, and the policies designed to deter and prevent it will hopefully increase and receive adequate funding and support. Much has been lost and much more is at stake.

The final chapter focuses attention on social forces that may facilitate a change in the nature of hate crime in the United States. There could be several conditions included on this list, but I limit it to three: the palpable growing disrespect of government both in and outside of the hate movement, the continuing problem of the militarization of the hate movement due to the involvement of military service men and women, and the changing face of the United States, which is becoming less White and more Brown. The chapter ends with a few public policy recommendations and other initiatives that have the potential to impact these developments.

An evolving landscape

The election of Barack Obama in 2004 as the first African-American President of the United States served to raise the ire of many in the hate movement. With his re-election in 2008, the Obama administration advocated for public policy changes in health care, immigration reform including the Dream Act, and for requiring background checks for the purchase of firearms along with other changes such as more nutritious menus in public schools. To many in the hate movement, these proposals merely served to justify (and solidify) their rancor against the federal government and this President in particular. In addition, the scandals involving the Internal Revenue Service alleged targeting of Tea Party and other conservative groups, the revelation of the National Security Administration's program to monitor mass communications in the US in addition to the Snowden revelations, all add fuel to these paranoiac worldviews. Neither should it be overlooked that there are voices in mainstream political discourse that are also suspicious and critical of the positions taken by the Obama administration. In fact, the disrespect shown by authority figures in Congress and elsewhere to the President may have actually encouraged and emboldened the fringe elements.

These developments in the political world may have energized the extremist movement. The Patriot Movement became more active since the first Obama election with over 1,300 groups by the end of 2012 (*Intelligence Report*, 2013). Patriot groups and Sovereign Citizens in particular view the government as the enemy; an entity that enacts and promotes laws that are designed to erode the civil rights of (White) American citizens and degrade the quality of life in this country. Sovereign Citizens are a subset of Patriot groups. They do not recognize the authority of government officials, politicians, federal, state, or local laws or the authority of law enforcement officers to enforce the law. They refuse to be subject to these laws. The Anti-Defamation League defines the Sovereign Citizen movement as:

> a loosely organized collection of groups and individuals who . . . believe that . . . existing government in the United States is illegitimate; . . . they seek to "restore" a . . . minimalist government that never . . . existed . . . sovereign citizens wage war against the government . . . using . . . harassment and intimidation tactics . . . occasionally resorting to violence.
>
> (ADL)

Individuals who identify themselves as sovereign citizens are capable of dangerous and violent acts. When officers performed a routine traffic stop in West Memphis, Arkansas on May 20, 2010, they were shot to death by one of the occupants. Jerry and Joseph Kane, a father and son pair were sovereign citizens and it was Joseph Kane, a sixteen-year old, that shot both officers with an assault weapon (ABC News, 2010). An excerpt from the ABC news article:

> When first responders arrived, they found the two officers dead. As the Kanes tried to escape, a fish and wildlife officer rammed his truck into their vehicle. The Kanes began firing at the wildlife officer's cab . . . he was unharmed, but both Jerry and Joe Kane died in the ensuing gun battle.
>
> (ABC News, 2010)

The Kane's were responsible for the deaths of two officers and the attempted murder of a third and yet some in the movement look upon them as *heroes*. The capacity for this movement to unify and pose a serious threat to law enforcement was shown in the recent Cliven Bundy incident.

Bundy, a cattle rancher and subscriber of the Sovereign Movement has been involved in a long-term dispute with federal agents from the Bureau of Land Management that recently became an armed confrontation. With media attention focused on the developing standoff, Bundy began to amass supporters from sovereigns and those from the anti-government and other extremist movements. But these supporters were armed and willing to use deadly force on federal law enforcement officers:

> According to the U.S. Capitol Police, Senator Majority Leader Harry Reid . . . has received death threats at his home from Bundy supporters. . . . local residents of the area have complained that armed militia men

have set up checkpoints on some of the roads, demanding proof of residency before allowing cars to pass.

(Forbes)

Sovereign Citizens have committed violent acts, including murder, against law enforcement officers carrying out their policing responsibilities. What is further worrisome is that the credo of Patriot and Sovereign Citizens groups coincides nicely with a central ideological belief in the hate movement, that the United States' government is Jewish-influenced and controlled and is therefore not legitimate (nor are its agents). This Zionist Occupied Government (ZOG) must be eventually overthrown even by violence.

Should the Patriot movement and groups within it such as Sovereign Citizens become more organized, coordinated with other extremist groups, agenda-driven and sophisticated, there could be more violent episodes pointed at targets beyond that of law enforcement. On June 8th, 2014 Jerad Miller, a reported supporter of Clive Bundy, and his wife Amanda Miller were responsible for the shooting deaths of two Las Vegas police officers who were having lunch at the time of the attack. The couple were also involved in the shooting death of a Walmart shopper (not law enforcement) who encountered the couple as they fled the earlier shooting. The Millers had expressed anti-government sentiments on social media. After killing the officers, the Millers draped the Gadsden "Don't Tread on Me" flag and a swastika on the body of one of the officer's. They also announced that this is the beginning of the revolution (CNN, June, 2014).

Another area of concern that could change the nature of hate crime in the United States involves radical extremists entering the US military or become adherents to hate ideology during active service. The realization that racist groups recruit military personnel and indoctrinate them with racist ideology became undeniable in the 1995 case of James N. Burmeister. At the time of the racially motivated shootings, Burmeister, an army private, was also a neo-Nazi skinhead. But additional incidents have since occurred. Wade M. Page, an army veteran, entered a Sikh temple in Oak Creek, Wisconsin on August 5, 2012 where he shot and killed six people thought to be Muslim. Page was described as a racially prejudiced individual while in the military, who spoke frequently about racial holy war (CNN, August, 2012). Sociologist Randy Blazak stated the following about extremist groups and the military:

They view the military as . . . opportunity to get shots in on non-whites. [In a] 2004 case in . . . Oregon . . . a group of soldiers came back from . . . war upset that they didn't get to kill . . . "brown people" and went on a crime spree . . . Officials also discovered Aryan Nation graffiti in Baghdad during the US occupation there.

(Carroll, 2012, paragraphs 11–12)

More recently authorities uncovered a plot to overthrow the government and to assassinate President Obama by a group that included military personnel from

Fort Stewart, Georgia. The group known as *Forever Enduring Always Ready* or FEAR, plotted a campaign of terrorist attacks, bombings, and assassinations in order to take over Fort Stewart, seize its ammunition, and disrupt and overthrow the government. Some members of the group pled guilty to burglaries, financial-transaction-card thefts and violations of the Georgia Street Gang Terrorism and Prevention Act. Four members pled guilty to the 2011 execution of two individuals, one of which was a member of FEAR. The group also purchased nearly $90,000 in weapons and bomb making materials (Terry, 2013). These are very serious crimes and they also show the potential of such groups, which are comprised of weapons-trained military personnel, to plot and carry out acts that could cost the lives of many.

The Pentagon has made efforts to educate commanding officers (and enlisted personnel) on what characterizes believers in the hate movement so that they may be identified (e.g. racist tattoos, ideological terminology, literature, symbols, paraphernalia) (Neiwert, 2010). It was announced in a recent directive issued by the Defense Department, that those who serve in the military "must not actively advocate white supremacist doctrine, ideology, or causes. This includes writing blogs or posting on Web sites" (Neiwert, 2010, paragraph 5). Depending upon their activities, these individuals could be subject to penalties such as demotions or being stripped of security clearance revoked or finally discharged. Recruiters are also trained to identify various indicators of extremism so that impacted individuals may be screened out and not accepted for enlistment.

The Defense Department continues policies to weed out or punish personnel who are involved with hate groups or the hate movement, but these policies are not foolproof and are only as effective as the personnel who carry them out. The Defense Department recently reported that through its efforts, 320 soldiers were found to be actively involved in extremist activity (Potok, 2006). The identification of these individuals is crucial. Once they are in the armed services, they make efforts to connect inside and begin to plan and coordinate activities. *Operation Vigilant Eagle*, a Department of Homeland Security program is designed to analyze and share information regarding Iraqi and Afghanistan war veterans whose involvement in white supremacy, militia or other extremist groups poses a domestic terrorism threat (Neiwert, 2010).

As encouraging as these policies and programs are, they only have a limited effect on those who are no longer in the military and targeted for recruitment by White nationalists. Since the 9/11 terrorist attacks until August 2011 over two million military personnel have served in Iraq, Afghanistan or both. Of that number, over one million have left the military (Martinez & Bingham, 2011). What must be recognized is the dark figure that represents the number of military-trained persons who are now actively participating in a hate group, a cell or who have become lone wolves. Considering the recent number of those who have left the service, there will be a number of them who will either become active participants in an extremist group, begin to adopt extremist ideology, or become merely sympathetic to the cause. Any of these developments could increase the violence potential of hate groups.

In 1999, I described a set of conditions that could be impactful of hate crimes in the US. These conditions included (a) a greater ability for perpetrators to cause massive injuries and or multiple deaths; (b) a growing acceptance of extremist ideology in the marketplace of political ideas, (c) the legal protection of extremists in the court system, (d) an increase in religious zealotry among hate crime perpetrators, and (e) an increased adoption of extremist agenda into the concerns of Middle-America (Petrosino, 1999). There is continued concerned for most of these conditions such as the capacity for determined offenders to hurt others and the mainstreaming of extremist perspectives. Others have loss some relevancy such as the increase in religious zealotry or the legal protection of extremists (or their non-violent activities) in the courts.

These and other conditions will likely be tested out as we approach what will be a marked sea change in American society. According to the US Census Bureau's population projections, by the year 2050, Whites will no longer be the majority in the United States. Racial minorities are expected to make up more than 50 percent of the total population and that no other advanced country will be as diverse (Kotkin, 2010). Latino and Asian populations are expected to nearly triple. Today 25 percent of children under the age of five in the US are Hispanic and by 2050, that number will be 40 percent. Hispanics will be 28 percent of the population; African-Americans will still be 13 percent; Asians will be 7 percent; multiracial persons 4 percent and Native Americans and Pacific Islanders will be 1 percent.

This change alone will have huge ramifications across multiple dimensions; certainly political, social, and economic. It will also have tremendous consequences for what will be the new majority and the new minority. According to several theoretical explanations for hate crime—particularly for "group-threat" theories, to the extent that such theories are accurate, hate crime and related acts of domination and control should peek before the demographics settle into its new configuration. Not only will the national majority be Brown and Black and not White, but the US population will expand by another 100 million going from 300 to 400 million by 2050. This will also impact the nation's economy, which may have implications for group conflict and possibly hate crime. Today, there are four states where this seismic demographic change of minorities as the new majority has apparently already occurred: California (60.3 percent), Hawaii (77.1 percent), New Mexico (59.8 percent), and Texas (55.2 percent). Other states will also see a gradual change in the racial and ethnic composition of their respective populations as well.

These changes may contribute to an increasingly uncomfortable and threatening social environment for racists. Anxieties stemming from the perception of *losing power* to those who are subhuman and unworthy might be enough to motivate more to lash out in hate crimes. Some Whites supremacists already see the "Aryan" people (or the White race) as "endangered and facing demographic and cultural extinction" brought by social institutions viewed as "anti-white" because they now include multicultural and diversity as aims and objectives (Blee, 2002). In a similar vein, the work of political geographer Colin Flint addresses the role of territoriality, contested space and perceived threats as issues which facilitate racial violence. In his article, United States Hegemony and the Construction of Racial Hatreds, he makes a seminal observation:

> Tensions of identity and geographical space laid the foundations for the xeno-phobia subsequently fueling, and fueled by, the KKK, and reflection in the self-proclaimed role of militias and other groups to defend a particular view of America.

(Flint, 2003, 169)

These current observations, as well as lessons learned from history, point to the likelihood of upcoming surges of hate crimes and hate incidents. Rini Sumartojo (2003) discusses hate crime as acts perpetrated by offenders who are contesting social place; places where victims were not expected or permitted to be. When perpetrators engage in these acts, they are doing so from their frame of reference or understanding as to who is "out of place" in a given location. Similar to Levin and McDevitt's (2002) defensive category of hate crime, the offender is motivated to address this breach by demonstrating to the victim that he or she is "out of place" and committing acts of harassment, assault or worse upon the victim to make the point. Sumartojo emphasizes the importance of understanding the meaning of social place to the offender, but not only himself or herself but also as it pertains to the victim.

We are reminded by Flint and others that adherents of hate ideology evaluate all human events through simplistic lens. Event A either threatens the dominance of the Aryan or White race or it does not. Therefore population shifts caused by an influx of non-White immigrants, an increased birth rate of Yellow, Brown, and Black babies, and population mobility and intermarriage would all be inter-preted as threats to White dominance. Those dedicated to the cause would feel it necessary to respond to such changes. Defending against a greater presence of minorities could signal the need for a serious and sustained violent response. Flint describes this reaction as, (the advocacy of) "an extremely violent kind of agency at the local scale to maintain an established view of local spaces. The resonance of the far right's message lies in its recognition of people's attachment to and dependence upon places" (Flint, 2003, 178). American history witnessed episodes of "white flight" and or "concerned citizen's councils," which reflected strategies regarding contested spaces. Many of these participants were not affiliated with hate groups.

Should ordinary citizens interpret these demographic changes in a man-ner similar to White nationalists and the like, the potential for violence could broaden. Subsequently, as the United States changes from a predominately White nation to a predominately Brown and Black one, it is likely that there will be more frequent contestations (as perceived by offenders) for social spaces and social dominance in areas previously controlled primarily by Whites. Hate crimes motivated by these demographic changes will likely play out over the next several decades.

Public policy recommendations

Embracing the new America

This anticipated surge in hate crimes and other community disorders are largely avoidable if sufficient and sustained efforts are shepherded by government officials who have prioritized the well-being of the American people, community leaders who seek well-functioning and healthy neighborhoods, and educators who seek to inspire students to be not only academically bright, but moral human beings. Leadership must come from all socializing institutions in society to prepare for the new social landscape.

Education initiatives

There are countless educational resources, training workshops, curricular materials, and best practices guidelines on incorporating cultural diversity, multicultural, and inclusion standards in instructional materials. These materials exist on every educational level, kindergarten through 12 and in higher education as well. School-based programs would have an important role in continuing to educate students on the importance of cultural understanding, appreciating the similarities and differences among people and respect for all human beings. The US Department of Education has funded programs that address issues of cultural diversity and could continue to incentivize such programs. There are many non-profit organizations which offer a variety of resources to meet the needs of schools and instructors (see for example: The National Association for Multicultural Education (NAME)'s Advancing and Advocating Social Justice and Equity or the American Institutes for Research and Learning Point Associates' Educating Teachers for Diversity websites.

Community-based initiatives

Community organizations also have the capacity to highlight different cultures, styles, customs and traditions—making them less foreign, or strange and more familiar and acceptable to the American palate. Social institutions and government agencies all have a stake in preparing for this transition. But learning and sharing these values in the community is more intimate and is grappled with in the environment that's closest to where day-to-day life is lived—the community. Again, there are countless numbers of community programs that seek to enlighten the public on issues of culture, religion, language, customs, and practices of different social groups. One example is *Multicultural BRIDGE.* One of the goals of this program, which is located in the Berkshires, in Massachusetts, is to integrate diverse groups through community activities and facilitate understanding. Social programs do not often advertise this purpose directly but this program does. Their website describes a number of services that it provides community stakeholders. I will just list a few here:

- **Cultural literacy and programs:** BRIDGE services include diversity training, cultural competence training, and multicultural awareness workshops. We design and facilitate forums, conferences, speeches, and retreats *focused on integrating diversity into the workplace and in communities.* We provide cultural proficiency assessments and planning for all organizations.
- **Facilitated community conversations:** BRIDGE *facilitates productive community dialogues* on sensitive topics such as gender race parenting, sexual identity, sexuality, bullying, and other dimensions of diversity and culture.
- **Multicultural presentations:** *Building community connections* by celebrating diversity for dancers, community dinners, education, performances, and art shows.
- **Recruitment, Placement, Integration, and Retention:** BRIDGE's omnibus approach *integrates diverse professionals* in to your workplace culture and the wider Berkshire Community. Bridge partners with recruitment agencies, internship programs, and colleges.

The mission statement of *Multicultural Bridge* reflects the type of program that could impact the occurrence of hate crime if there are an adequate number of them especially in geographical areas where demographic changes are inevitable. Their mission statement is admirable:

> We promote mutual understanding and acceptance among diverse groups serving as a resource to both local institutions and the community at large. We serve as catalysts for change through collaboration, education, training, dialogue, fellowship and advocacy.

(Multicultural Bridge)

Criminal Justice System initiatives

Hate crime offenders who are not steeped in ideology may be good candidates for alternative treatment in the criminal justice system such as diversion programs, restorative justice initiatives and community-service options. Several years ago, a search of such interventions for youthful offenders involved with hate crime by this author found fewer of these services offered. The reason given was budget cuts. Here we have an opportunity to make these programs available again and to ensure that they are sustained by permanent funding. As mentioned in Chapter 7 on criminal justice responses, we noted that the UK and Australia utilize restorative justice measures for hate crime offenders far more than the US. There is opportunity to learn what is effective in these programs that can be adapted in this country. Those who belong to extremist groups and who identify with hate ideology must also be reached by these initiatives. Essentially, their hatred is born out of fear and ignorance and these things can and must be addressed.

These few suggested policy areas have the capacity to make a real impact on how people of different groups view one another. These initiatives are clearly not just for minorities, but for everyone; and they should be presented in that way.

The ultimate aim is to strengthen the fabric of American society by recognizing, respecting, and incorporating the many different voices, insights, and contributions of a diverse populace. Replacing fear and suspicion with the recognition that people are more similar than dissimilar will help build resistance to the *us vs. them* paradigm. The new United States will be comprised of a diverse people, yes; but these diverse people will share similar values as reasonable human beings, desiring security, peace, and liberty.

If we are determined to see our common humanity, the US and all other nations can be strengthen by being unafraid of its own diversity.

Bibliography

ABC News (July 1, 2010). Deadly Arkansas Shooting by Sovereigns Jerry and Joe Kane Who Shun U.S. Law. Available from http://abcnews.go.com/WN/deadly-arkansas-shooting-sovereign-citizens-jerry-kane-joseph/stop [Accessed June 17, 2014].

American Institutes for Research and Learning Point Associate's Critical Issue: Educating Teachers for Diversity. (n.d.) Available from http://www.ncrel.org/sdrs/areas/issues/educatrs/presrvce/pe300.htm [Accessed March 6, 2015].

Anti-Defamation League (ADL). (n.d.). Extremism in America. Sovereign Citizens Movement. Available from http://archive.adl.org/learn/ext_us/scm.html?xpicked=4 [Accessed June 16, 2014].

Blee, K. M. (2002). *Inside Organized Racism: Women in the Hate Movement.* Los Angeles, CA: University of California Press.

Carroll, W. (2012). Are Military Hate Groups on the Rise? Military.com. Available from www.military.com/daily-news/2012/09/12/hate-groups-and-the-military.html [Accessed June 27, 2013].

CNN. (August 6, 2012). Police Identify Army Veteran as Wisconsin Temple Shooting Gunman. Available from www.cnn.com/2012/08/06/us/wisconsin-temple-shooting [Accessed June 26, 2013].

CNN. (June 12, 2014). Authorities Had 3 Encounters This Year With Couple in Las Vegas Shootings. Available from www.cnn.com/2014/06/12/justice/las-vegas-shooting [Accessed June 17, 2014].

Flint, C. (2003). United States Hegemony and the Construction of Racial Hatreds. In C. Flint (ed.) *Spaces of Hate: Geographies of Discrimination and Intolerance in the U.S.A.* (pp. 165–82). New York: Routledge.

Forbes. (April 30, 2014). Context Matters: The Cliven Bundy Standoff. Available from www.forbes.com/sites/jjmacnab/2014/04/30/context-matters-the-cliven-bundy-standoff [Accessed June 17, 2014].

Intelligence Report. (2013). *The Year in Hate and Extremism.* Issue 149.

Kotkin, J. (2010). The Changing Demographics of America. Smithsonian.com. Available from www.smithsonianmag.com/specialsections/40th-anniversary/The-Changing-Demographics-of-America.html?c=y&page=1 [Accessed June 24, 2013].

Levin, J. & McDevitt, J. (2002). *Hate Crimes Revisited.* Boulder, CO: Westview Press.

Martinez, L. & Bingham, A. (2011). U.S. Veterans: By the Numbers. ABC News. Available from http://abcnews.go.com/Politics/us-veterans-numbers/story?id=14928136 [Accessed June 17, 2014].

Multicultural Bridge. (n.d.). Available from www.multiculturalbridge.org [Accessed June 17, 2014].

National Association for Multicultural Education (NAME): Advancing and Advocating Social Justice and Equity. (n.d.). Available from www.nameorg.org/resources/teaching-resources [Accessed June 17, 2014].

Neiwert, D. (April 15, 2010). Pentagon Decides It's Time to Clamp Down on the Right-Wing Extremists Infiltrating Ranks of U.S. Military. Available from http://crooksand liars.com/david-neiwert/pentagon-decides-its-time-clamp-down [Accessed June 25, 2013].

Petrosino, C. (1999). Connecting the Past to the Future: Hate Crimes in America. *Journal of Contemporary Criminal Justice*, 15(1), 22–47.

Potok, M. (2006). Extremism and the Military. *Intelligence Report*, Summer, Issue 122. Available from www.splcenter.org/get-informed/intelligence-report/browse-all-issues/2006/summer/extremism-and-the-military [Accessed February 8, 2015].

Sumartojo, R. (2003). Contesting Place. In C. Flint (ed.) *Spaces of Hate: Geographies of Discrimination and Intolerance in the U.S.A.* (pp. 87–107). New York: Routledge.

Terry, D. (2013). Army Veteran Pleads Guilty in Fort Stewart Militia Case. Southern Poverty Law Center. Available from www.splcenter.org/blog/2013/01/23/army-veteran-pleads-guilty-in-fort-stewart-militia-case/ [Accessed June 27, 2013].

Wisconsin v. Mitchell (92–515), 508 U.S. 47 (1993). Legal Information Institute. Available from www.law.cornell.edu/supct/html/92-515.ZO.html [Accessed June 17, 2014].

Index

Aboriginal people 199
absence of capable guardians 85, 86, 87
Adorno, T. 80, 81
advocacy groups 113
affirmative action 82, 95, 112
African-Americans 138–43, 164, 165;
  campus hate crimes 24; Cracker Barrel
  case 10–11; demographic changes 225;
  economic and educational disadvantage
  89–90; history of hate crime 33, 35–8,
  42, 45; laws 53; location of hate crimes
  21–2; lynchings 35, 54, 118; minority
  group perpetrators 15, 118–20, 127, 128,
  220; Moudry case 187; prison gangs
  183; prosecution of hate crimes 177;
  social learning theory 90, 91; "sundown
  towns" 92; thrill hate crimes 85; urban
  areas 36–7, 54, 70
Afrikaner Resistance Movement (AWB)
  197
AIDS 121–2
Alabama 4–5, 38
Albania 209
Allen, Darrel James 15
Allport, Gordon W. 78–80, 96
Altemeyer, B. 81
Amedure, Scott 179
American Prosecutor's Research Institute
  (APRI) 175
Ancheta, Angelo 146
Anderson, James 92–3
Andorra 209
Andrade, Allen 177
Anti-Defamation League (ADL) 7,
  156; community programs 158;
  data collection 16; hate groups
  109; information on hate crime 20;
  model statute 8–10, 57–8, 65, 67, 71;
  Sovereign Citizens movement 222;
  youth involvement 40–1

anti-immigrant groups 113, 123, 192, 193;
  see also xenophobia
anti-mask laws 62–4
anti-Semitism 3, 6, 154, 155–7, 164,
  184, 220; ADL role 20; authoritarian
  personality 80; belief systems 123;
  campus hate crimes 24; Canada 206;
  Christian Identity theology 124; France
  200–1; Franklin 88; Germany 202, 203;
  hate groups 112; history of hate crime
  36, 45; LCCREF report 192; social
  learning theory 81; Ukraine 216–17;
  United Kingdom 204, 205; see also Jews
anti-statism 124
Aoki, Keith 146
apartheid 196, 197
arbitration clauses 72
Arizona 123, 141–2, 144, 148, 149, 150,
  172
Arkansas 57, 177, 222
Armenia 209
Armenians 192
Aryan Brotherhood (AB) 182, 185, 186
Aryan Nations 78, 123, 124, 223
Aryan Youth Movement 115
Asian-Americans 20, 120, 143–7, 164;
  demographic changes 225; history of
  hate crime 34–5, 42, 45; legal defenses
  against hate crime 178; location of hate
  crimes 21–2; prison gangs 183; thrill
  hate crimes 85
assault 13, 15, 31; anti-Asian hate crime
  34, 146; hate groups 110; India 194; Ku
  Klux Klan 38; slavery 33; statistics 18;
  see also violence
asylum seekers 192, 202, 216
Australia 184, 198–9, 228
Austria 209
authoritarian personality 80, 81
Azerbaijan 209

White Wolves 195
Widner, Bryon 114
Wilkinson, W. W. 81
Willems, H. 106
Winston, Theodore 108
Wisconsin 59–60, 67, 223
Wisconsin v. Mitchell (1993) 58, 59–60,
  67, 68, 69, 220
Wolf, Robert 3
women: corrective rape 197, 198; female
  infanticide 193–4; hate groups 117–18,
  130; prosecution of hate crimes 174–5,
  186; victimization of 142; *see also*
  gender
Wooden, W. A. 111
workplace settings 22–3
Wright, Malcolm 40, 139
Wyoming 10, 177

xenophobia 106, 107, 115, 226; anti-
  Asian hate crime 145; anti-immigrant
  sentiment 148; Christian Identity
  theology 124; France 200; Germany
  202; LCCREF report 192; Russia 196;
  United Kingdom 205

Yoon, Won-Joon 145
youth 40–1; neo-deprivation theory 112;
  perpetrators 104, 105, 106, 129; racism
  107; sentencing of offenders 181–2
Yuki 32

Zapata, Angie 177
Zionist Occupied Government (ZOG) 123,
  124, 223